IMAGES
of America

GARDINER
ON THE KENNEBEC

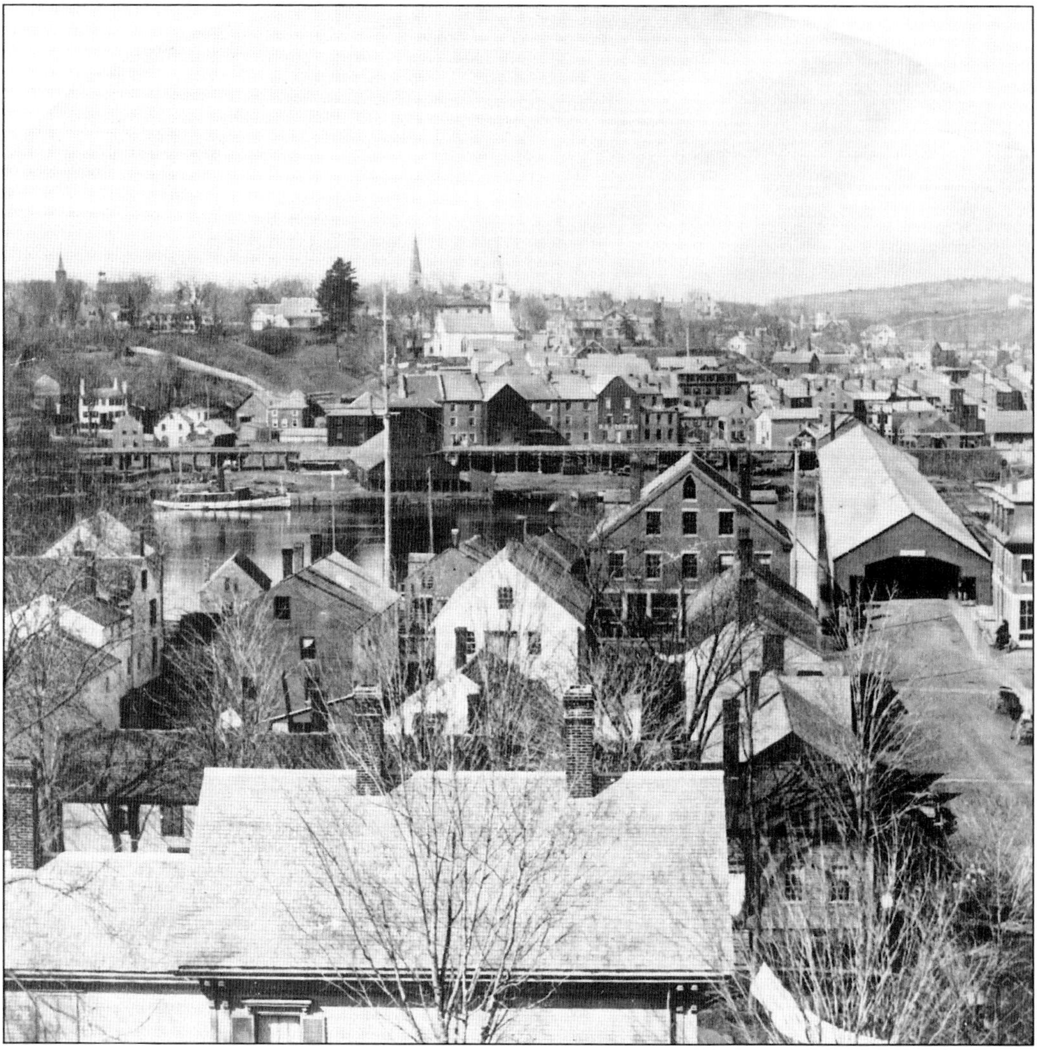

Every building stands out clearly in this 1877 photograph of Gardiner from Randolph. Downtown Randolph is in the foreground, with the present IGA block and covered bridge at the right. Built in 1853, the bridge was destroyed in the 1896 flood. Across the Kennebec, the backs of the buildings along the southern end of Water Street can be seen. The horizon is pierced by the spires of St. Joseph's Catholic Church (at the left) and Christ Church and the Universalist Church, now Congregational (in the center).

IMAGES of America

GARDINER ON THE KENNEBEC

Danny D. Smith and
Earle G. Shettleworth Jr.

ARCADIA PUBLISHING

ISBN 978-0-7385-8965-7

Published by Arcadia Publishing
Charleston, South Carolina

Printed in the United States of America

For all general information contact Arcadia Publishing at:
Telephone 843-853-2070
Fax 843-853-0044
E-mail sales@arcadiapublishing.com
For customer service and orders:
Toll-Free 1-888-313-2665

Visit us on the Internet at www.arcadiapublishing.com

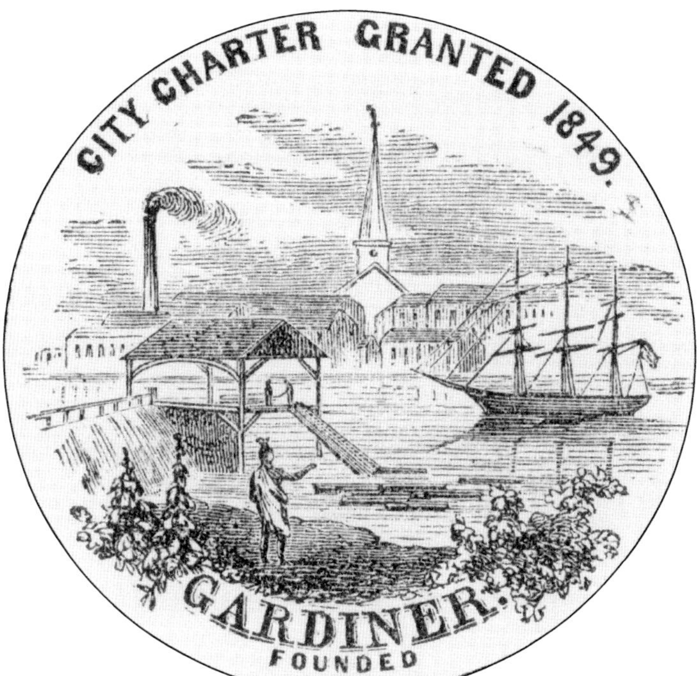

When Gardiner was incorporated as a city in 1849, this seal was designed to symbolize various aspects of community life. In the foreground stands an Indian, a reminder of the Native American heritage of the Kennebec River. On the river are falls, which power a sawmill, reflecting the thriving lumber industry. A vessel represents shipbuilding, transportation, and trade. An idealized city in the background is comprised of prosperous factories and commercial buildings which are presided over by a lofty church tower, emblematic of the central position of religion in nineteenth-century society.

Contents

Bibliographical Note

The only attempt to write a comprehensive history of Gardiner is its earliest one, John W. Hanson's *History of Gardiner* (1852), which is sadly out-of-date. The next history appeared as a chapter in Henry D. Kingsbury and Simeon L. Deyo's *Illustrated History of Kennebec County* (1892, pp. 601–667), which contains good accounts of the industrial history of the second half of the nineteenth century but is very unbalanced by the inclusion of paid biographies. *Leading Business Men of Lewiston, Augusta and Vicinity* (1889, pp. 141–170) contains a good account of the commercial activity and merchants at the end of the nineteenth century. *Picturesque Gardiner* (Gardiner Board of Trade, 1896) preserves many good views of the city at the time. *The Centennial of Gardiner* (1903), edited by Josiah S. Maxcy, preserves the ceremonial addresses given in celebration of the town's incorporation in 1803. Evelyn L. Gilmore's *History of Christ Church* (1893) provides much of the context that is lacking in the foregoing authors' works. Henry S. Webster edited many volumes of the vital records of Gardiner, West Gardiner, Randolph, Farmingdale, and Pittston as well as monographs on the early land titles and Dr. Gardiner which are an essential beginning point for research in original records. Robert Hallowell Gardiner I, at the request of his children in 1860, wrote his *Early Recollections*, which gives an eye-witness account of the transformation of Gardiner from a frontier town to a prosperous city. This account was published by the author's great-grandchildren in 1936. In the 1980s, James Connor compiled massive indexes to the names published in the many local newspapers. His indexes and microfilm of the papers are in the Community Room at the Gardiner Public Library where a good vertical file preserves much local history. *Ninety Years On* (1940), the autobiography of Henry Richards, and *Stepping Westward* (1931), the autobiography of his wife, Laura E. Richards, evoke many local personalities of the period from 1876 to 1940. *The Gardiner Story* (1949) is a brief summary of local history for the centennial of the city charter. *Gardiner and Bostonians* (1951) relates mid-twentieth-century industrial history. Notable houses appear in *An Architectural and Historical Survey* (1984), edited by Leroy Congdon and Joanne Clark. Danny D. Smith, in both his *Gardiner's Yellow House* (1988) and *Yellow House Papers Inventory* (1991), gives account of the founding families of the community.

Introduction

The recurring theme in the history of Gardiner, Maine, is the alternation of control, by economic and political forces, between leaders outside and from within the community. The earliest presence of Europeans is vitally linked to the competing interests of the English and French crowns to gain control of the North American continent. Gardiner was in the center of that contested arena. The King of England declared his sovereign interest in all of North America, and granted the territory from coast to coast between latitudes 40 and 48 to the Great Council of Plymouth. The council then divided that vast territory into smaller proprietary companies. The Pilgrims who arrived on the *Mayflower* opened the Kennebec Valley.

Plymouth Colony nearly collapsed at the end of the first decade. John Allerton, who had connections at the English court, lobbied for a grant in Maine where the Pilgrims could trade in fish and furs with the Indians. Although Allerton's grant embracing the Kennebec Valley proved to be the temporary economic salvation of the Pilgrims, a combination of poor management and exhaustion of beaver and sturgeon resources ended the Pilgrims' hope. In 1660, shortly before their absorption into the Massachusetts Bay Colony, they made one last attempt to raise money by selling their Kennebec Valley lands to four Boston merchants.

The four Boston merchants almost made a commercial success of their acquisition, but a series of wars soon convulsed the American colonies between 1675 and 1763. The struggle between the French and English was resolved only when the English conquered Quebec in 1759. Then Indian raids ceased in Maine, and for the first time the Massachusetts businessmen could envision practical possibilities for expansion into the central Maine area. A well-capitalized group of investors in Boston bought out the heirs of the earlier investors and organized a joint stock company, initially consisting of 192 shares. One-tenth of the shares was soon in the investment portfolio of Dr. Silvester Gardiner, leading surgeon of Boston, who had amassed one of the largest fortunes in the colonies through the importation of medical supplies. He presided over the affairs of the company and secured a monopoly of the stores on the frontier and the operation of the supply sloop which constantly sailed between Boston and the settlements on the Kennebec River. When subdivisions of company land were made, Dr. Gardiner always secured the best lots.

The best land in the 1.5 million-acre grant held by the Kennebec Proprietors was located at the confluence of the Cobbosseeconte Stream and Kennebec River—right here in Gardiner, Maine. That choice site drops 130 feet during the last mile of the Cobbosseeconte Stream. Dr. Gardiner soon exploited this prime stretch of water power by erecting two sawmills, a fulling mill, potash factory, and a gristmill. The gristmill was the only place within a 50-mile radius that the pioneers could grind their corn. Therefore, Gardinerston, as this area was known after 1754, became an economic center for the entire region. This community was also at the head of tide, and as a consequence, ships which sailed on the ocean could come only this far north before dragging on the river bottom. Economically, Gardiner commanded the best site for numerous wharves, one of which jutted out 1,250 feet into the river. The practical outcome stemming from the combination of prime mill sites and good wharves was tremendous.

Let us try to envision the appearance of the community at the time Dr. Gardiner carved a little settlement out of the howling wilderness. Let us walk along the parking lot between Cobbossee Stream and the back of the buildings on Water Street. Let us look up to the Yellow Church, now the Congregational Church, halfway up the hill. Imagine Water Street with a few rude huts skirting the walled palisade halfway up the hill. If you imagine away the man-made landscape, you will understand that the fort had a commanding view of the confluence of the stream with the river. That important site controlled all traffic—before the roads were blazed through the woods to back lots, travel was only by water.

Dr. Gardiner, an ardent Tory and adherent of the Church of England, remained loyal to the King of England when the American Revolution broke out. As a result, his 100,000-acre grant, which included the present municipalities of Gardiner, Pittston, Randolph, West Gardiner, and part of Farmingdale, was confiscated by the provisional government and was going to be sold until, at the last minute, his lawyer son-in-law discovered a technical flaw in the legal proceedings. In the meantime, Dr. Gardiner had been exiled from the United States upon pain of imprisonment and possible death. The year before he died in 1786, he obtained a reversal of his exile and was ready to reassert the claim to his landed estate. He left a will leaving the entire estate to his grandson with the stipulation that his grandson change his surname from Hallowell to Gardiner. The estate was a vast tract of land which under terms of the will could never be divided but would descend from eldest son to eldest son forever.

The undivided and indivisible inheritance set the stage for another economic disaster for this area. Because the land could not be divided into settlers' lots, prospective pioneers could not obtain titles to the land. No legal remedy was in sight until 1803, when the young grandson came of age and claimed his inheritance, which had been held in trust by absentee executors. The bright young Robert Hallowell immediately complied with his grandfather's will and changed his surname to Gardiner. He is known in history as Robert Hallowell Gardiner I (1782–1864), for whom this city is named.

Robert Hallowell Gardiner found chaos as he entered into his vast landed inheritance. No responsible pioneer would settle here without prospect of obtaining secure land title in a community where he would risk his life's fortunes. Consequently, the mills and wharves had fallen into decay during the time of the absentee proprietor. There were at least sixty families illegally squatting on the land. But Robert found solutions. His lawyer broke the entail on the estate so that the land could be divided and sold in fee simple parcels, the best ownership possible in land. He settled with the squatters by allowing them to discount the improvements they had made on the land against the purchase price. He also brought in good engineers and managers to rebuild the wharves and mills. He supervised the repair of the several dams on Cobbosseeconte Stream. He invested his own capital to build up the main street and start several stores. Most importantly, he commissioned Solomon Adams to survey the entire estate, and that act allowed for the systematic sale of house lots and the laying out of streets and roads.

The larger needs of the community were also promoted by Robert Hallowell Gardiner. In 1834 he chartered the Gardiner Savings Institution, thereby providing for the regulated circulation of money. He built, at his own expense, the large stone church at the summit of Church Hill, Christ Church, which has been a community center since its erection in 1819. Since 1824, the Common opposite the church has set a proper tone for the ornamental residences in the heart of the community. His leadership in establishing the Gardiner Lyceum, the first vocational college in the nation, brought additional economic advantage to the region. His great stone mansion, Oaklands, designed by America's foremost architect of the time, Richard Upjohn, has been an important symbol of the city's cultural links that extend well-beyond state lines. Two American presidents, as well as many other historic figures, have been guests there.

By 1820, when the Squire of Oaklands was making substantial improvements in the community, Maine was poised to begin a six-decade period of unparalleled economic growth. We have never recovered from our relative strength vis-à-vis the nation since 1880. The excitement of this golden era is summed up by Maine novelist Robert P. Tristram Coffin in *Captain Abby and Captain John* (New York: MacMillan, 1939):

> The years from 1820 to 1880 were the only years when the State of Maine was able to keep her smartest children home and give them all something to do, and not have to breed them for states farther west, Illinois and Michigan, Wisconsin and Minnesota, Oregon and Washington. Those states had to look elsewhere, during that spell, for good farmers and fishermen and boatbuilders and lumbermen, and not rob the Maine cradle of its best lumbering and fishing babies.

During the fifty years from 1772 to 1820, Maine's population increased more than fivefold; from 29,080 in 1772 to 298,335 in 1820. The implications of these figures are tremendous. The economic and social ferment released in the wake of the American Revolution boded a change in the character of the nation, and of this social movement, in New England, we will see the mirror image of the westward expansion. Active economic forces meant land speculation and rapidly expanding markets for timber, but the actual amount of land placed for agricultural use was still relatively small.

From the time of Robert Hallowell Gardiner's assumption of leadership until the Civil War, shipbuilding and trading were the basis of the community's economy. Agriculture, so important in surrounding towns, was only marginally important here. Gardiner's great-granddaughter, Rosalind Richards, evoked that spirit of the shipbuilding trade and the city's links to world enterprise during that golden era in her book, *Northern Countryside* (New York: Holt, 1916):

> Ship-building was the chief industry of the place. There were four principal ship-yards. The skippers as well as the lumber came from close at hand. It seems a wonderful thing, in these stay-at-home times, that keen young lads from the farms could have been, at twenty-one, in command of full-rigged ships, fearlessly making their way, in prosperous trade, to places that might as well be in Mars, for all most of us know of them today: but Java and the spice Islands, Shanghai, Tasmania, and the Moluccas were household words in those days, and you still hear a sentence now and then which shows the one-time familiarity of ways which have passed from our knowledge.

In 1849, the town of Gardiner obtained a charter from the state legislature and became a city. At this time, the area boasted busy shipyards: the Cooper, Agry, and Stevens and Kimball yards in Pittston; the Bradstreet and Pierce yards in Gardiner; and the S.C. Grant yard in what would become Farmingdale in three years. Farmingdale split from Gardiner because of a tax revolt. Mrs. Chadwick, wife of a powerful lawyer, insisted that her husband push legislation through to break with the city fathers of Gardiner, who would not build sidewalks to her corner where Maine and Northern Avenues join. During the 1840s, eight barks, brigs, and schooners, as well as twenty ships, three steamers, and two clipper ships were turned out by these yards. Ten large wharves served as the shipping point for lumber and other manufactured goods. Many mills, tanneries, and a large pottery lined the Cobbossee. Two rows of stores, mostly wooden structures which would perish in the city's great fire of 1860, lined Water Street. Church Hill, rising abruptly 125 feet, is aptly named because the spires of the Congregational, Universalist, and Episcopal churches answered to the other very visible steeple of the Methodist church on Highland Avenue.

The sense of community in the nineteenth century was strong. Upon his return from Boston in 1878, Henry Richards (1848–1949), grandson of Robert Hallowell Gardiner, described the commercial district as a series of shopping trips which were like neighborly calls:

> . . . all the stores in those days were kept by Gardiner men and women, every one of whom had a stake in the town and a position in the social, religious and

philanthropic groups in which the whole heart and soul of the place found expression, not only in manifold good works, but in rivalries and competitions which gave Gardiner the name of a fighting town, though the fights seemed to bind us all closer and closer together, after the dust they raised had settled.

These conditions had changed drastically by the close of Henry's long lifetime in the late 1930s, when he described "the change that has come over Gardiner and the whole country, as mass production and incipient state capitalism have crowded small, individualistic enterprises off the stage."

The merchants whom Richards encountered in the 1870s were dealers in wool and hides, West India goods, and patent medicines. The grocery store was a small operation with pickle and apple barrels by the front door. There were no packaged goods. The professional buildings housed a surgeon-dentist, notary public, surveyor, and many attorneys. Physicians came in many categories: allopathic, homeopathic, botanic, and physopathic.

Although Savels Paper Mill was established as early as 1807 in Gardiner, the paper industry started to assume undoubted importance in the 1860s, when the S.D. Warren Copesook Paper Mill began the century-long dominance of the local economy by the paper companies. Among the companies to spring up were the Hodgkins Paper Company, Richards Paper Company, and the Hollingsworth and Whitney Paper Mill. During the second half of the nineteenth century, Joshua Gray presided over the other large industry, the sawmills. Steamboat passenger ships, typified by those in the command of Captain Jason Collins, provided another important link to the outside booming economy. Another industry, as remarkable for its sudden appearance and rapid end as its source of great wealth, was the ice industry, active from the 1880s to the 1920s. At the turn of the nineteenth century into the twentieth, Gardiner's last major industry, which even stabilized the local economy during the Great Depression, became fully established: the shoe manufacturers. The Commonwealth Shoe and Leather Company and the R.P. Hazzard Shoe Company, in conjunction with the paper mills, provided a firm economic base until well after World War II.

The philanthropic interests of the Richards family brought cultural and social stability to the community. Through the efforts of Henry and Laura E. Richards, the high school was built in 1920, the hospital established in 1919, the Gardiner Public Library in 1881, and the Gardiner Water District in 1885, along with many other institutions such as the local chapter of the Red Cross, and the establishment of a public health nurse and complete overhaul of the city charter. These important institutions, the lengthened shadows of single individuals, all sprang into existence when the city's social and political life was organized in hierarchical circles, focused around the Gardiner and Richards families at the apex. Slightly below them were a larger group of the mill management oligarchy, whose links to the principal bankers, attorneys, and larger store owners forged a strongly-bonded caste.

Although Gardiner, in 1878, was small enough so that everyone knew everyone with some intimacy, traditional bonds gradually gave way to the impersonal forces of the late twentieth century. High-rise capitalism redefined the economic landscape. Since the 1960s, industry has generally left the northeastern United States, and Gardiner found itself in the same unfortunate sweep of events which have left all communities in the region largely in the control of outside interests. The process described by Richards in the 1930s has entered its final stage of development. Nearly all the stores we patronize are owned by chains; for the most part based outside the state. Much local policy is a distillation of Federal mandates. Gardiner is largely a bedroom community for state government workers in Augusta and employees of the Bath Iron Works. Many residents commute to Portland daily because the real estate market here is still within the reach of young middle-income couples. The creative innovations which this city will have to devise in order to mold these conditions to our advantage will be the greatest challenge to Gardiner's leaders at the beginning of the twenty-first century.

Danny D. Smith, March 1996

One

Patterns of Settlement 1754–1802

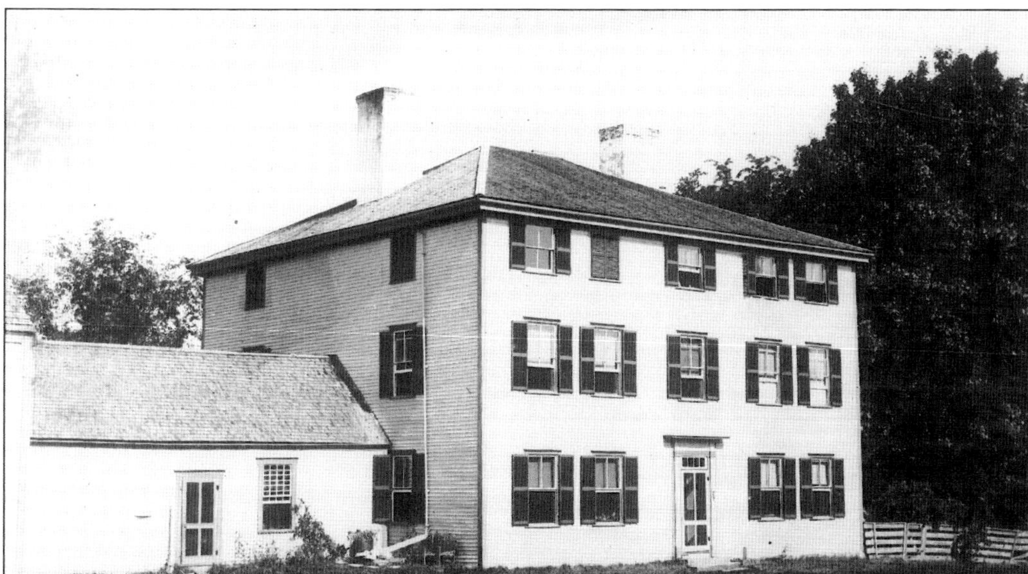

The Pownalborough Court House on the Kennebec River at Dresden was constructed in 1761 by the Kennebec Proprietors to accommodate the courts of the new Lincoln County as well as to provide a tavern and inn. Erected by Boston architect-builder Gershom Flagg, this three-story building was duplicated in the Great House which Dr. Silvester Gardiner built at Water and Church Streets, now the site of Fleet Bank.

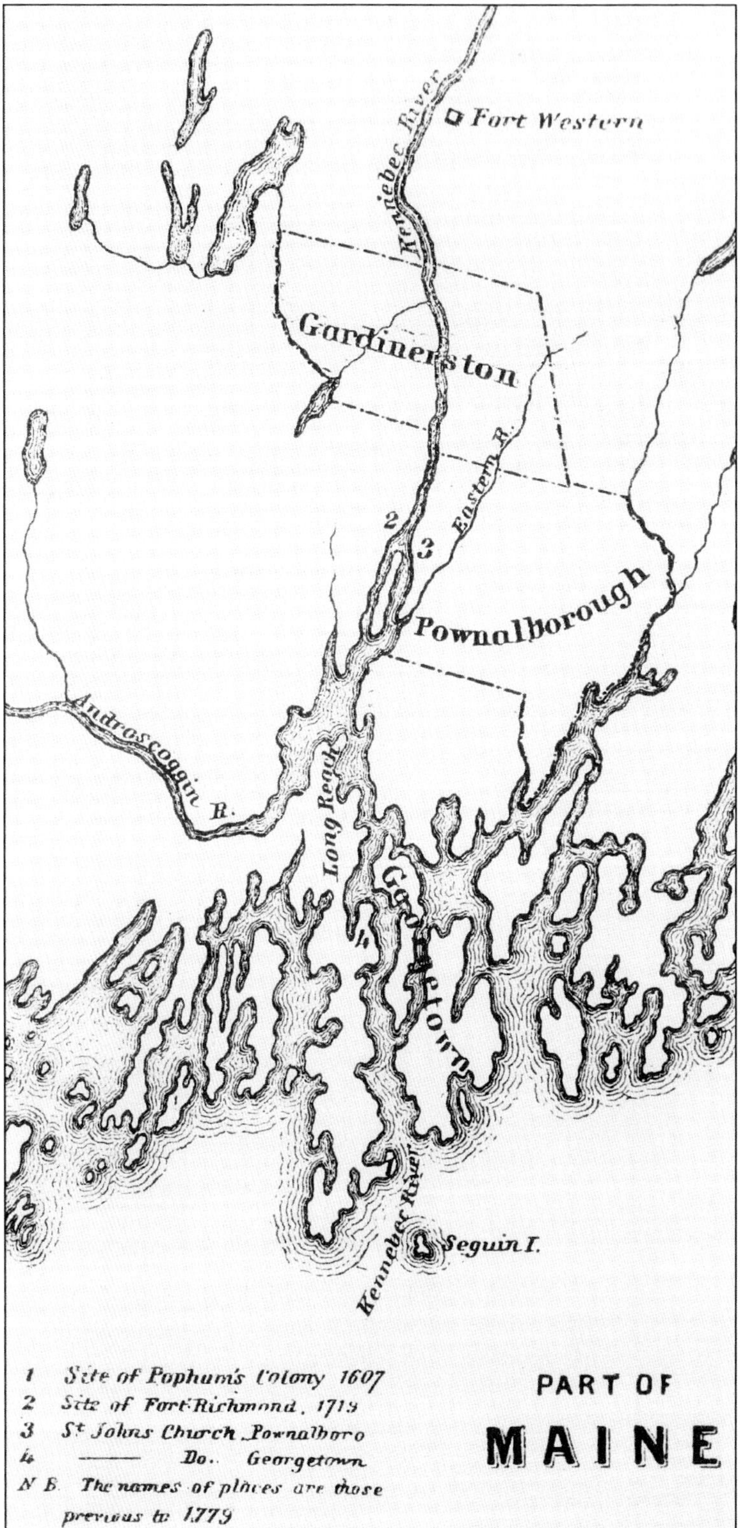

Gardinerston was the principal allotment for Dr. Silvester Gardiner from the Kennebec Proprietors, it being much of his one-tenth interest in the 1.5 million acres of land stretching 15 miles on each side of the Kennebec River from the north line of Bath to Skowhegan. Ancient Gardinerston included, in addition to the present city of Gardiner, the present towns of Pittston, Randolph, a small section of Chelsea, West Gardiner, and Farmingdale.

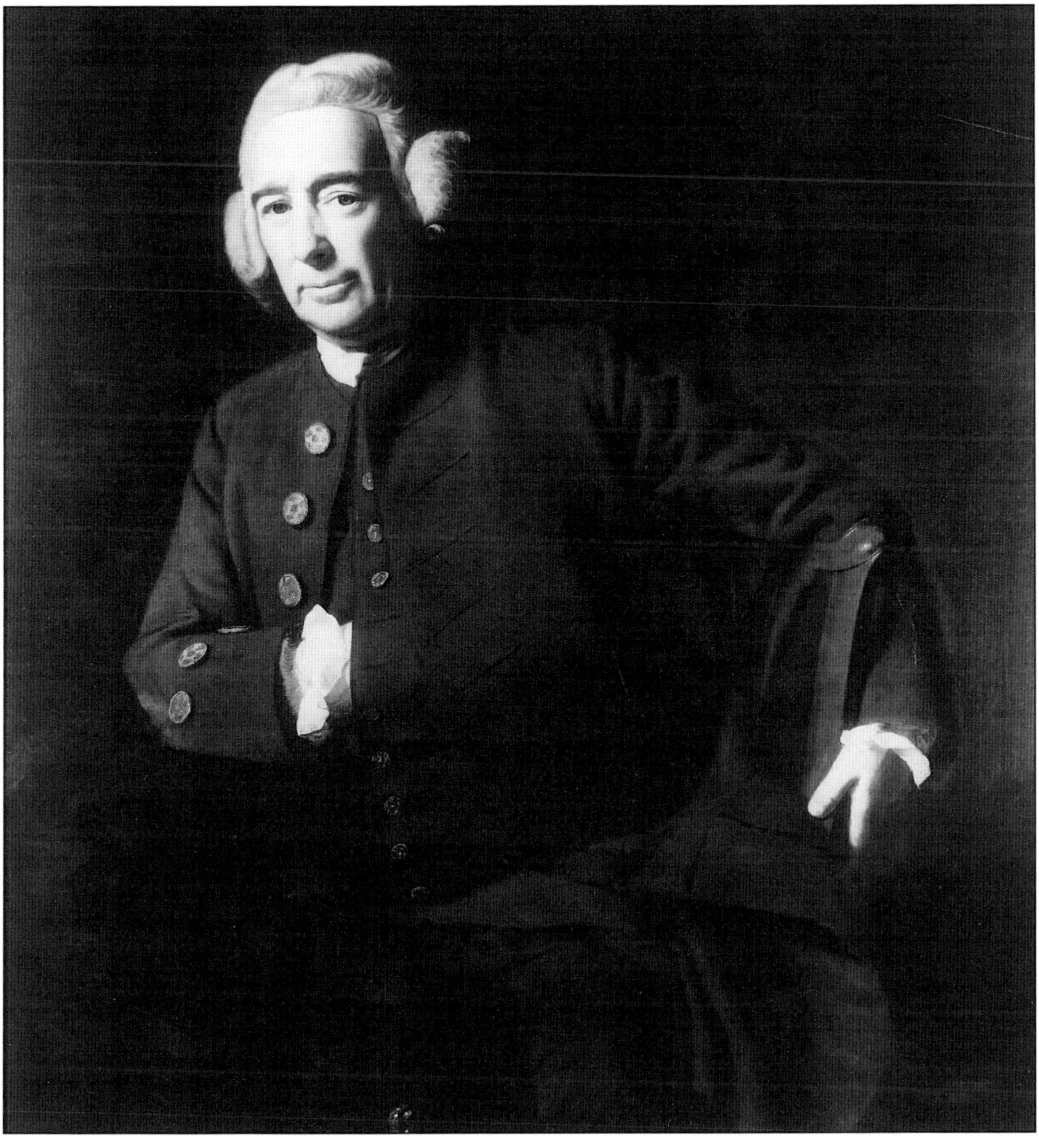

Dr. Silvester Gardiner (1708–1786) appears in this portrait by J.S. Copley at the age of sixty-four in1772 at the height of his career as a successful doctor and businessman who by some accounts was the was the wealthiest man in America. Born into a prosperous land-owning family in South Kingston, Rhode Island, he went abroad in 1727 to study medicine in Paris and soon after his return established himself as the leading surgeon in the American colonies. He performed the first successful surgery for the removal of kidney stones in Boston and became the largest importer of pharmaceutical supplies in New England. With other prominent Boston merchants, he became a large investor in the Kennebec Proprietors, the land company which brought settlers to the Kennebec River valley. As a staunch supporter of the King and the Church of England when the American Revolution began, he cast his lot with the established order and soon entered exile in England when his lands were confiscated. His son-in-law found a flaw in the legal proceedings taking away his land and reversed the doctor's sentence of banishment. In 1786 he returned to Newport, Rhode Island, ready to reclaim his lands; but broken in health, he soon died, leaving the large estate in Maine to his four-year-old grandson.

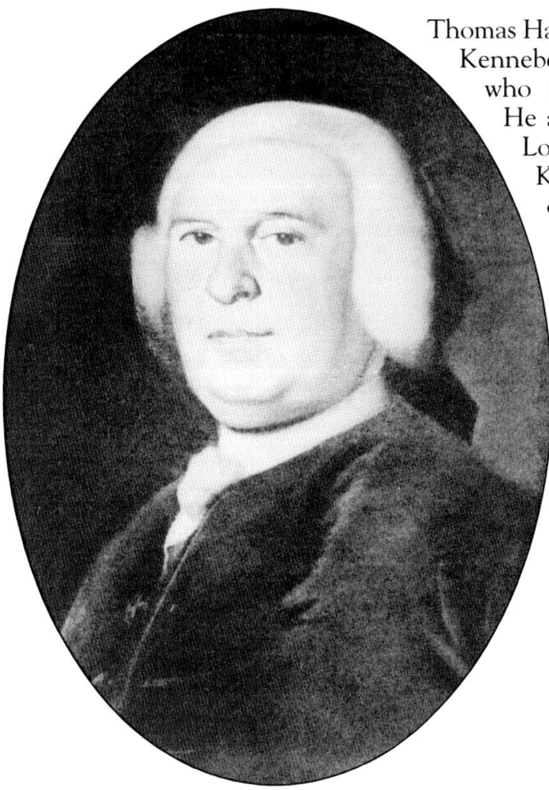

Thomas Hancock (1703–1764) was a Boston merchant, Kennebec Proprietor, and the uncle of John Hancock, who signed the Declaration of Independence. He and Dr. Gardiner exchanged parts of Great Lots 11 and 20 extending 5 miles in from the Kennebec River, consolidating Gardiner's lot on Cobbossee Stream and Hancock's lot in present-day Richmond and Farmingdale.

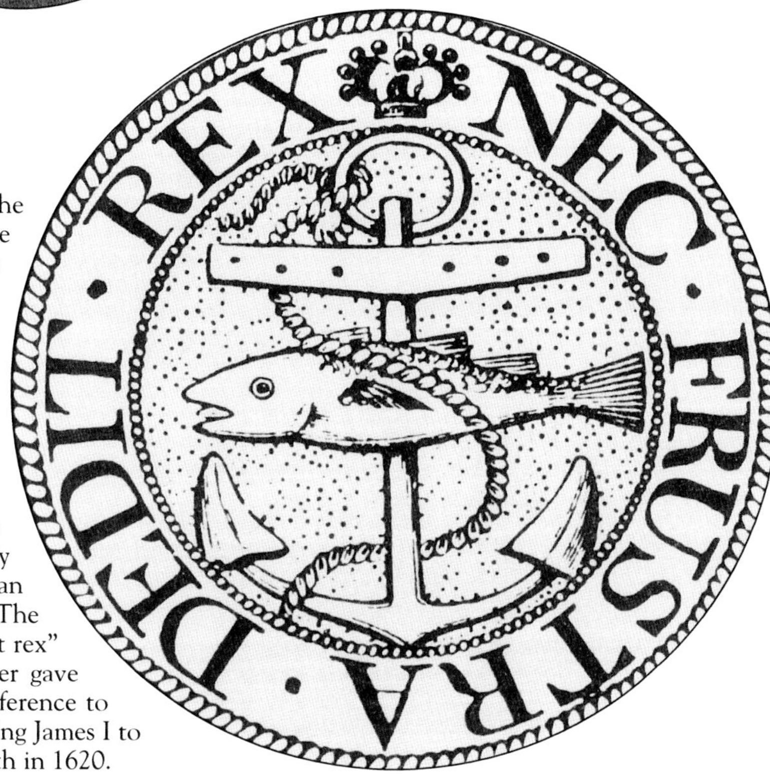

This seal of the Proprietors of the Kennebec Purchase from the late Colony of New Plymouth was affixed to all legal papers of the company, from 1749 until its dissolution 1816. The device on the shield recalls the principal sources of wealth in the early days of settlement: an anchor and codfish. The motto "Nec frusta dedit rex" means "The King never gave anything in vain," a reference to the original grant by King James I to the Council of Plymouth in 1620.

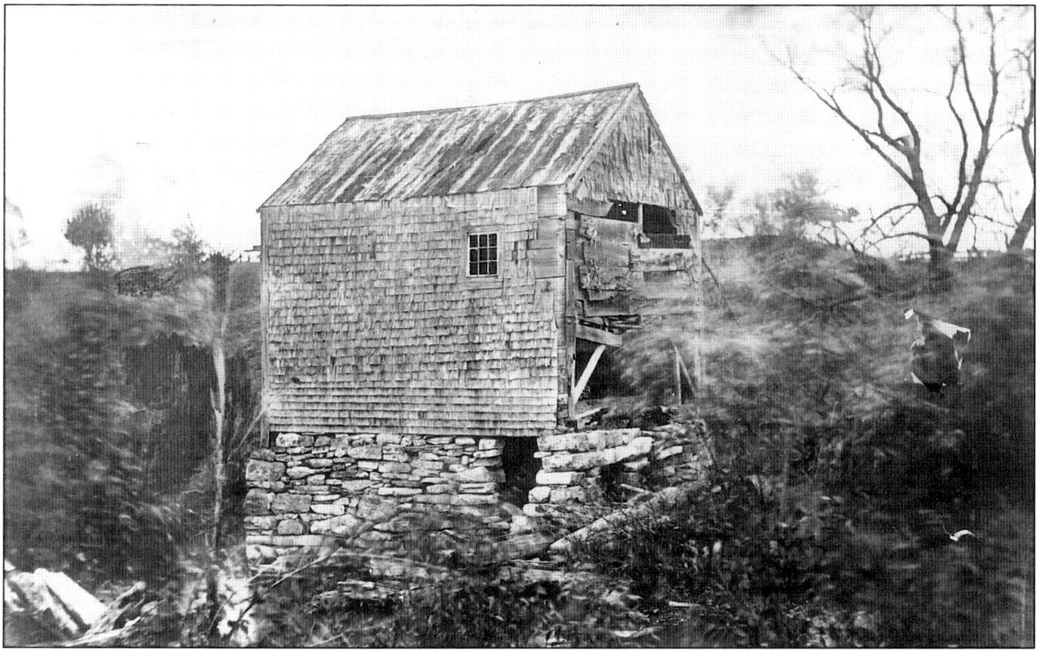

This gristmill, erected under the supervision of Dr. Silvester Gardiner in 1753, became one of the chief attractions drawing settlers to the area. It stood on the mill stream north of Dresden Mills and was powered by water from a flume near the dam. This and the sawmill below helped Dr. Gardiner to reap extra dividends from the Boston-based Kennebec Proprietors.

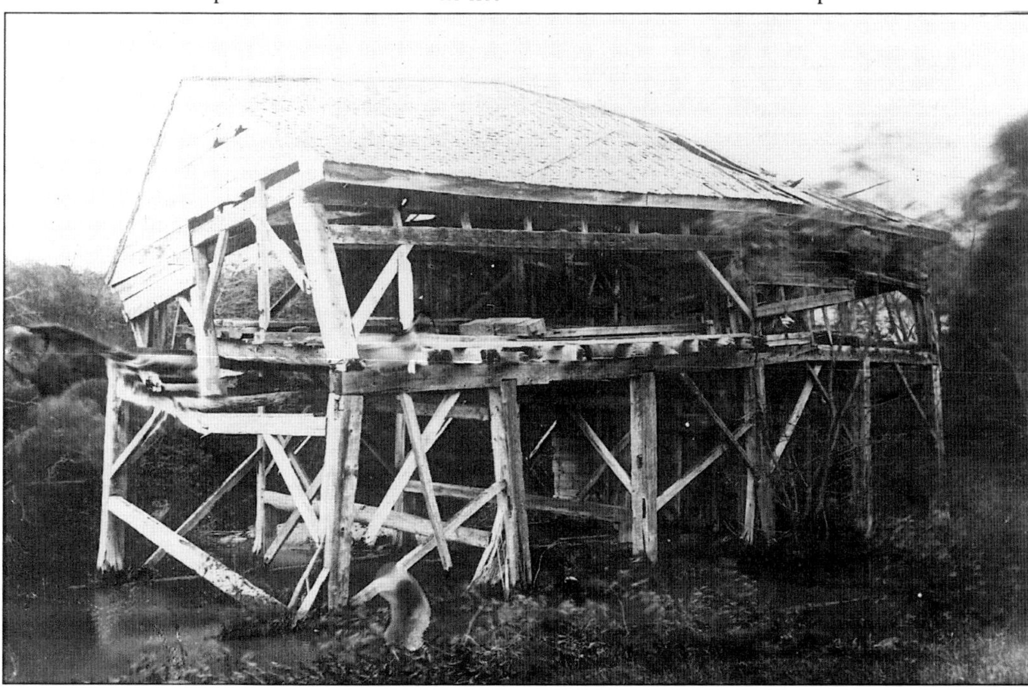

Dr. Gardiner built this sawmill near the mouth of the mill stream at Dresden Mills in 1753. Fortunately, in 1860, Aaron B. Houdlett photographed it and the gristmill at the top of the page before they collapsed.

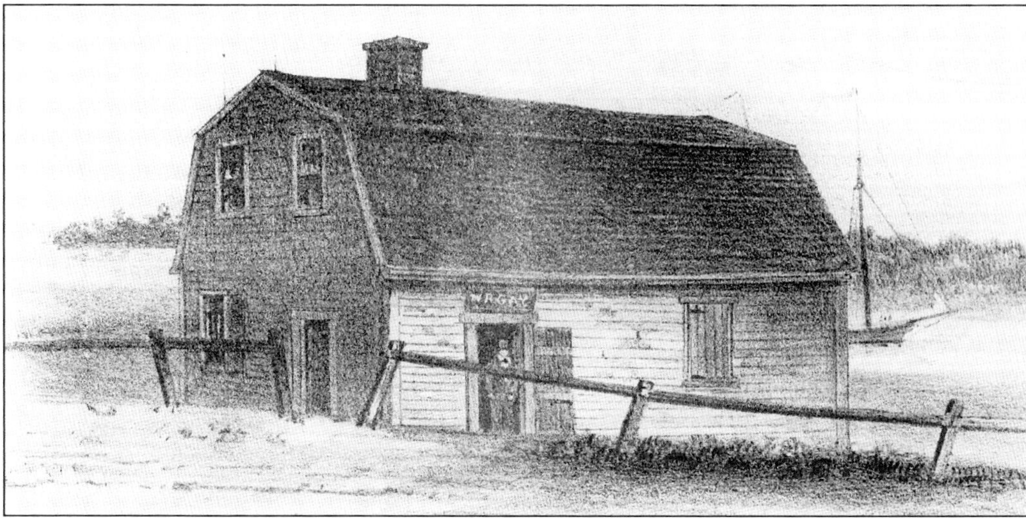

Gardiner's "Old Post Office" was built in 1763 by Dr. Silvester Gardiner at the foot of Vine Street. At the time of its demolition in May 1882, it was the oldest building in the city. This gambrel-roofed house became a post office in the 1790s, when its owner, Seth Gay, became postmaster. Originally, mail came by packet up the river in summer and monthly in winter by a man on snowshoes. In 1803, it took a rider on horseback three and a half days to bring the mail from Boston by way of New Gloucester and Wiscasset; in 1799, it took eighteen days for news of Washington's death to reach Gardiner.

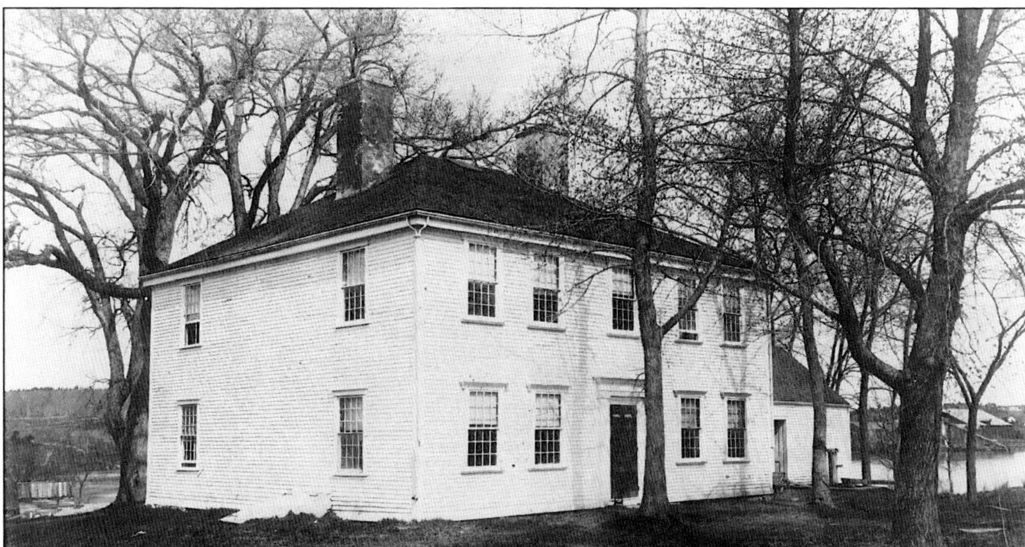

Among those who settled in the Kennebec Valley was the young Jonathan Bowman, a 1755 Harvard graduate and nephew of the powerful Thomas Hancock of Boston. Hancock's influence probably resulted in Bowman's appointments as collector of excise, register of probate, register of deeds, clerk of the court of common pleas, and justice of the peace for Lincoln County. In 1762, Bowman commissioned Gershom Flagg of Boston to build this fine Georgian-style house on the Kennebec River a short distance below the Pownalborough Court House in Dresden. The elegance of the Bowman House reflects Flagg's talent as a Colonial designer and builder.

This silhouette depicts Reverend Jacob Bailey (1731–1818), the "Frontier Missionary" who was a major factor in Dr. Gardiner's colonizing efforts. A bright lad from rural Rowley, Massachusetts, Bailey found his way, despite poverty, to Harvard, where he graduated in 1755. In 1760, he was ordained in London to serve the missions on the Kennebec River. He first conducted services for Dr. Gardiner's band of settlers in the fort on Church Hill in April 1763 and established St. Anne's Church in Gardinerston in 1771. When the Revolution broke out, he refused to omit prayers for the King of England and fled to Nova Scotia, where he served as rector of Annapolis until his death.

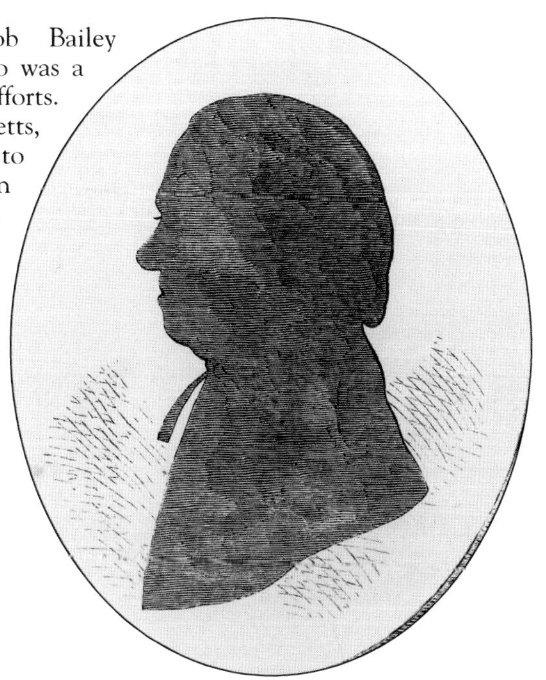

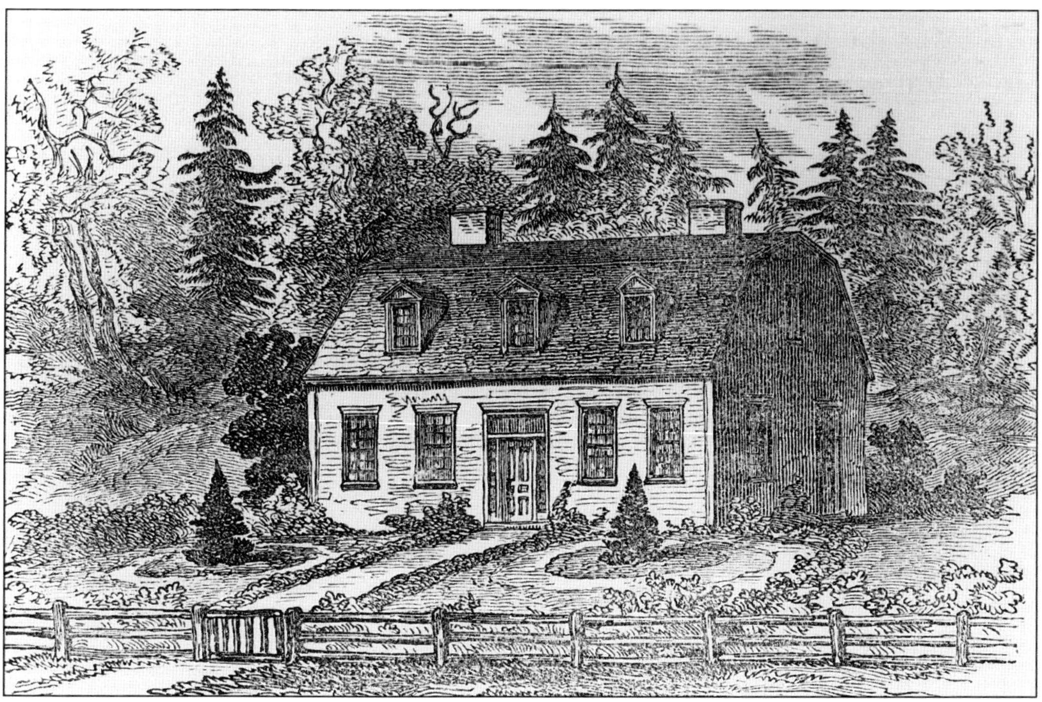

The parsonage of Reverend Jacob Bailey was in Dresden and attached to St. John's parish, which he helped to establish in 1770. From this outpost, he traveled regularly to many congregations gathered along the Kennebec from Georgetown to the "Fort," now Augusta. In rare moments of leisure, he composed poetry and bred flowers which still bear his name. Now only a marker indicates the parsonage site in Dresden, which has been reclaimed by the forest.

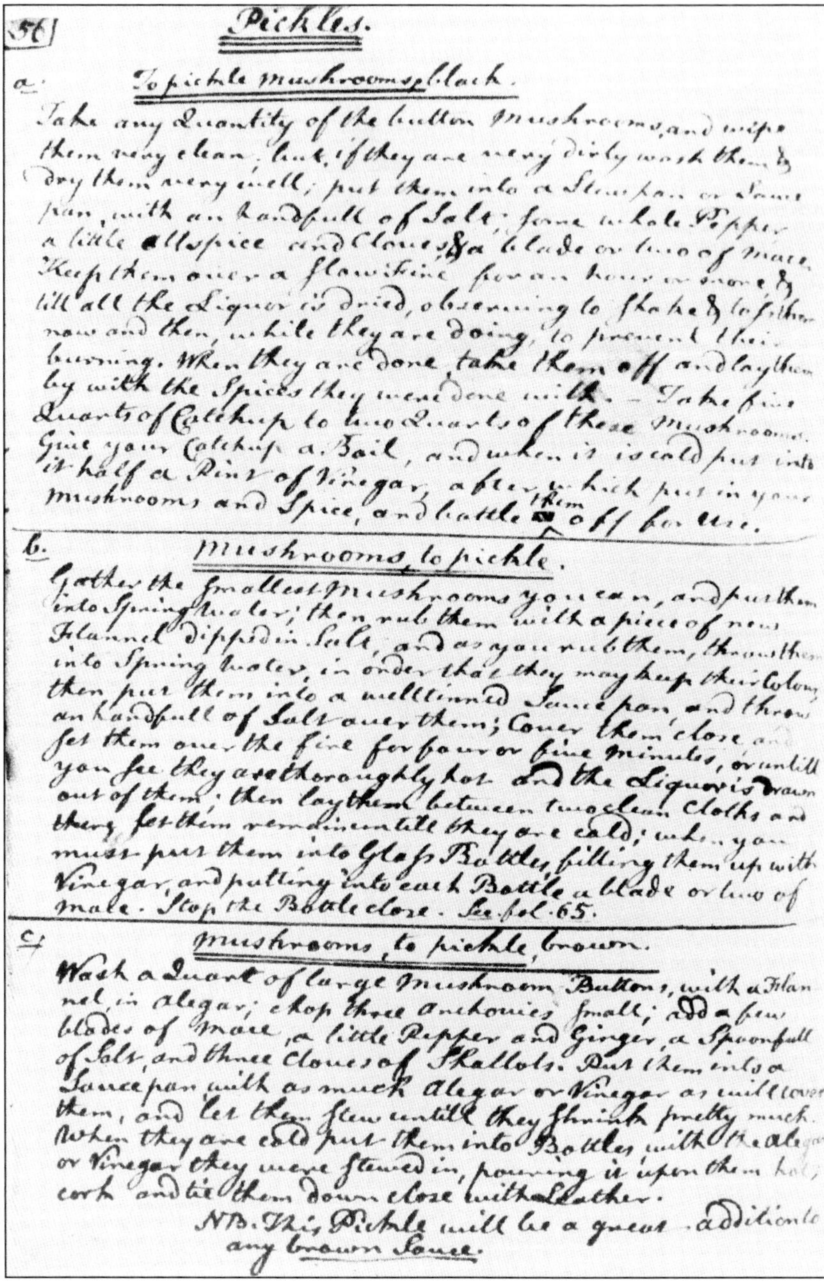
56 Pickles.

a: To pickle mushrooms black.

Take any Quantity of the button Mushrooms, and wipe them very clean, but, if they are very dirty wash them & dry them very well; put them into a Stewpan or Saucepan, with an handfull of Salt, some whole Pepper, a little Allspice and Cloves, & a blade or two of mace. Keep them over a slow Fire for an hour or more & till all the Liquor is dried, observing to shake & to stir them now and then, while they are doing, to prevent their burning. When they are done, take them off and lay them by with the Spices they were done with. — Take five Quarts of Catchup to two Quarts of these mushrooms. Give your Catchup a Boil, and when it is cold put into it half a Pint of Vinegar, after which put in your mushrooms and Spice, and bottle them off for use.

b. Mushrooms, to pickle.

Gather the smallest Mushrooms you can, and put them into Spring water; then rub them with a piece of new Flannel dipped in Salt, and as you rub them, throw them into Spring water, in order that they may keep their Colour; then put them into a well tinned Saucepan, and throw an handfull of Salt over them; Cover them close and set them over the fire for four or five minutes, or untill you see they are thoroughly hot and the Liquor is drawn out of them: then lay them between two clean Cloths and there let them remain untill they are cold; when you must put them into Glass Bottles, filling them up with Vinegar, and putting into each Bottle a blade or two of mace. Stop the Bottle close. See fol. 65.

c. Mushrooms, to pickle, brown.

Wash a Quart of large Mushroom Buttons, with a Flannel, in Alegar; chop three Anchovies small; add a few blades of mace, a little Pepper and Ginger, a Spoonfull of Salt, and three Cloves of Shallots. Put them into a Saucepan with as much Alegar or Vinegar as will cover them, and let them stew untill they shrink pretty much. When they are cold put them into Bottles with the Alegar or Vinegar they were stewed in, pouring it upon them hot; cork and tie them down close with Leather.

N.B. This Pickle will be a great addition to any brown Sauce.

A page from Mrs. *Gardiner's Receipts from 1763* for pickled mushrooms ("receipts" is the old term for recipes). This cookbook reflects the relentless efficiency of Anne Gibbins Gardiner as she presided over a busy doctor's household of nine children and a vast array of celebrated guests. She included receipts for soups, broths, gravies, sauces, fish, shellfish, pickles, hams, vinegars, mushrooms, catsups, pies, puddings, and cider wines. Her receipt for Portable Soup, the forerunner of today's soup mixes, rendered dried soup cakes which her husband took with him on his extended trips to the Kennebec River. Another interesting receipt is for Ox Cheek Soup. Never one to leave anything to chance, she even included instructions for the proper cultivation of mushrooms.

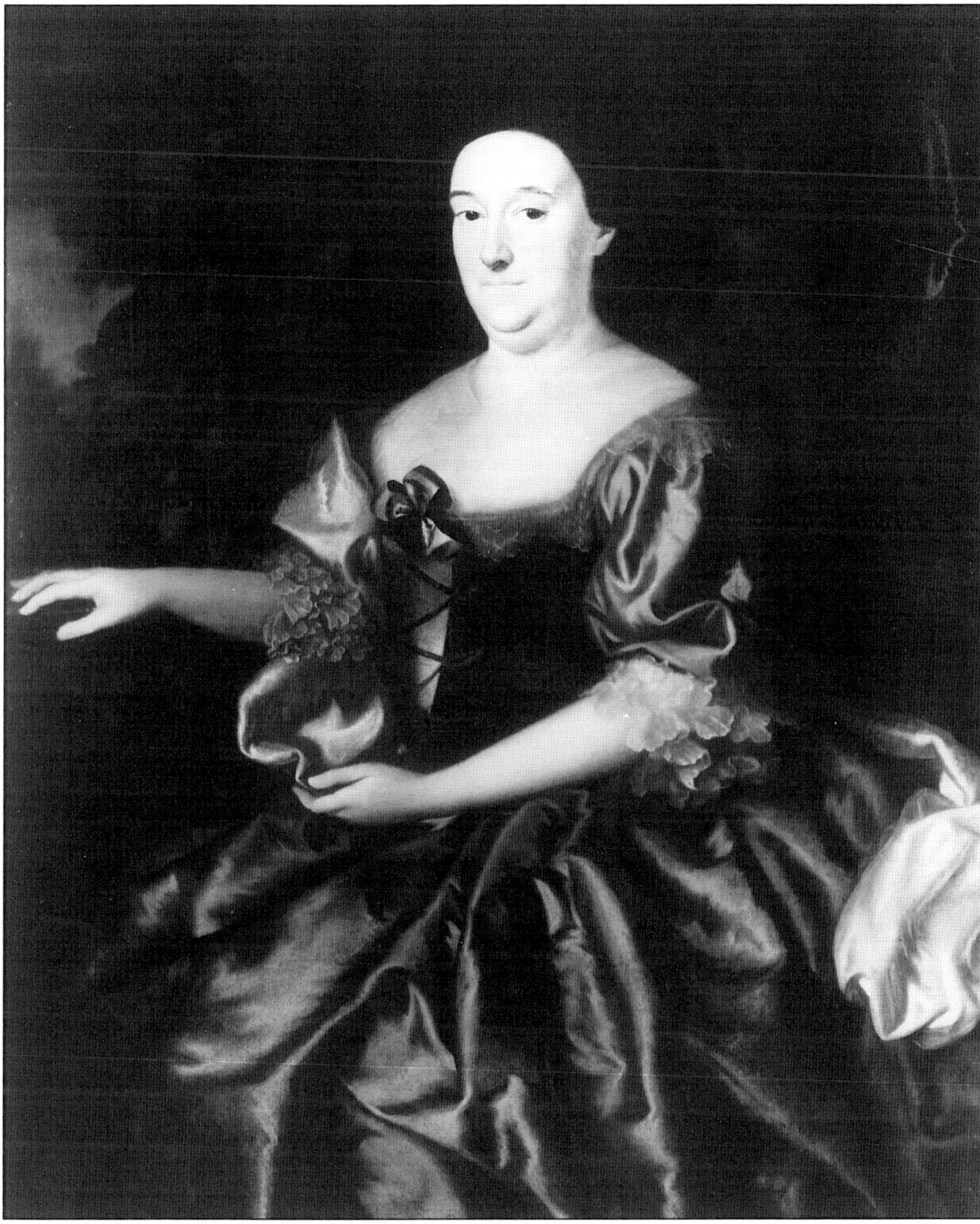

Anne Gibbins Gardiner (1712–1771) was the first of Dr. Silvester Gardiner's three wives, and the mother of all his nine children. This portrait, although long-attributed to Copley, is now recognized as the work of Joseph Blackburn. The subject was the daughter of Dr. John Gibbins, who was, previous to Dr. Gardiner, the leading physician in Boston. With the death of her only brother, John Gibbins, a youth of great promise who had graduated from Harvard in 1740, Anne became the sole heiress to her family's fortune, which consolidated her husband's position in the business and social circles in Boston.

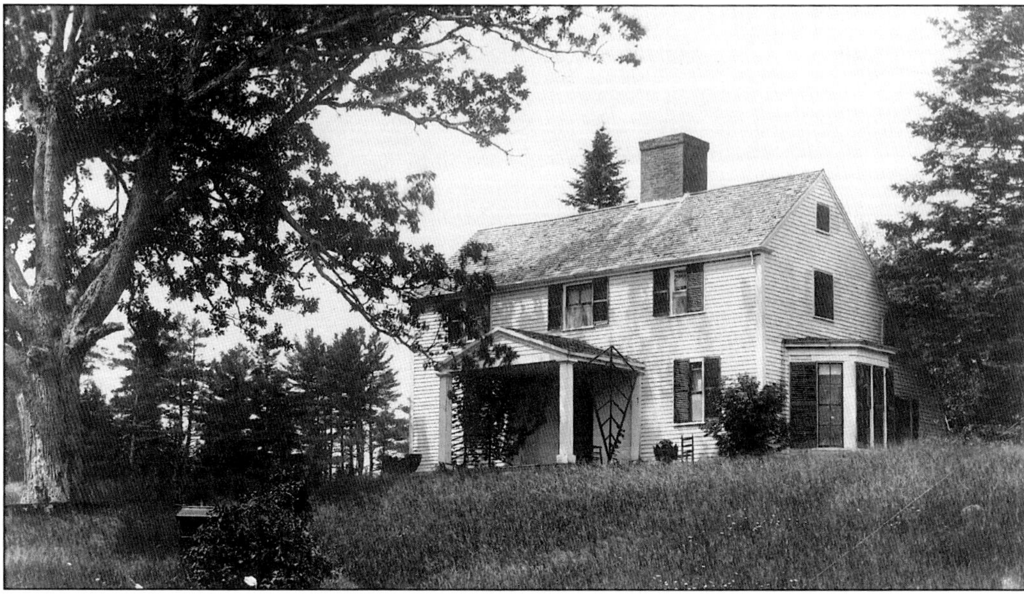

The Dumaresq House, on Swan Island in the Kennebec River, was built by Dr. Silvester Gardiner in 1763, as one of his residences when he came to Maine during the summers to develop his vast land holdings. He bequeathed it to his daughter Rebecca, who married Philip Dumaresq. Their descendants in the Perkins line bestowed their name onto the town comprising the land area of the island. This house and others on the island are now preserved in a state wildlife refuge area.

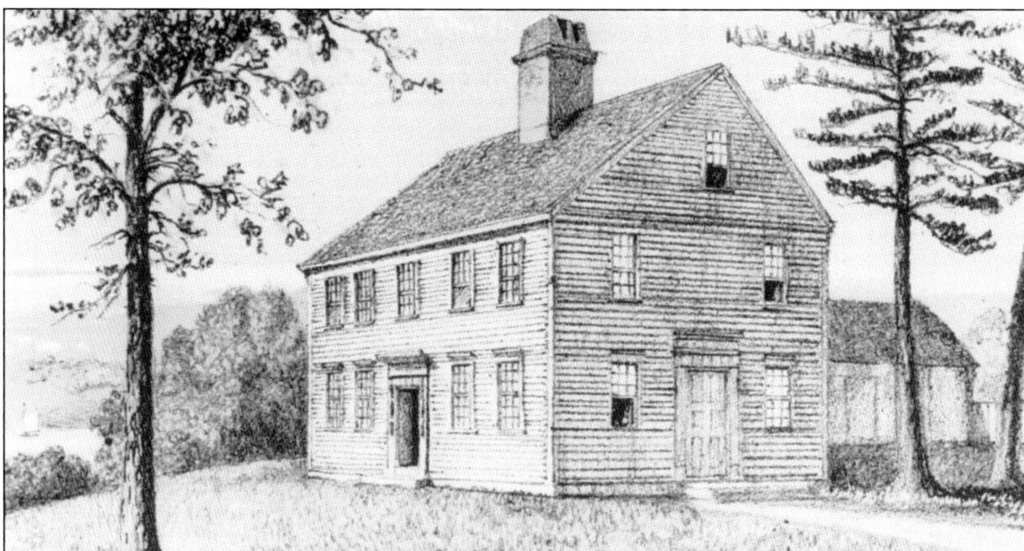

Artist Edwin Whitefield included this view of the Major Reuben Colburn House in Pittston in the 1886 edition of his book, *The Homes of Our Forefathers*. Located just off Route 27, this substantial central-chimnied Colonial house was built in 1765. Acquired by the State of Maine in 1973, the Colburn House is the headquarters of the Arnold Expedition Historical Society. The Colburn boatyard, behind the house on the Kennebec River, was commissioned by George Washington to build the 220 bateaux used by Colonel Benedict Arnold and his army of 1,100 on their ill-fated march to Quebec in 1775.

Robert Hallowell (1739–1818) was the son of Benjamin Hallowell, for whom the city of Hallowell is named. In 1772, when this wealthy Boston merchant and collector of customs married Hannah Gardiner, daughter of Dr. Silvester Gardiner, he united the two largest land interests in the Kennebec Valley. After Dr. Gardiner's death, Robert managed the Gardiner estate until his son Robert, the sole heir of the estate, came of age and changed his surname to Gardiner.

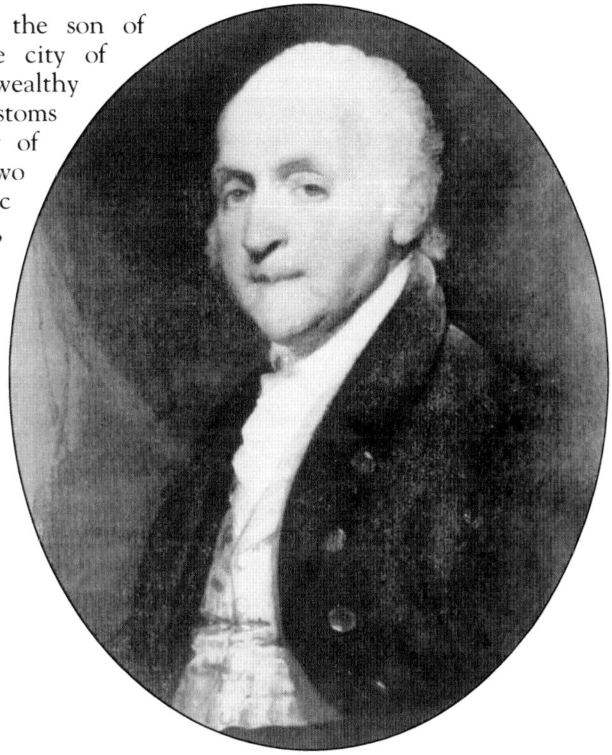

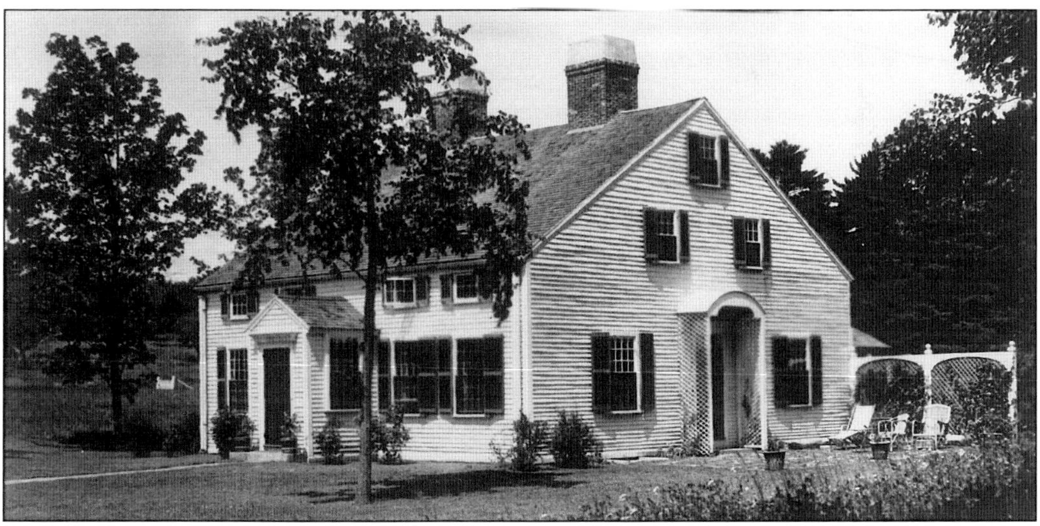

Built in 1796, in what is now Randolph, this large cape was designed by Charles Vaughan for Dr. Silvester Gardiner's son-in-law, Robert Hallowell. Hallowell used the house during the summer visits which brought him from Boston to manage the Gardiner holdings. When his son, Robert Hallowell Gardiner, inherited his grandfather's property in 1803, the house became the family residence until the first Oaklands was constructed in 1810. At that time, the Hallowell House left the family, only to be reacquired in 1927, dismantled, and rebuilt across the Kennebec River at Oaklands, where it stands today. This photograph shows the house a few years after the 1927 move, which was supervised by Henry R. Shepley of the Boston architectural firm of Coolidge, Shepley, Bulfinch, and Abbott.

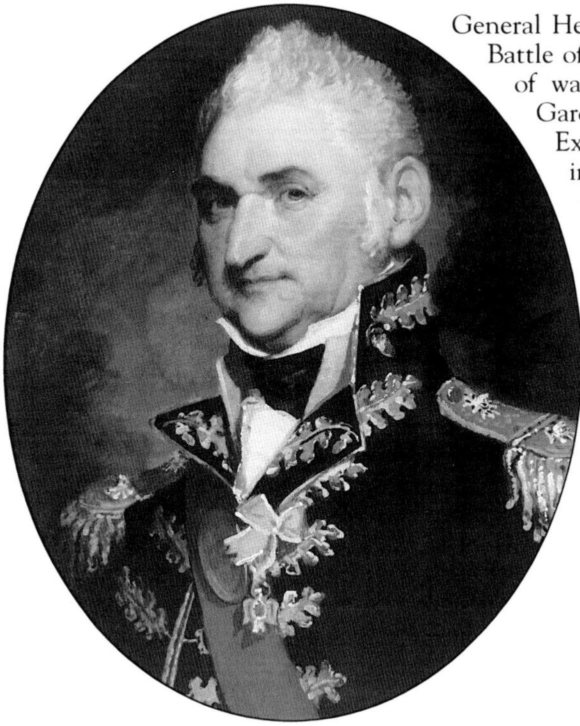

General Henry Dearborn (1751–1829), hero of the Battle of Monmouth, congressman, and secretary of war under Thomas Jefferson, first visited Gardiner while an officer in the Arnold Expedition to Quebec. In 1783, he settled in Gardiner, building a house on the site of the present library. He was known as a "law and order man," erecting a whipping post at a point midway between the sites of the future library and city hall. In 1793, when he became active in national affairs, his association with Gardiner faded, although many of his step-children and their families remained prominent in the community for decades.

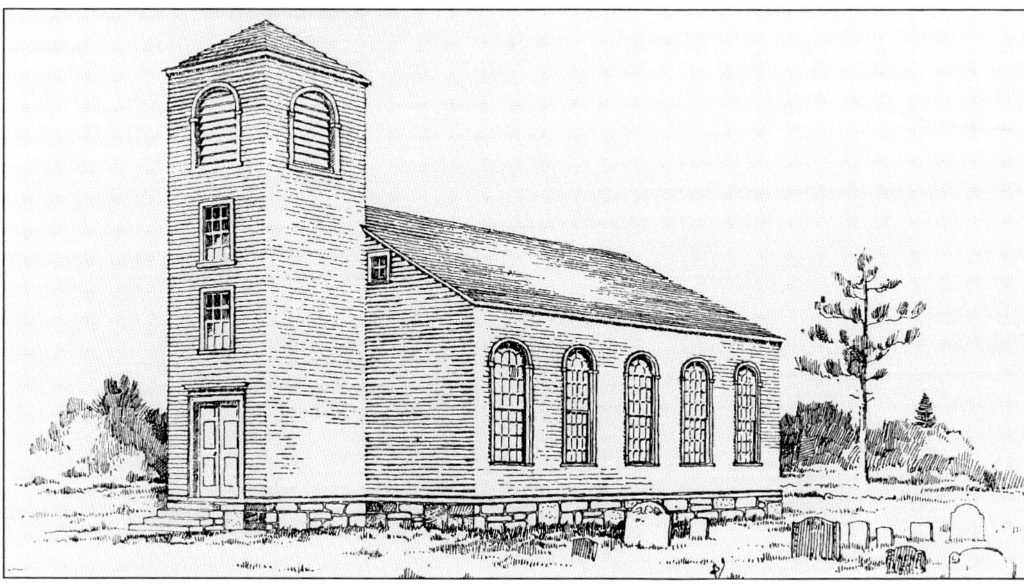

St. Anne's Church was the original name of Christ Church parish, and this second building, erected in 1793, stood about 200 feet south of the present stone building. In 1772, Jacob Bailey dedicated the first St. Anne building, but it was left uncompleted during the Revolution. Dr. Gardiner's will provided for its completion, which was nearly done when it was destroyed by fire. The congregation rebuilt the above church, which continued to be used until 1820, when the stone building was built for an expanded congregation. The parish leased the old building to the town of Gardiner for use as the town hall. On July 4, 1834, drunken merrymakers burned this building, and the land on which it stood reverted to Christ Church.

Two

Squire Gardiner's Town 1803–1849

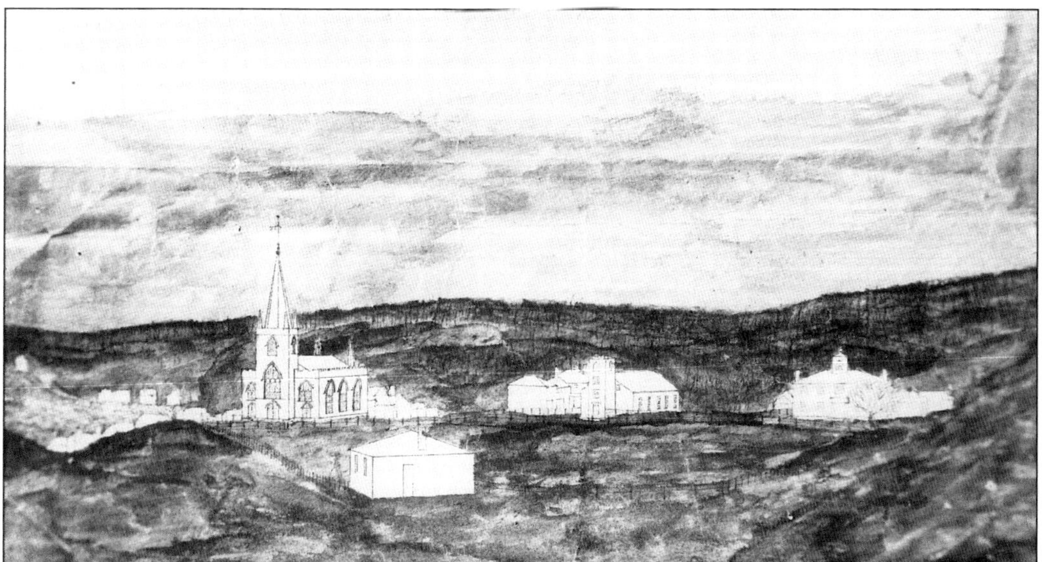

In 1824, Robert Hallowell Gardiner I gave a 5-acre Common to the community with the stipulation that it be well-maintained for public use. Four years later, Allyn Holmes made this drawing of the Common, showing, from left to right: Christ Church, a schoolhouse, the Silas Holman House, St. Anne's Church, and the Lyceum. Gardiner reclaimed the Common in 1843 because of the town's failure to meet the terms of his gift. After some work, the Common was soon reinstated to municipal ownership and still serves as the community's principal park.

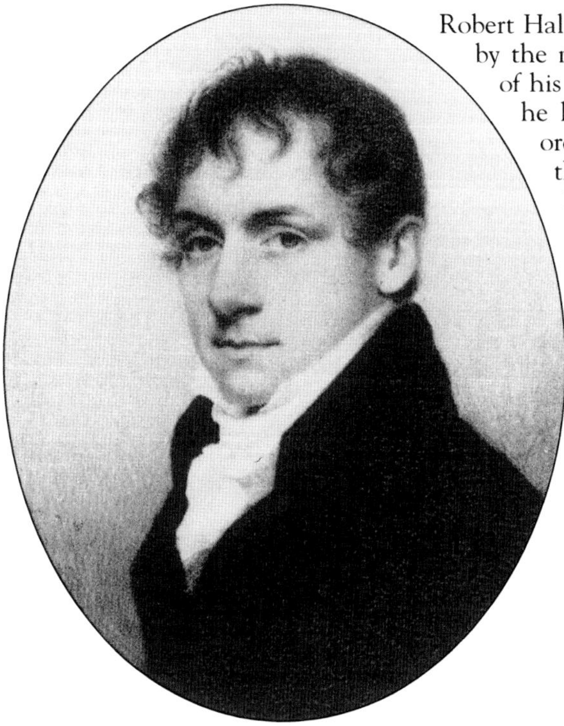

Robert Hallowell Gardiner I (1782–1864), as painted by the miniaturist E.G. Malbone, about the time of his marriage to Emma Tudor. Shortly before, he had changed his surname to Gardiner in order to inherit his grandfather's estate, and this portrait depicts the young squire as he started his six-decade-long career to develop his namesake community.

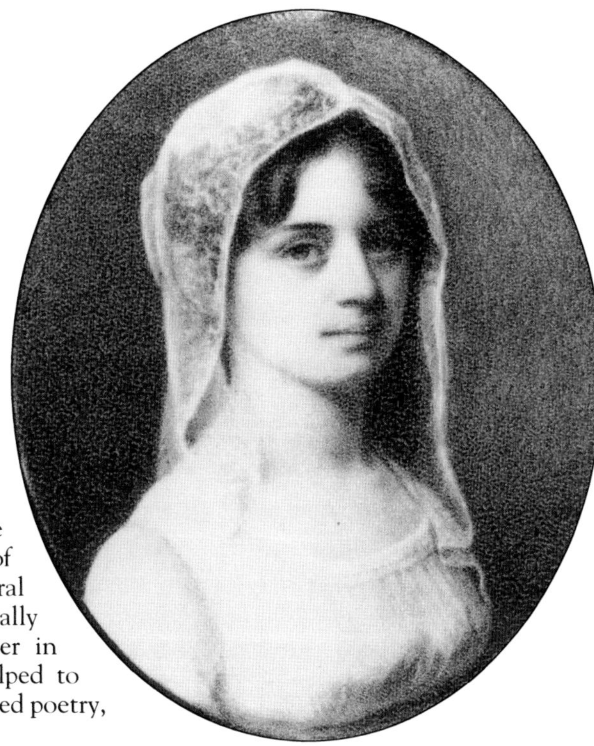

Emma Jane Tudor Gardiner (1785–1865), the wife of Robert Hallowell Gardiner I and the mother his nine children. She was the daughter of William Tudor, judge advocate general of the Continental Army who personally handed the commission as commander in chief to George Washington. She helped to design the interior of Oaklands, composed poetry, and painted in pastels.

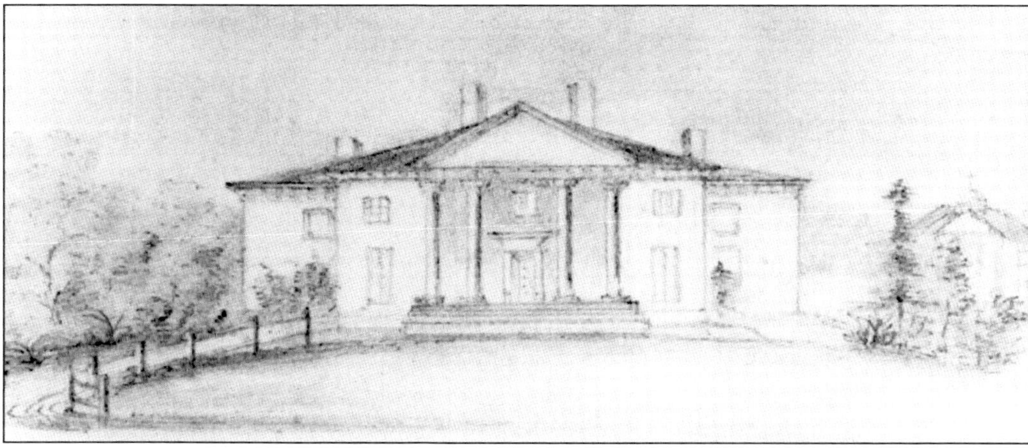

With a growing family and increasing social responsibilities, Robert Hallowell Gardiner I and his wife felt the need for a larger home than the Randolph cape where they had resided since their marriage in 1805. Gardiner framed his new home on 40 acres of land by the Kennebec, holding a traditional house-raising. Neighbors were rewarded for their help with generous amounts of food and drink. Named Oaklands, the stately, columned mansion, shown in this drawing by Emma Jane Gardiner, was completed in 1810. It served as the family residence until it burned in November 1834, to be replaced by the present house.

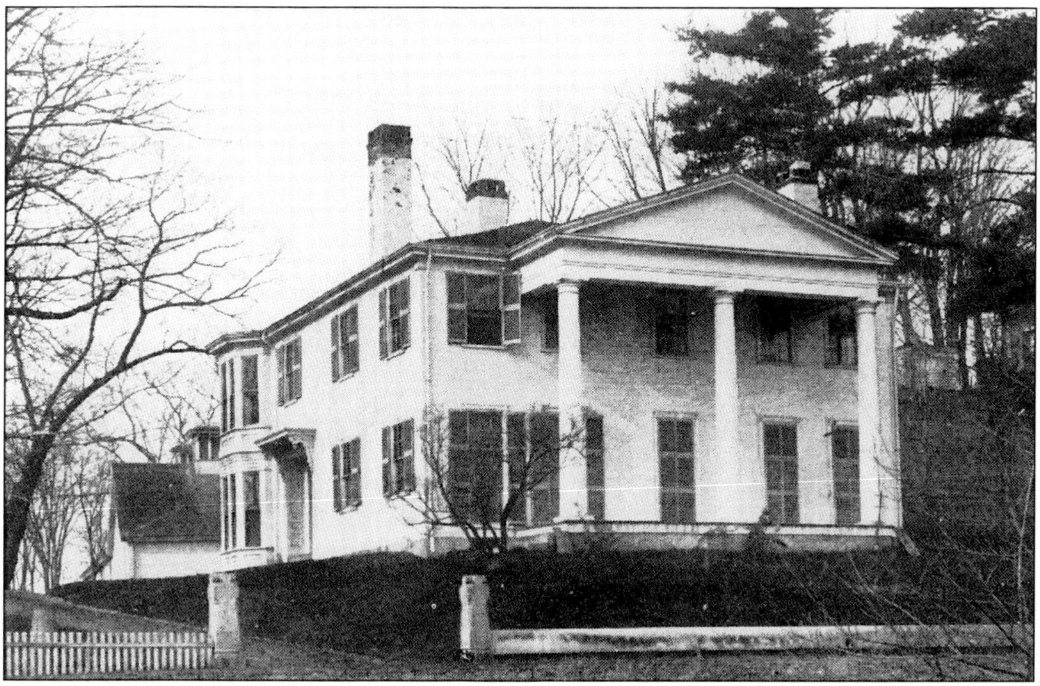

This *c*. 1806 Federal-style mansion with a graceful portico near the intersection of Bridge Street and Maine Avenue was torn down in 1966. Built for Barzillai Gannett (1764–1835), the district's congressman and ancestor of the newspaper family of that name, this impressive landmark was known as the Allen Mansion after its purchase in 1812 by Frederic Allen (1780–1865). He married Hannah Whipple, a lady of scientific and literary fame and a granddaughter of Dr. Silvester Gardiner. They and their six talented children drew many famous visitors to this city, including General Winfield Scott.

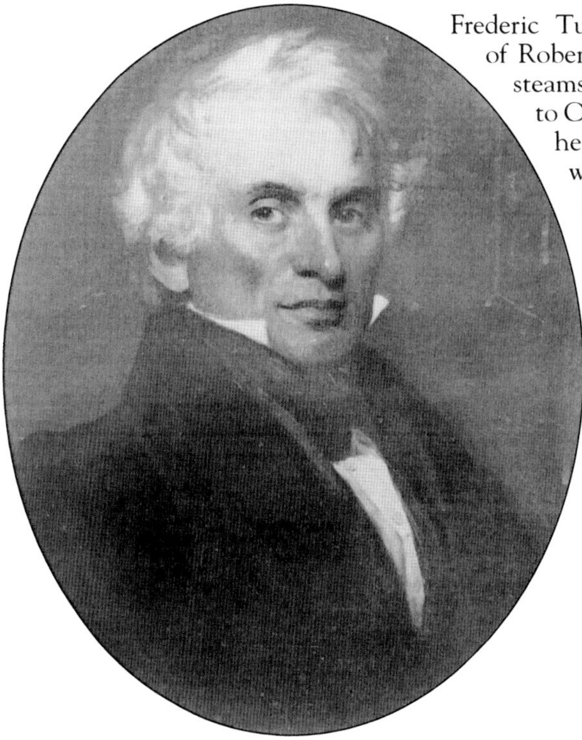

Frederic Tudor (1783–1864), brother of the wife of Robert Hallowell Gardiner I, was owner of a steamship which raced and beat one belonging to Commodore Vanderbilt. As the "Ice King," he started the export of ice to warm climates when people thought the idea crazy, but he persevered and acquired a fortune.

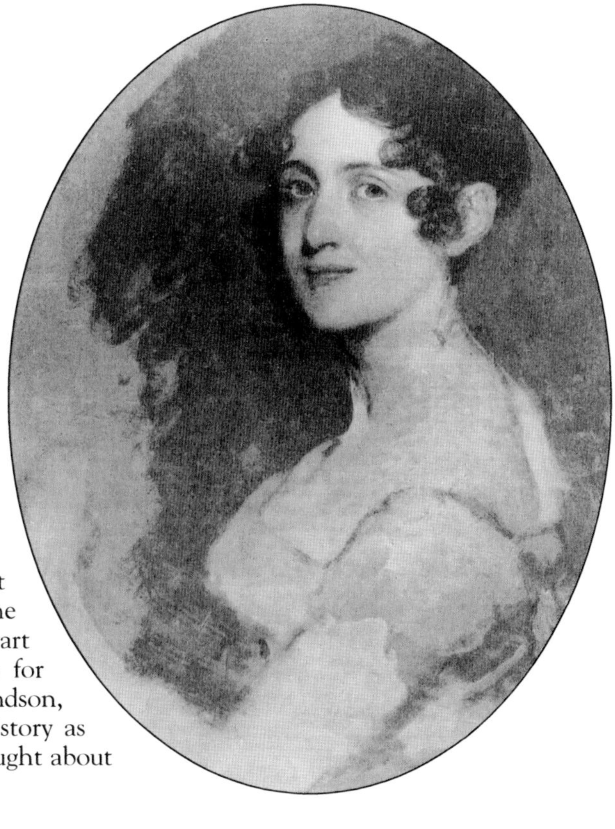

Delia Tudor (1787–1860), a sister of the wife of Robert Hallowell Gardiner I, married Commodore Charles Stewart of the U.S. Navy, in whose ship (and unknown to him) she smuggled the deposed president of Peru. After his court martial for the international crisis, Commodore Stewart divorced her. She fled to Oaklands for refuge with the Gardiners. Her grandson, Charles Stewart Parnell, known in history as the "Uncrowned King of Ireland," brought about many political reforms there.

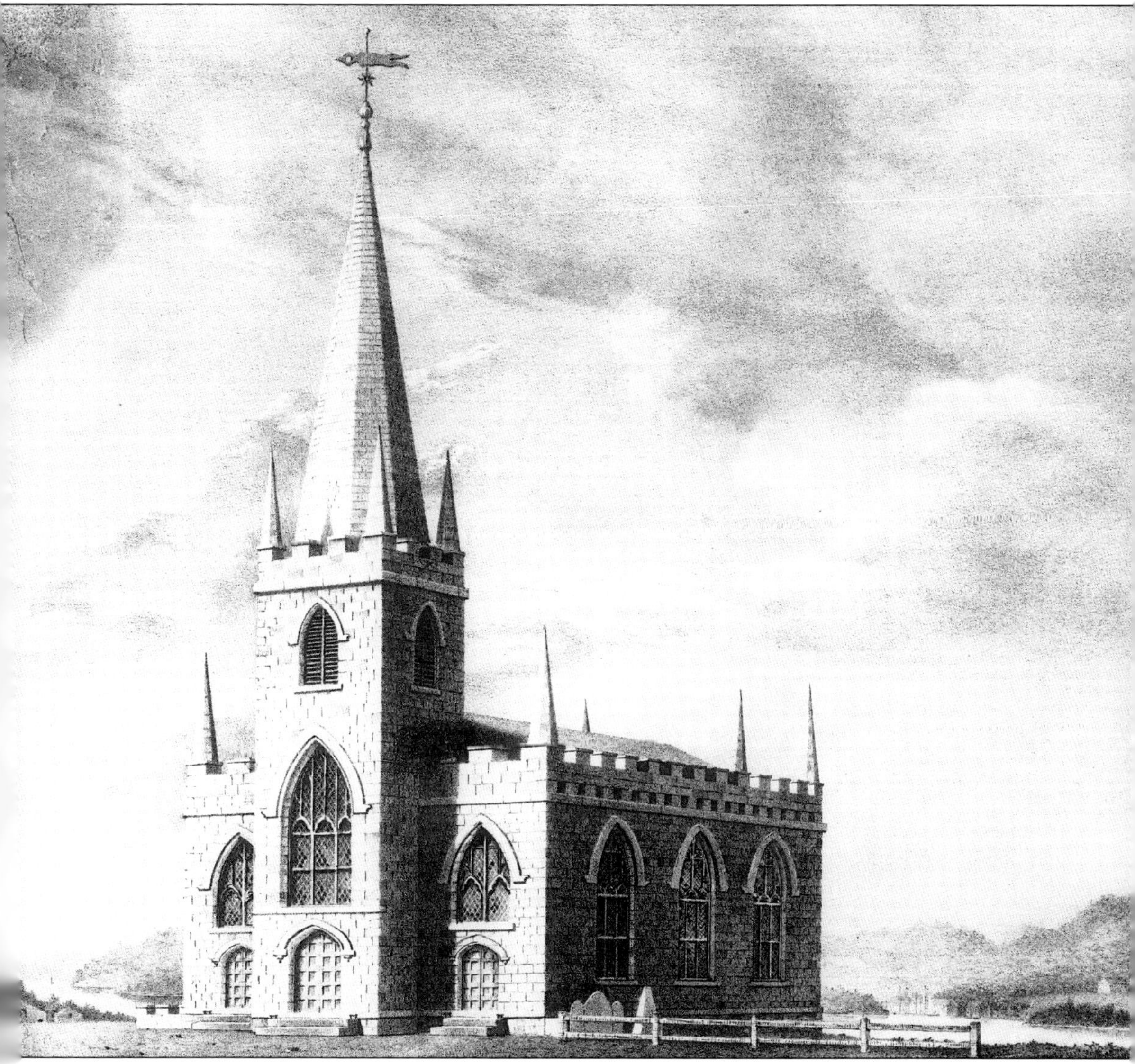

Facing the Common from its location at Dresden Avenue and Church Street, Christ Church is shown in this early lithograph as it appeared upon its completion in 1820. This Gardiner landmark is Maine's first stone church, its first example of ecclesiastical Gothic Revival architecture, its oldest Episcopal church in continuous use, and the original seat of the Diocese. The building was constructed at a cost of $14,571 through the efforts of Robert Hallowell Gardiner I, who obtained the plans from Reverend Samuel Farmar Jarvis of New York and furnished the granite from a quarry at Litchfield Neck on Cobbossee Stream. Both Gardiner and the Right Reverend George Burgess, the state's first Episcopal bishop, are buried in the adjacent churchyard.

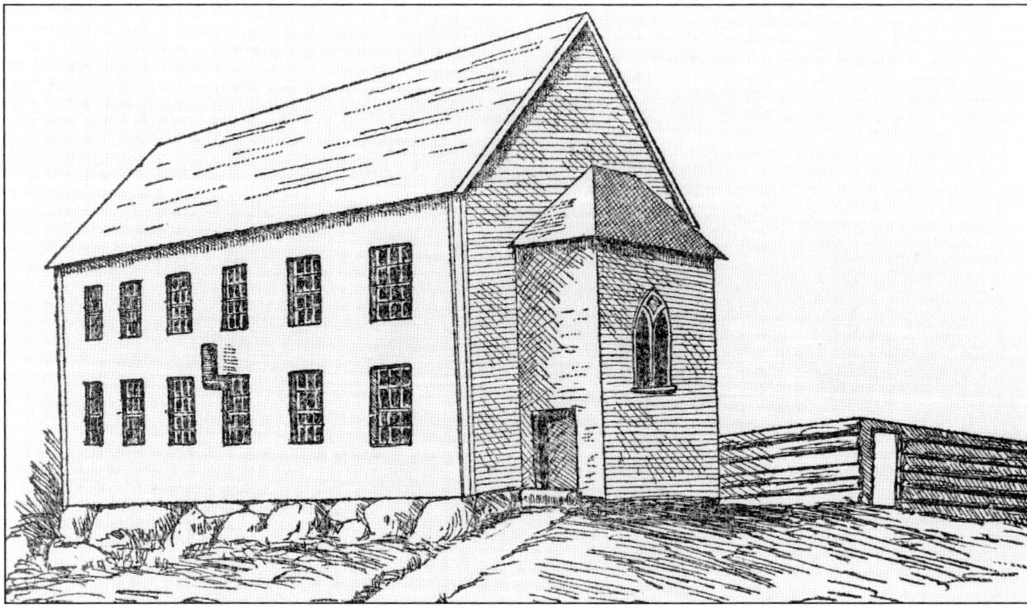

Within ten years after Jesse Lee preached the first Methodist sermon in Hallowell in 1793, Methodism had gained sufficient popularity in the area to erect a meetinghouse on Bowman Point opposite the end of Bowman Street in Farmingdale. Built in 1803, this two-story frame structure was clapboarded and shingled on the outside, but left unfinished on the inside. By 1828, flood damage and a population shift in the community forced the abandonment of the meetinghouse in favor of the new Methodist church on Highland Avenue.

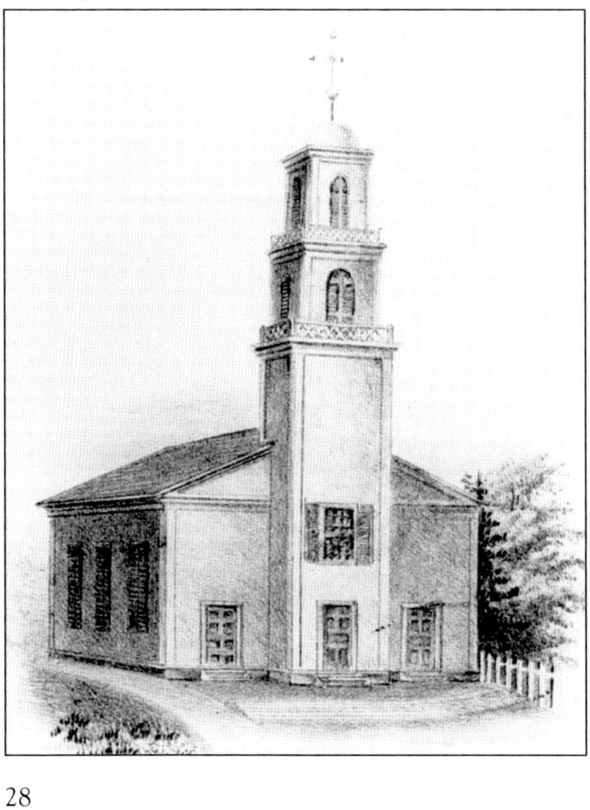

The Congregationalists built this Federal-style meetinghouse in 1836, across from the north side of the Common on land donated by Robert Hallowell Gardiner I. Extensively remodeled in 1889–90, the building was destroyed by fire in 1915. The site is now occupied by Christy's Convenience Store on Brunswick Avenue.

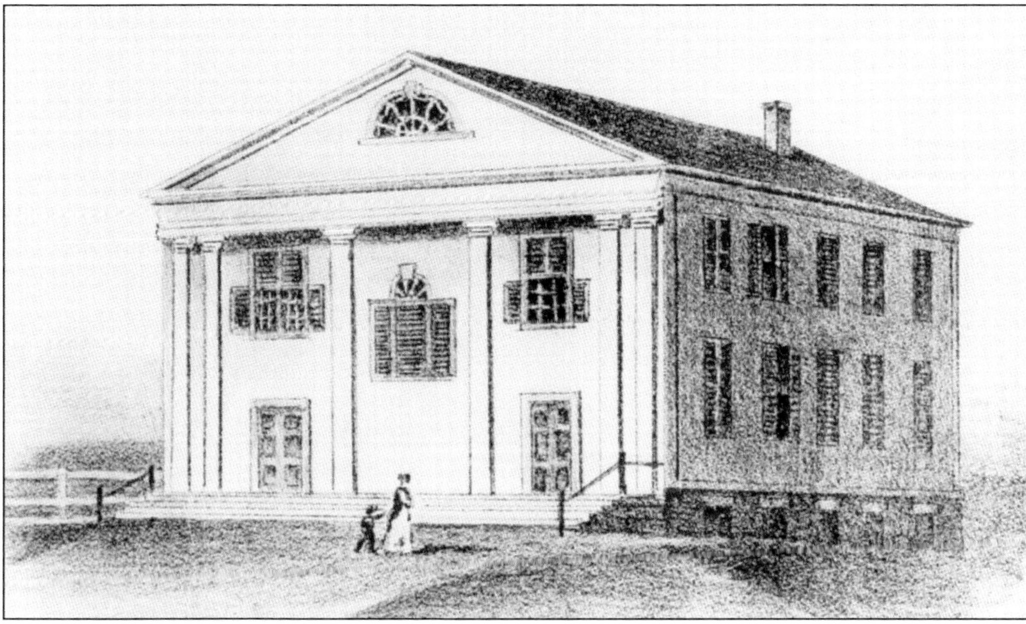

In 1828, the Methodists erected this transitional Federal-Greek Revival-style church on Highland Avenue. The master builder was Michael Woodward, who constructed the building for $3,500 on land donated by Robert Hallowell Gardiner I. The present clock tower and belfry were added in 1854, and the spire in 1867.

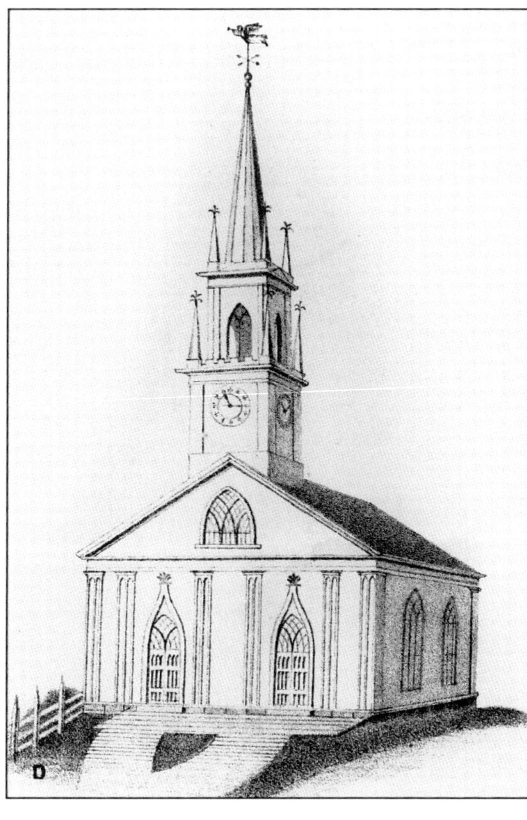

Since 1964, "The Yellow Church" on Church Street has been the home of the United Church of Christ-Congregational. Built in 1842 as a Universalist church, this handsome Gothic Revival building was probably the work of Anthony C. Raymond, a Bath architect and builder. The belfry and spire were removed in the 1920s.

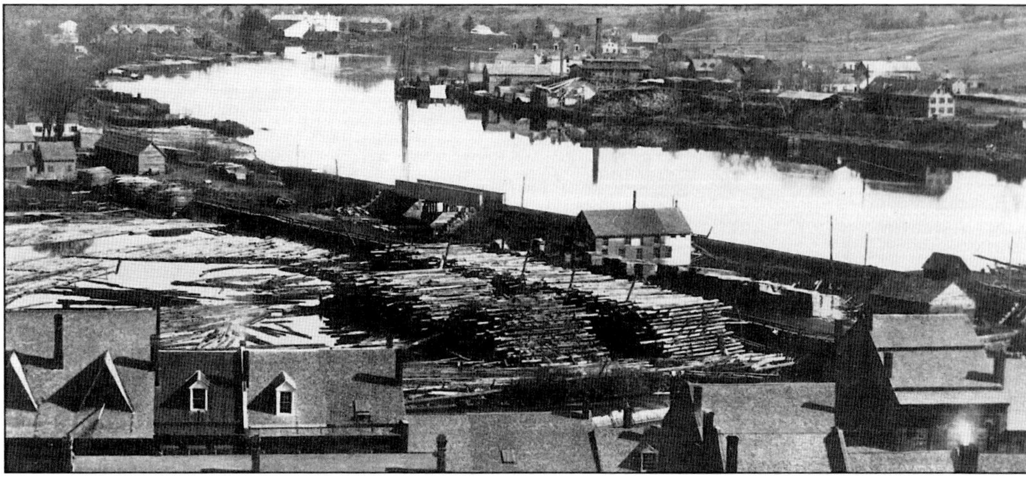

While this sweeping photograph of Gardiner's business district, the mill pond, the Kennebec River, and Randolph was taken in 1877, it pictures a scene largely unchanged since the 1840s. By that time, Water Street was lined with substantial brick commercial buildings, the roof tops of which appear in the foreground. At the center is the mill pond (now the Shop and Save parking lot), the holding area for thousands of logs which were floated down the Kennebec for processing in Gardiner's sawmills. The pond was separated from the river by a causeway which became Maine Avenue. The river banks are dotted with large ice houses, reflecting another of Gardiner's major industries.

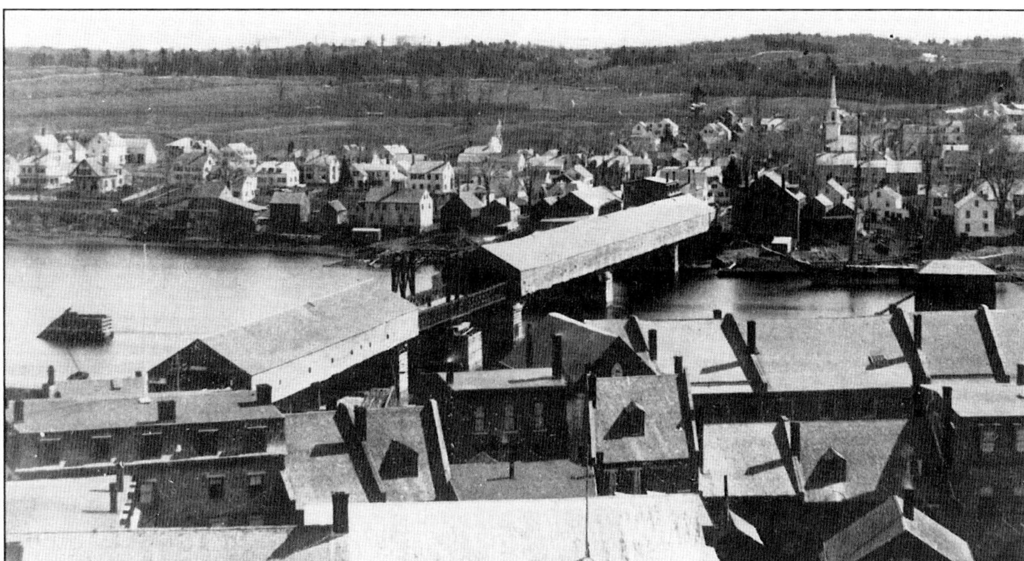

Taken in 1877, this panoramic photograph shows the south end of the Water Street commercial district in the foreground, the 899-foot covered bridge spanning the Kennebec, and the village of Pittston, now Randolph, on the opposite shore. The swing section on the 1853 bridge allowed vessels to pass upriver to Hallowell and Augusta. In 1860, Coolidge and Mansfield's *History and Description of New England* noted that "the village of Pittston is beautifully located on the bank of the Kennebec, has good water power, and is celebrated for the thrift and energy of its people. The principal occupations of the inhabitants are shipbuilding and agriculture."

During the 1830s and '40s Water Street became lined with three-story brick commercial blocks such as the ones shown here. This May 4, 1850 advertisement for George M. Atwood's bookstore appeared in a local newspaper, the *Kennebec Transcript*. Five years later, another Gardiner paper, the *Northern Home Journal* of January 4, 1855, commented on the growth of Water Street during the previous decade: "Thus the changes which have been accomplished by brick and mortar amount to something. The mercantile business, if the number of stores is a criterion, is much larger."

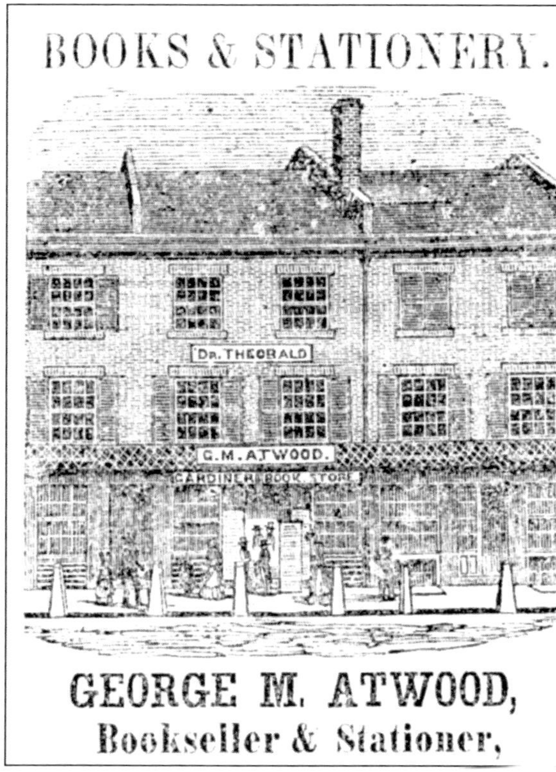

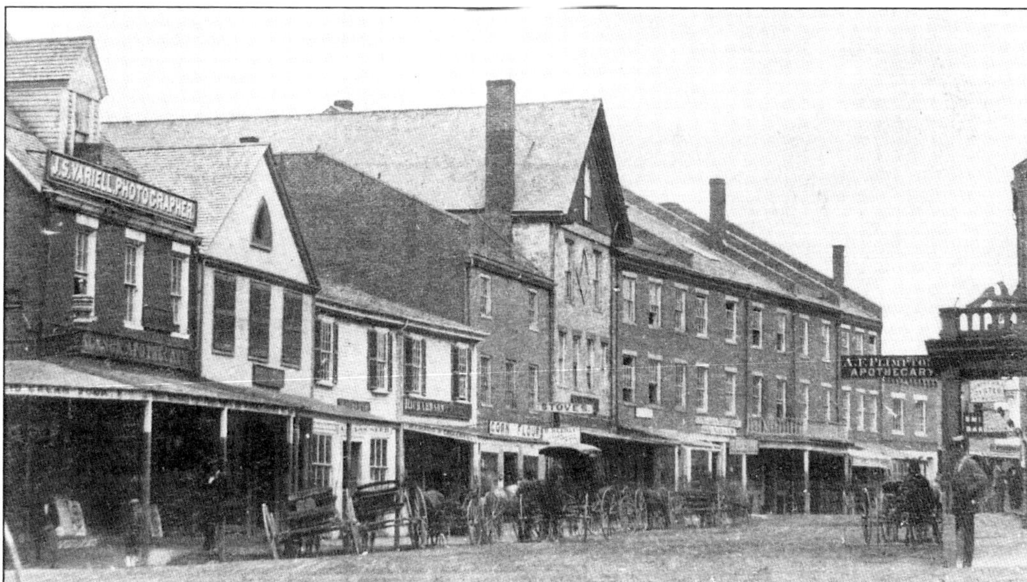

This 1870s photograph of the river side of Water Street from the intersection of Maine Avenue and Church Streets captures the business district's pre-Civil War appearance. At the left, the four modest frame and brick structures typify the commercial architecture of the first half of the nineteenth century. These structures, along with the adjacent Masonic Hall of 1855, were replaced in the 1890s. Only the row of three-story brick buildings from the 1840s at the right remains today.

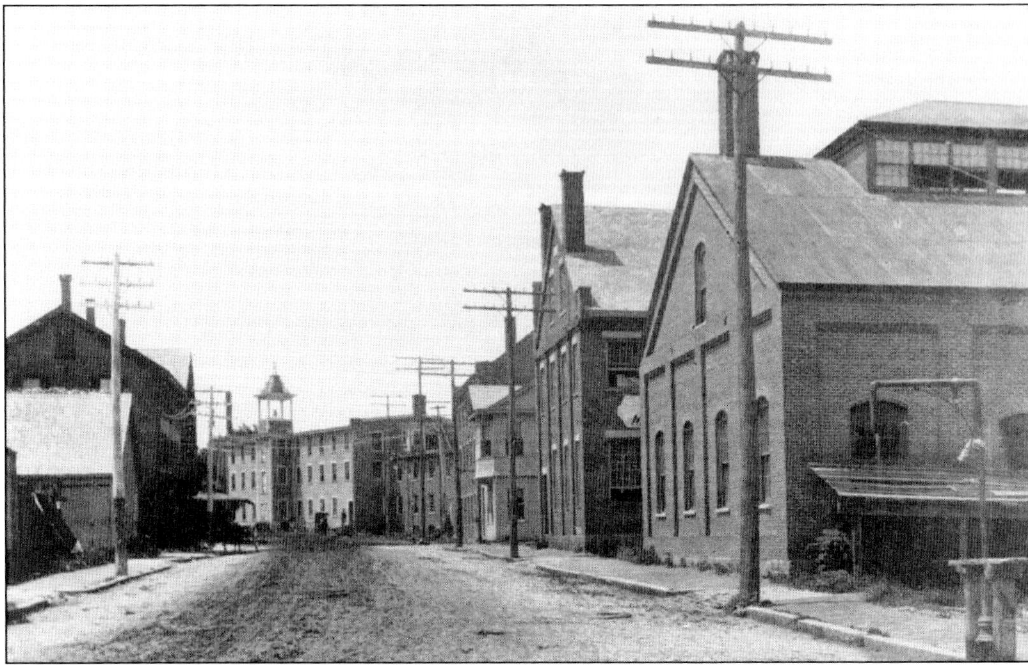

Major industries developed in the 1840s along this section of Water Street from Bridge Street to Winter Street, the location between Dams No. 1 and No. 2. This 1896 photograph shows the brick buildings of the Holmes and Robbins Machine Shop and Foundry at the right, and the Tucker Woolen Mill with its belfry in the background.

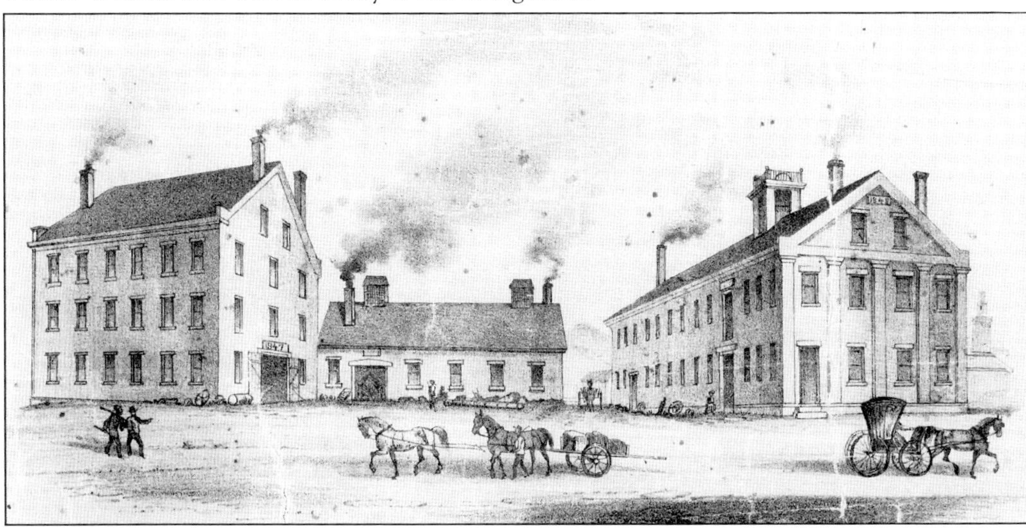

In 1832, Philip C. Holmes and Charles A. Robbins started a small machine shop and foundry, which burned in 1846. The following year they began building a group of substantial brick Greek Revival-style structures at Water and Winter Streets. This 1856 view shows the patten shop and storehouse of 1847 (left), the foundry (center), and the machine shop of 1848 (right). During the 1850s, the firm employed between thirty and forty workmen, making mill machinery and parts for sailing vessels. In 1874, Philip H. Holmes, a talented artist and inventor, assumed the management of the company from his father and ran it until the early 1900s, when the buildings became part of the Snow-Hazzard Shoe Factory.

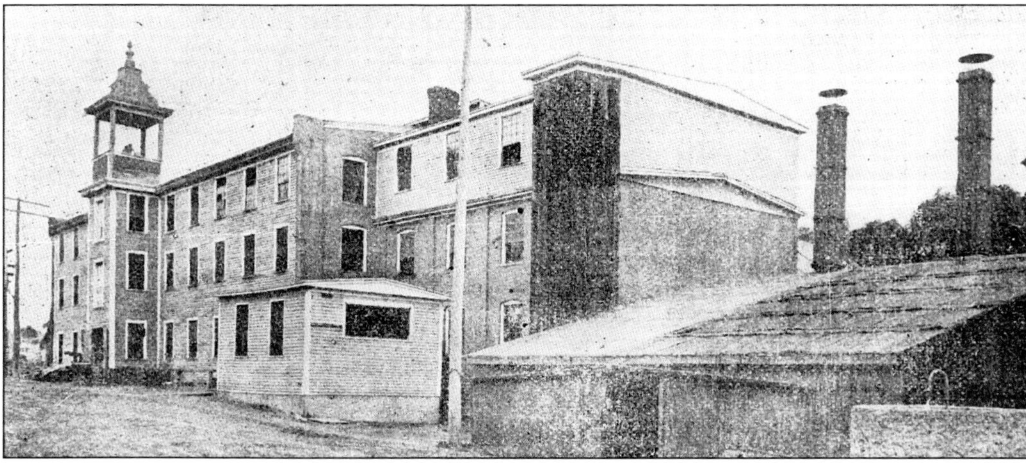

About 1838, I.N. Tucker started a woolen mill on the west side of Cobbossee Stream. In 1846, he moved to this factory on the east side, where the firm of I.N. Tucker & Company manufactured textiles until the late nineteenth century. A January 7, 1858 article in the *Northern Home Journal* noted that the mill produced "some 3,000 yards of cassimeres, satinets, and flannels a month, besides doing a large amount of dressing and carding. Their goods are sold principally to persons residing in the vicinity."

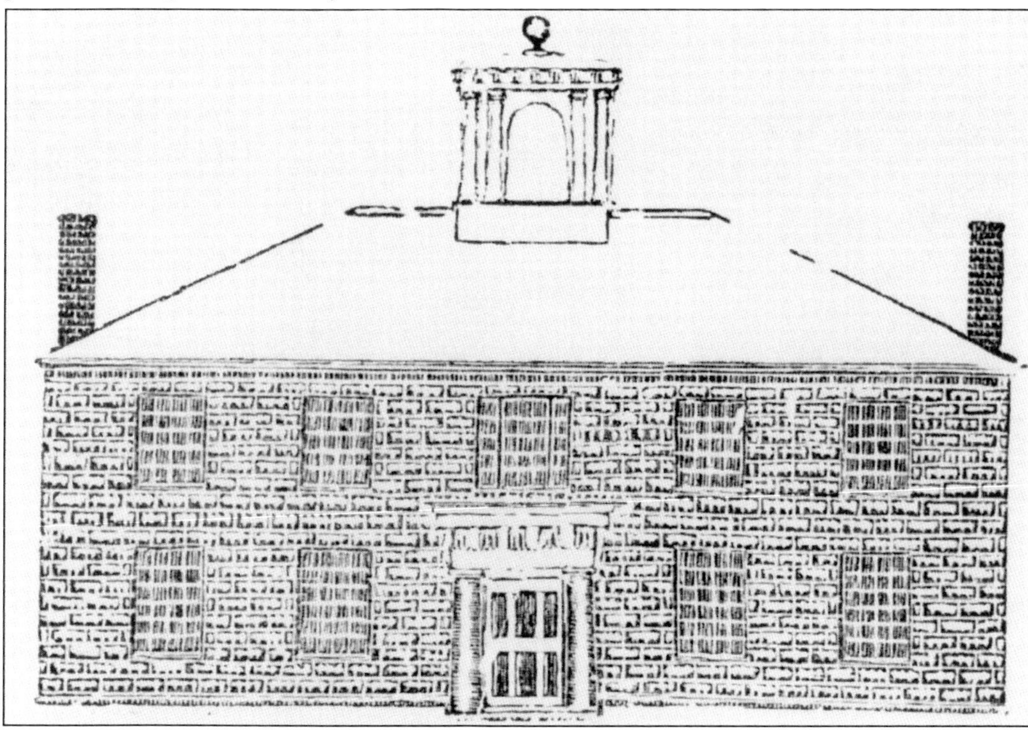

In 1822, Robert Hallowell Gardiner I founded the Gardiner Lyceum in this granite building at the corner of Dresden Avenue and School Streets. Gardiner envisioned the Lyceum as one of the nation's first technical schools, providing "a school for teaching mathematics, mechanics, navigation, and those branches of natural philosophy and chemistry which are calculated to make scientific farmers and skillful mechanics." Acquired by the city in 1857, the building served as Gardiner's high school until its destruction by fire in 1869.

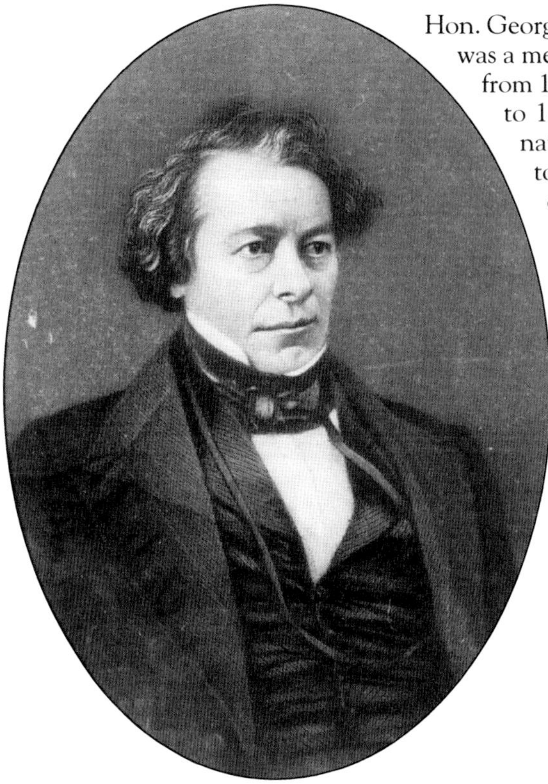

Hon. George Evans (1797-–867), resident of Gardiner, was a member of the U.S. House of Representatives from 1829 to 1841 and the U.S. Senate from 1841 to 1847. One of the leading politicians in the nation at the time, he brought President Polk to visit here in 1847. John Quincy Adams called him "one of the ablest men and most eloquent orators in Congress."

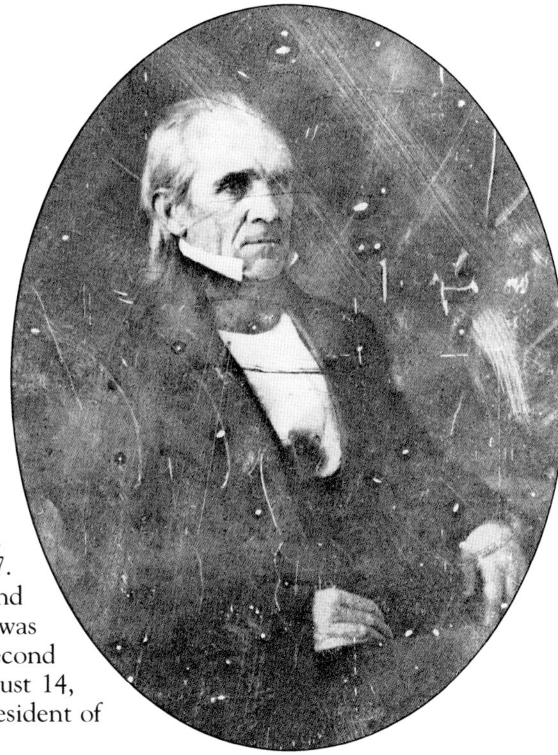

At the behest of George Evans, James Knox Polk (1795–1849), the eleventh president of the United States (1845–1849), visited Robert Hallowell Gardiner I at Oaklands on July 3, 1847. James Buchanan, the secretary of state and future fifteenth president (1857–1861), was among other cabinet members present. A second sitting president visited Oaklands on August 14, 1873: Ulysses S. Grant, the eighteenth president of the United States (1869–1877).

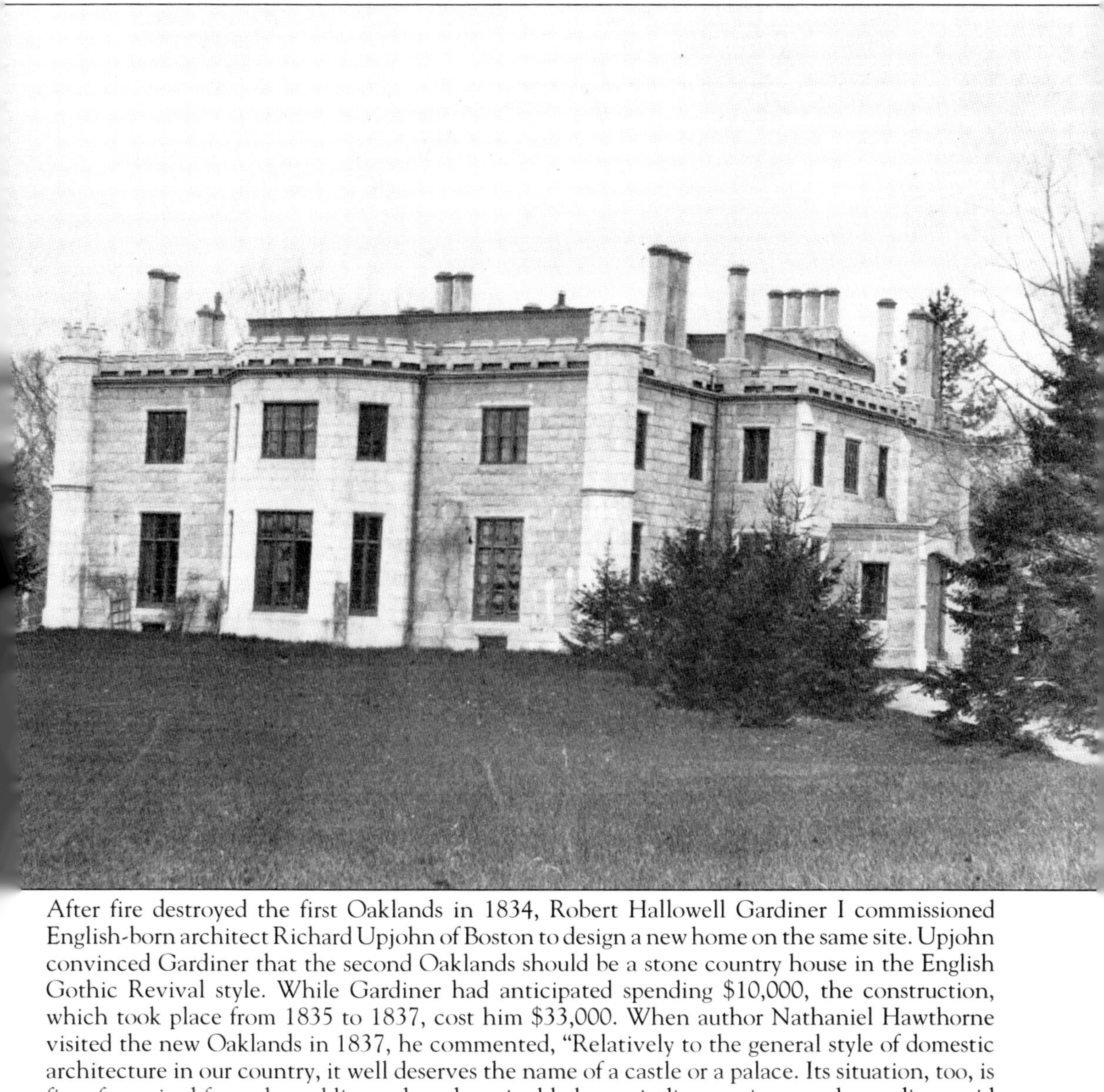

After fire destroyed the first Oaklands in 1834, Robert Hallowell Gardiner I commissioned English-born architect Richard Upjohn of Boston to design a new home on the same site. Upjohn convinced Gardiner that the second Oaklands should be a stone country house in the English Gothic Revival style. While Gardiner had anticipated spending $10,000, the construction, which took place from 1835 to 1837, cost him $33,000. When author Nathaniel Hawthorne visited the new Oaklands in 1837, he commented, "Relatively to the general style of domestic architecture in our country, it well deserves the name of a castle or a palace. Its situation, too, is fine, far retired from the public road, and attainable by a winding carriage-road, standing amid fertile fields, and with large trees in the vicinity." Word of Oaklands spread quickly, for by 1841, Andrew Jackson Downing stated in his influential book, *Landscape Gardening*: "In Maine, the most remarkable seat, as respects landscape gardening and architecture, is that of Mr. Gardiner, of Gardiner."

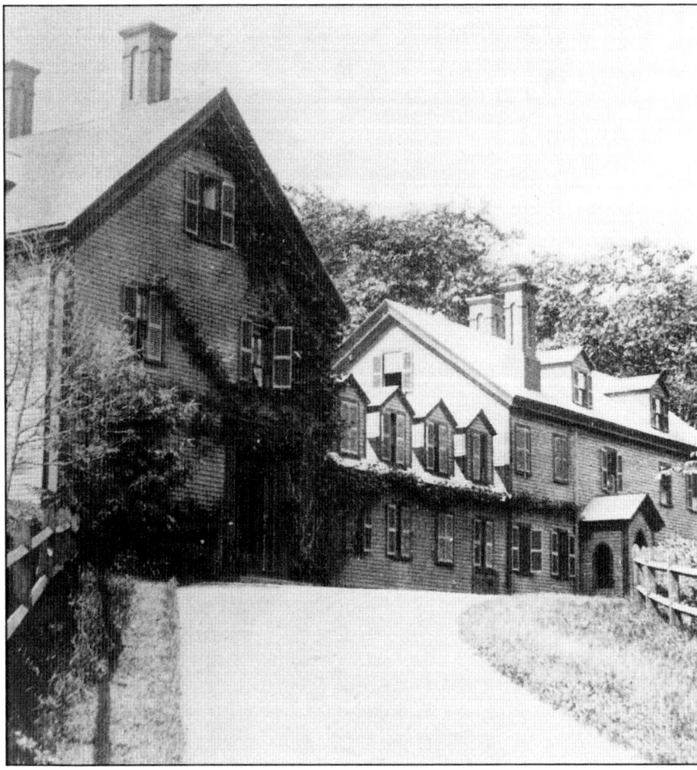

The Cove was the Richards family mansion, carved out of the Oaklands estate in 1844 by Robert Hallowell Gardiner I, as a gift to his daughter Anne and her husband, Francis Richards. It remained in the family until 1901, when heirs sold it to Weston Lewis. Laura E. Richards described the place in 1932 as a much-altered rambling structure with two parlors facing the river with bedrooms and nurseries over them; a long waist, lower-studded, containing a dining room and gun room, connected with a second block where the great kitchen was. The house was razed in 1949, and the land reunited with Oaklands.

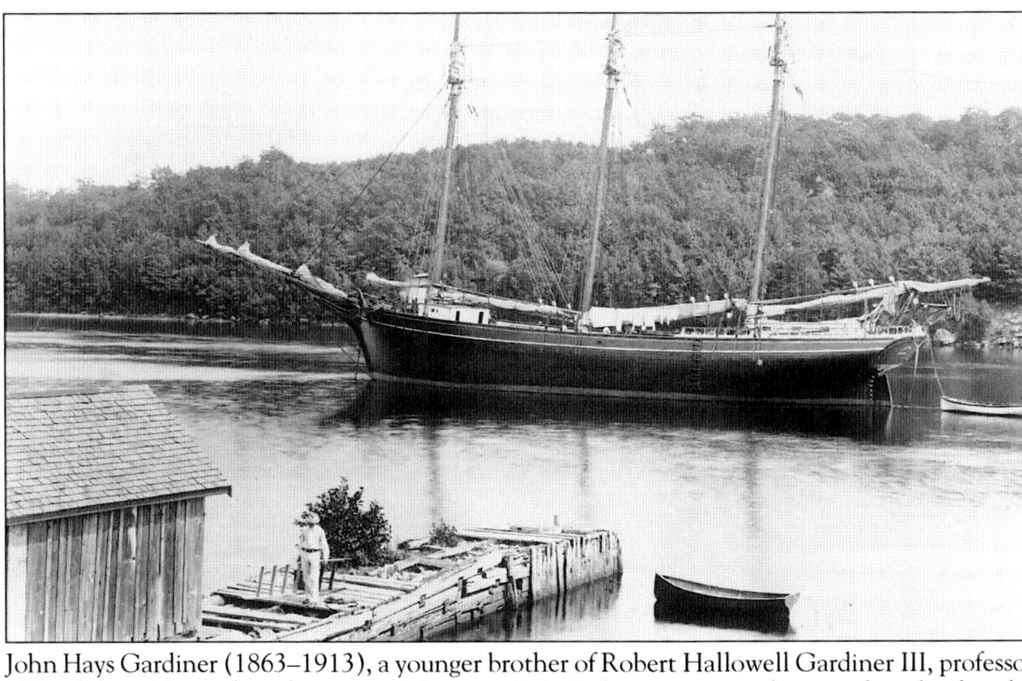

John Hays Gardiner (1863–1913), a younger brother of Robert Hallowell Gardiner III, professor of English at Harvard, and patron of the poet E.A. Robinson, is standing on the wharf at the Cove, the Richards estate. With 150 acres of pasture and woodland, the estate had frontage on the river where a deep indentation made a cove or small harbor.

The Right Reverend George Burgess (1809–1866) became first resident bishop of the Episcopal Diocese of Maine in 1847, when the limited finances of his new position required him to serve both as bishop and as the rector of Christ Church in Gardiner. During the next nineteen years, he expanded the number of parishes in Maine from five to nineteen and published many critically acclaimed theological works. He is buried beneath a massive marble cross designed by E.T. Potter at Christ Church.

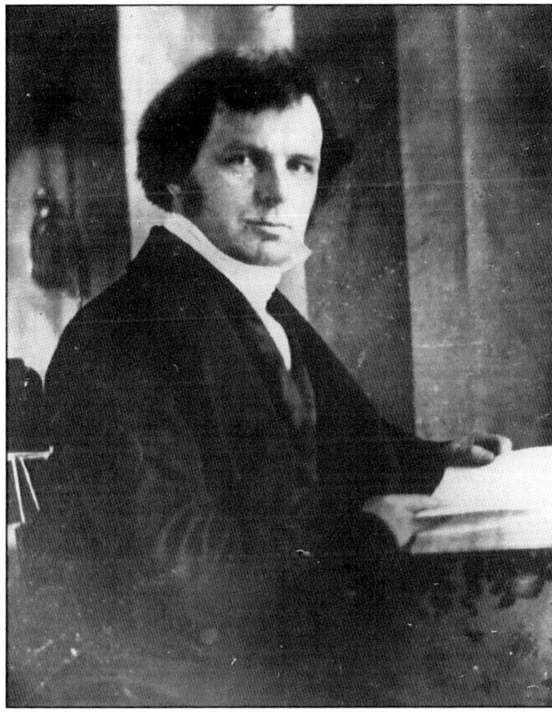

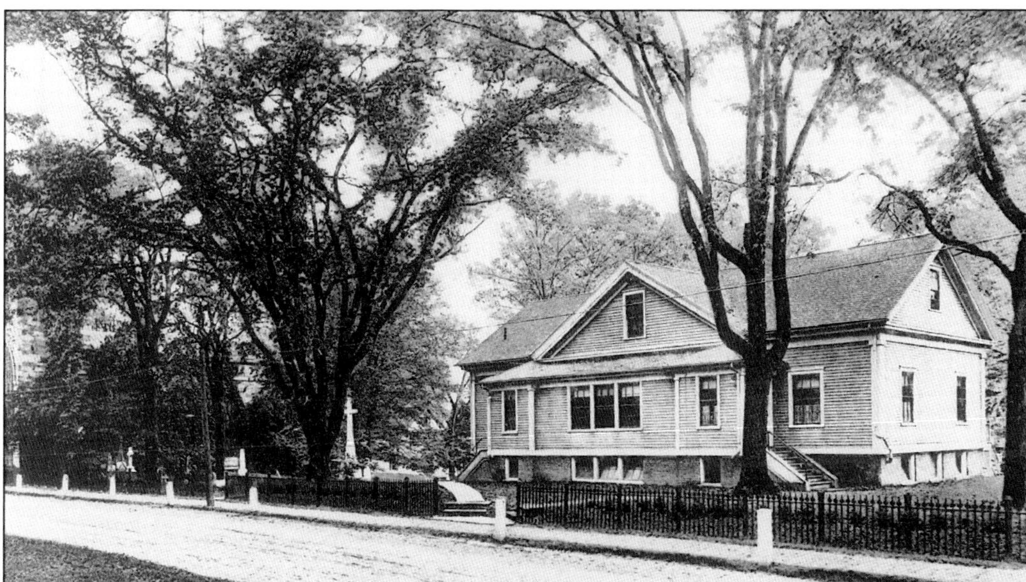

When Reverend William R. Babcock became rector of Christ Church in 1840, this Greek Revival-style parish house was constructed on Dresden Avenue between the churchyard and the Lyceum. Called the Lecture Room, the building was used originally for Sunday school classes and minor religious services. Designed by Francis Richards, a son-in-law of Robert Hallowell Gardiner I, the Lecture Room was completed in 1841 at a cost of approximately $1,000 and served Christ Church until its replacement by the present parish house in 1965. The large white cross to the left of the building marks the grave of the Right Reverend George Burgess, Maine's first Episcopal bishop.

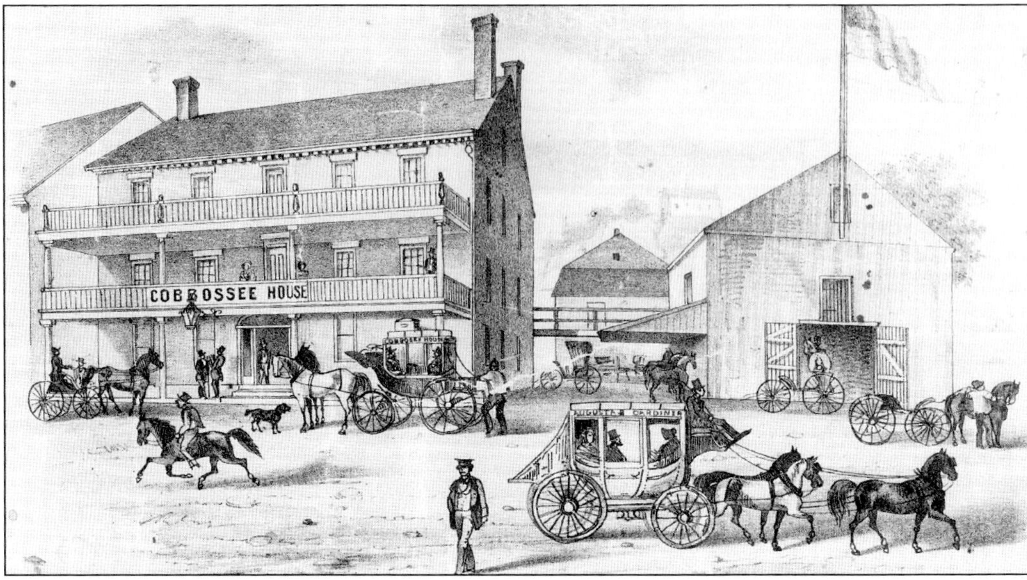

Gardiner's growth during the second quarter of the nineteenth century is reflected in the establishment of two hotels within a decade of each other. The first of these was the Cobbossee House of 1827, the three-story brick Federal-style building shown in this 1856 view. That year, Benjamin Johnson acquired the hotel and renamed it the Johnson House. In 1863, Johnson enlarged his establishment by adding a mansard roof. The following year, the wooden stable at the right was replaced by Johnson Hall. The hotel was a Water Street landmark until its demolition in 1972.

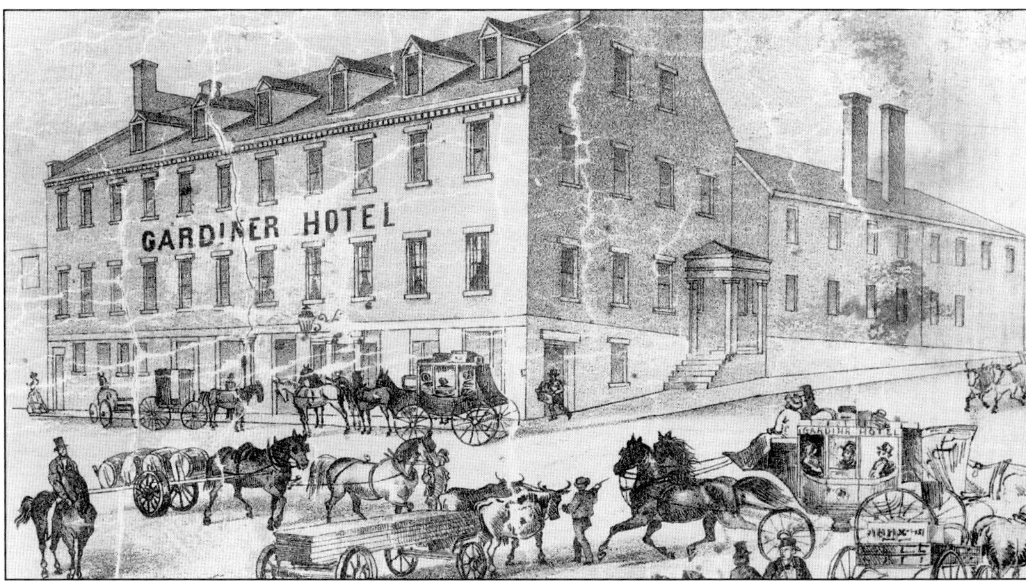

Erected in 1837 at Water and Church Streets, the Gardiner Hotel was an imposing late-Federal-style brick building based on the Hallowell House of 1834. This 1856 view shows the Gardiner Hotel as it appeared from 1837 until 1870. That year, a third story and a mansard roof were added, and the name was changed to the Evans Hotel in honor of Gardiner politician George Evans. The Evans Hotel was damaged by fire in 1901 and was replaced in 1903 by the Gardiner Real Estate Association Block, now the Fleet Bank.

Three

Mills and Ships 1850–1860

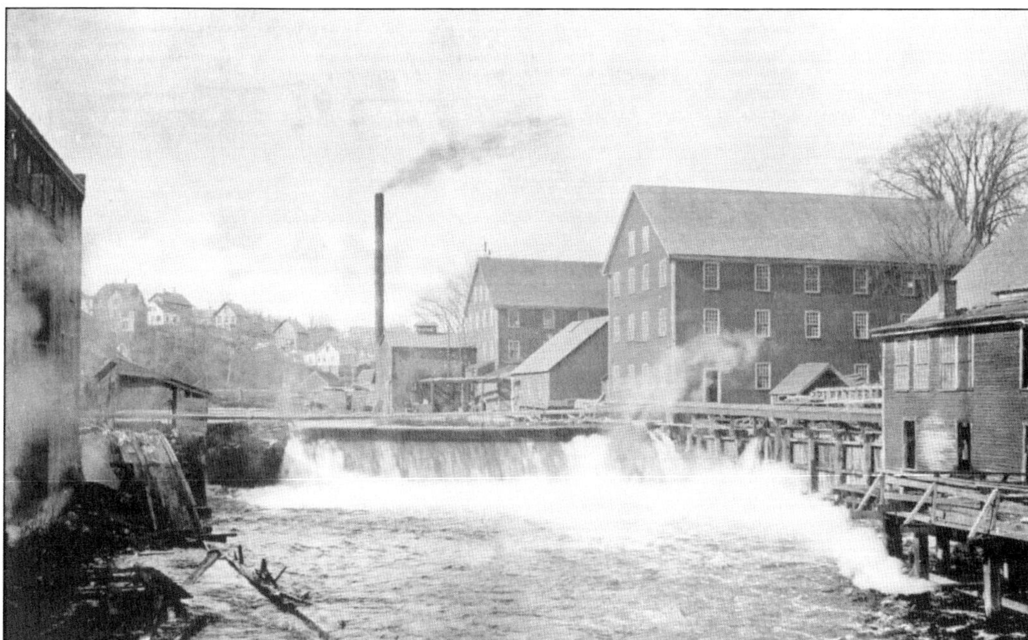

In the early nineteenth century, Robert Hallowell Gardiner I recognized the economic potential of harnessing the water power of Cobbossee Stream. Eight stone dams were built at intervals across the stream, transforming the area. This view from *Picturesque Gardiner* shows Dam No. 2 in 1896, with mills on the north side of the Cobbossee. The scene is described as follows: "The dam is owned by Joshua Gray, and is occupied by Joshua Gray & Sons' lumber mills, the Oakland Manufacturing Company's woodworking mills, the Gardiner Woolen Company, and Bartlett & Dennis' grist mill. The dam supplies about 400 horse power, which is about all in use."

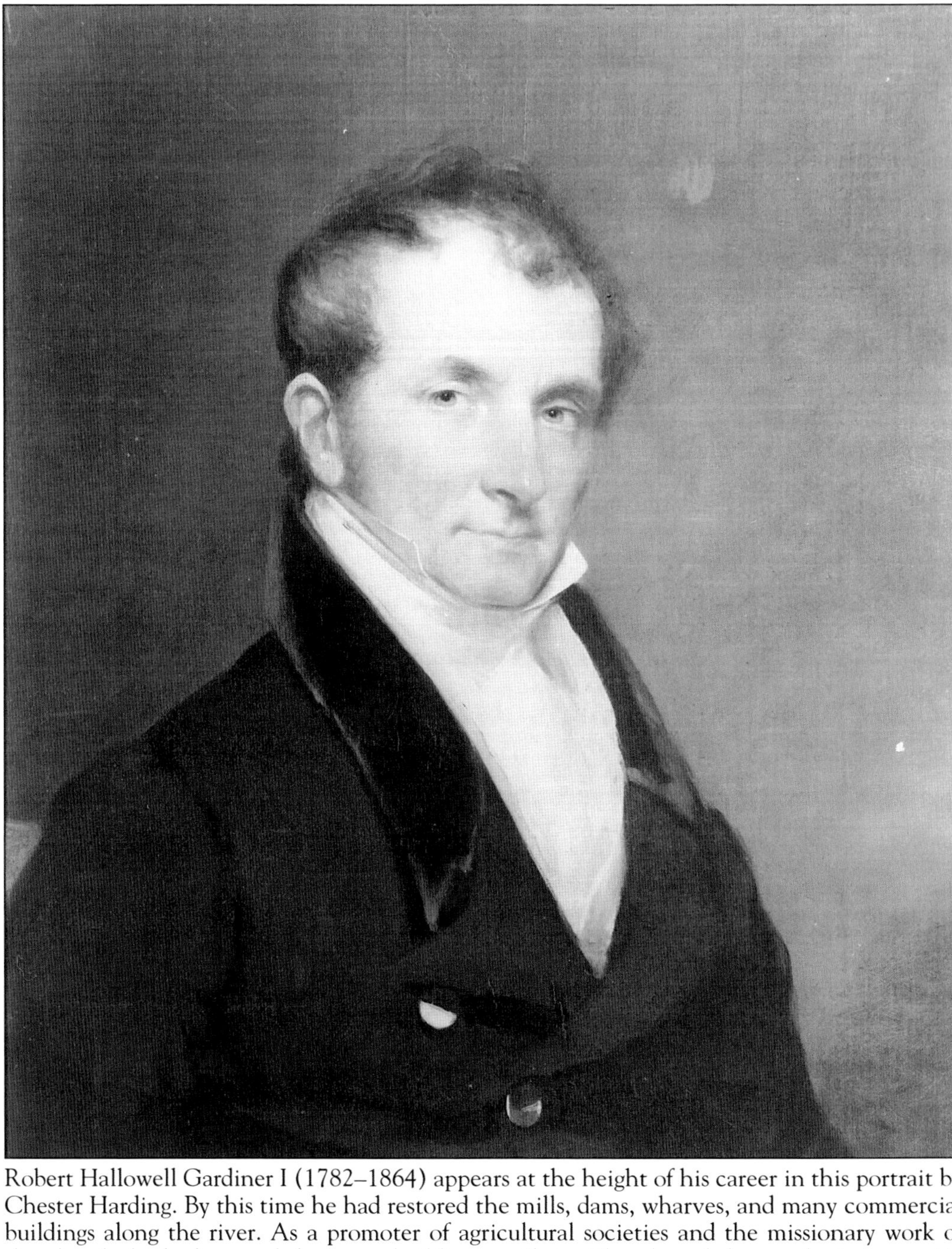

Robert Hallowell Gardiner I (1782–1864) appears at the height of his career in this portrait by Chester Harding. By this time he had restored the mills, dams, wharves, and many commercial buildings along the river. As a promoter of agricultural societies and the missionary work of the church, he had erected the stone building at Christ Church and the nearby Lyceum. He established the Gardiner Savings Bank in 1834, ten years after he had given the people of Gardiner their Common. By 1851, he had brought the railroad through Kennebec County. He reached beyond the city to incorporate the Episcopal diocese of Maine, become a co-founder of the mental hospital in Augusta, and become a founding member of the Maine Historical Society. He also promoted the post road to Brunswick (now Route 201), and was a founding member of the Boston Athenaeum.

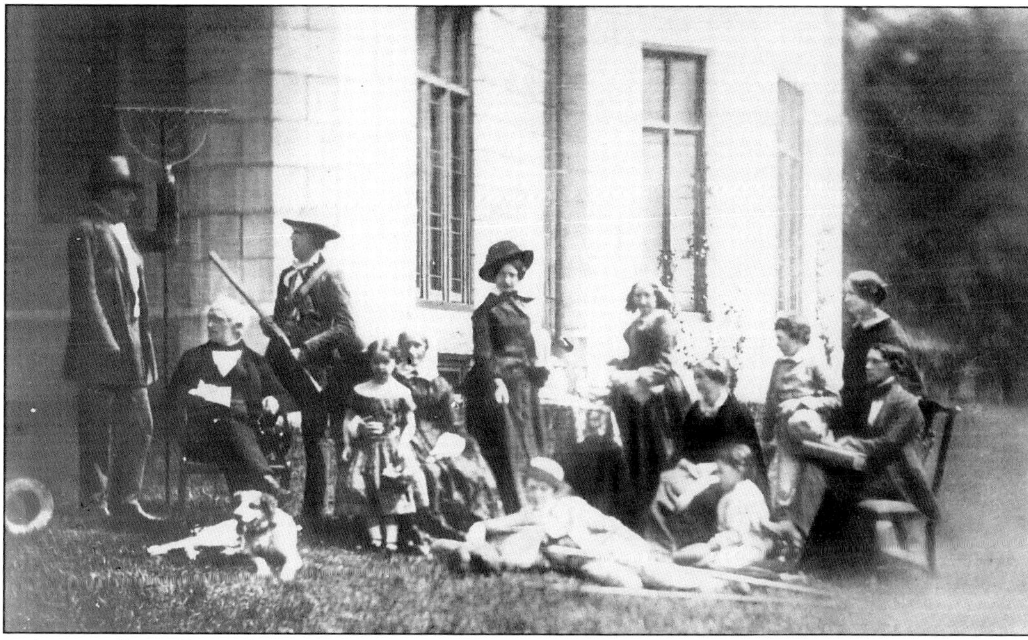

Robert Hallowell Gardiner I and his wife Emma celebrated their golden wedding anniversary at Oaklands on June 25, 1855, in the midst of their children and grandchildren. From left to right are: Francis Richards (1805–1858), Mr. Gardiner, Robert Hallowell Gardiner II (1809–1886), Emma Jane Gardiner (1847–1930), Mrs. Gardiner, Eleanor Harriet Gardiner (1825–1920), John Tudor Richards (1841–1920), Anne Hallowell (Gardiner) Richards (1807–1878), Henry Richards (1848–1949), Robert Hallowell Richards (1844–1945), Caroline (Vaughan) Gardiner (1825–1906), and Reverend Dr. Frederic Gardiner (1822–1889).

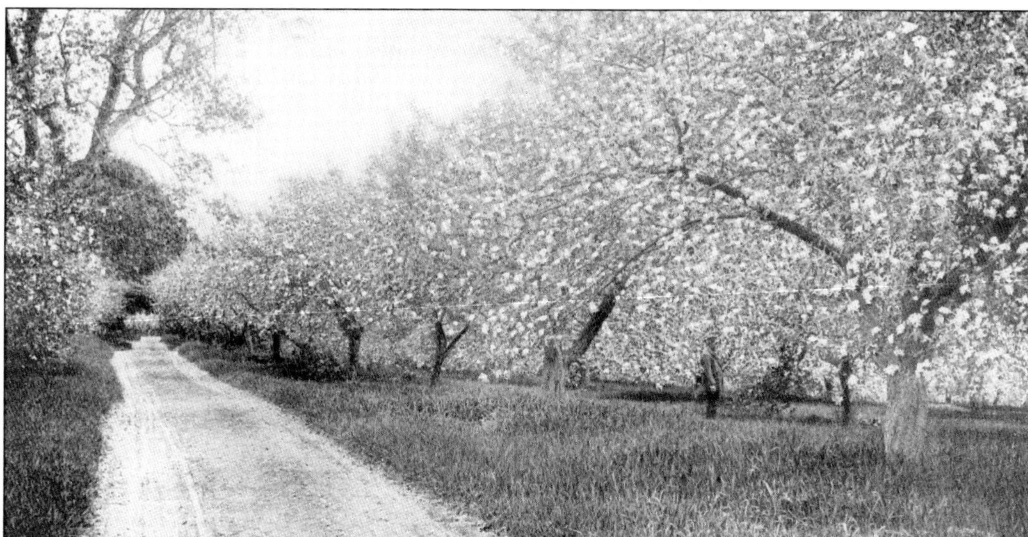

The Gardiner family and their Vaughan cousins in Hallowell introduced apples into Maine. Previously, it was supposed that the climate of Maine was too cold. Robert Hallowell Gardiner II actively promoted their cultivation, became president of the Maine Pomological Society, and developed a new species known as "Belleflowers," for which he established this extensive orchard at his Oaklands farm.

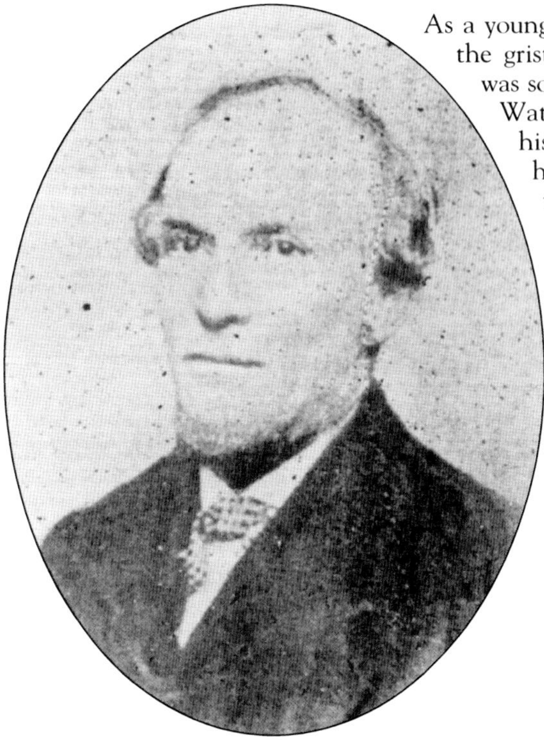

As a young man, Josiah Maxcy (1820–1878) managed the gristmill for Robert Hallowell Gardiner I, and was so successful that he built a block of stores on Water Street, saying that he wanted to invest his money where he had earned it. In 1864, he assumed management of all the Gardiner family properties and continued in that job until death. Later, his namesake son held the same position. He was the first of three generations to manage the Josiah Maxcy & Sons Insurance Agency, a firm founded in 1860 and closed in 1988.

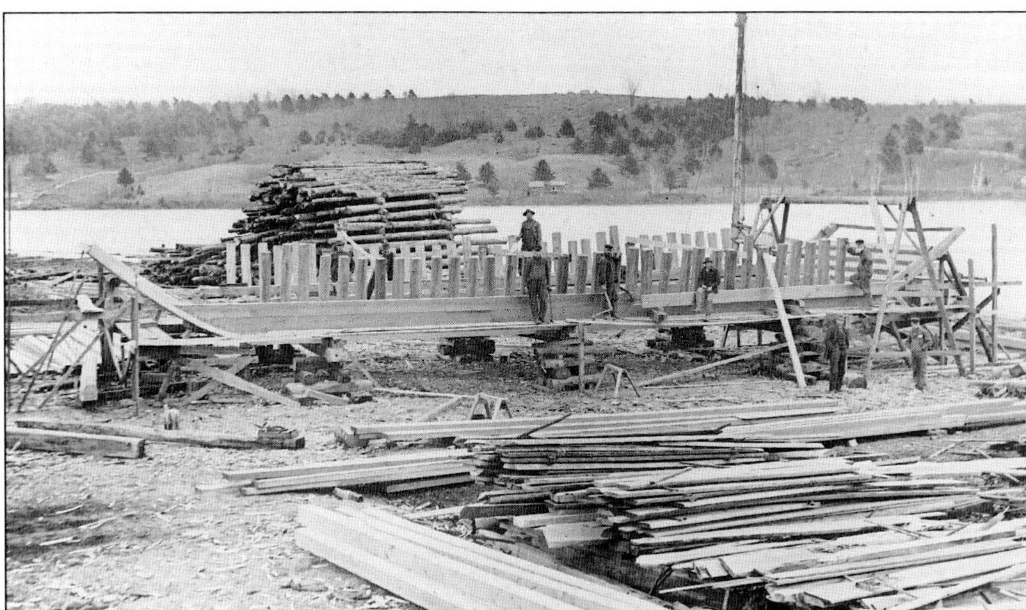

From the eighteenth century into the early twentieth century, ships were built on the banks of the Kennebec River. The long tradition of this industry is symbolized in this *c.* 1900 photograph by Herman Bryant of the construction of a scow, or "gondola," at South Gardiner. Scows were built either as sloop-rigged sailing vessels or as unrigged barges. Strictly working boats, they carried lumber, bricks, and other commodities on the water highway of the Kennebec.

The decorated stoneware produced in Gardiner and Farmingdale's nineteenth century potteries is highly prized today by museums and collectors. This covered jar made *c.* 1855 by Ballard and Brothers is owned by the Maine State Museum in Augusta. Collections of Gardiner pottery may be seen at the state museum and the Gardiner Public Library.

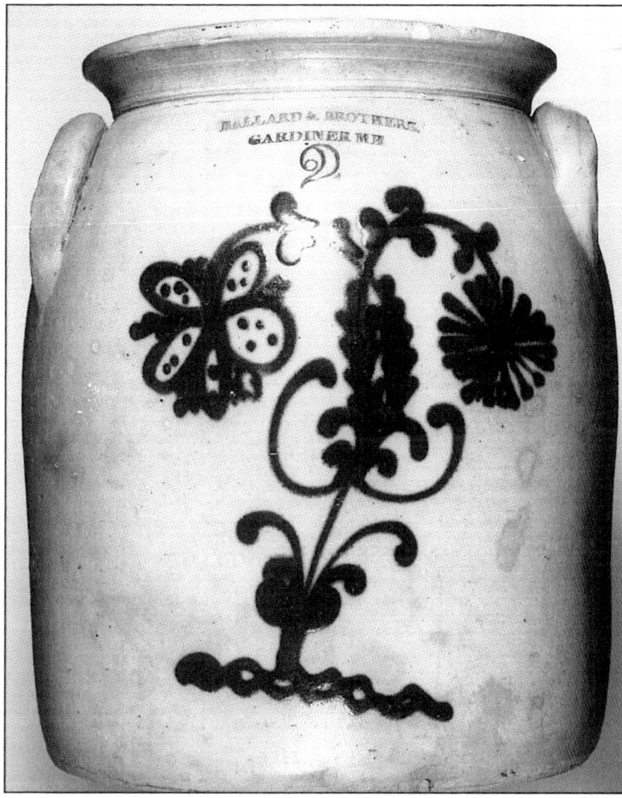

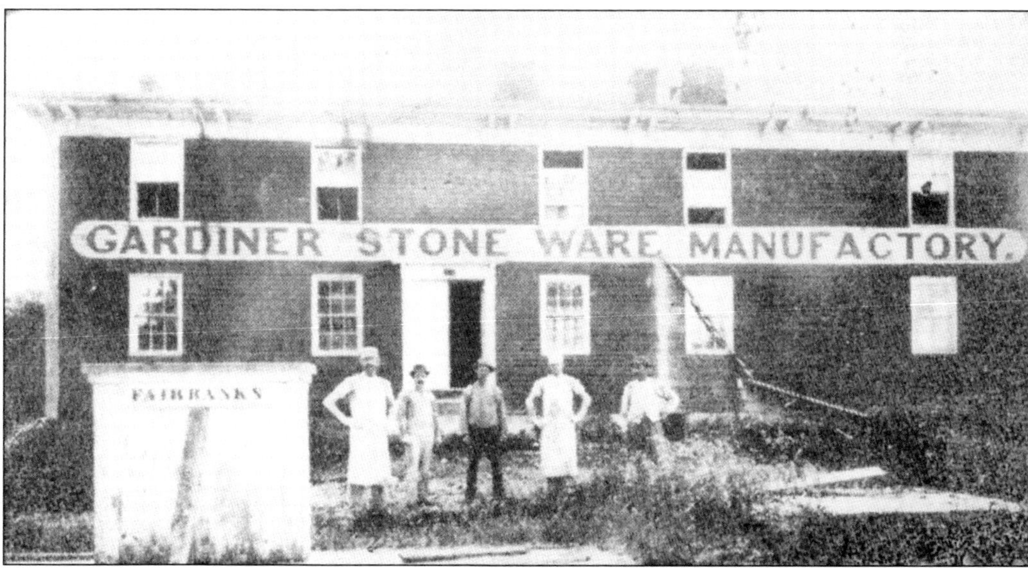

For twenty-three years, this factory in Farmingdale made thousands of pottery items for commercial and household use. In 1867, Gardiner potter Francis A. Plaisted built this plant south of Gould Brook on Maine Avenue between North and Sheldon Streets. Upon Plaisted's retirement in 1876, the business became known as the Gardiner Stone Ware Manufactory, the name under which it operated until it closed in 1890.

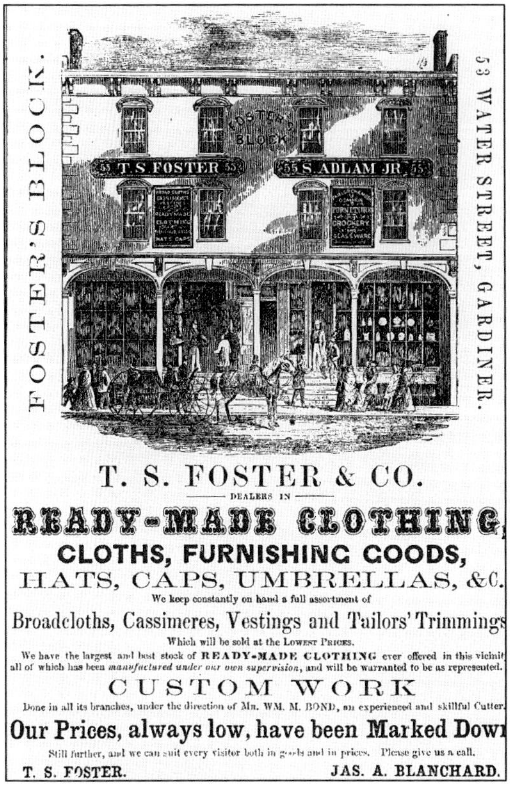

In 1856, the Foster Block was built on Water Street from designs by Peleg S. Robinson, a local architect and builder. Italianate in style, the facade displayed a series of cast-iron pillars and arches across the first story, behind which were recessed two shop fronts and the entrance to the upper floors. The *Northern Home Journal* of October 2, 1856, spoke admiringly of the Foster Block: "The heavy iron pillars and arches on its front give it a grand look that is rarely seen in Down East architecture." Much altered, the building still stands on Water Street.

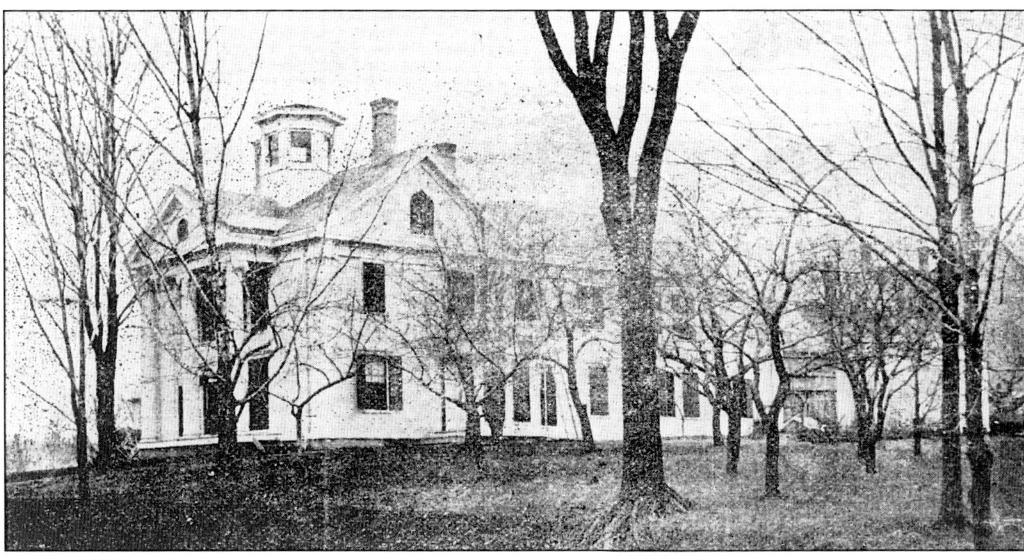

Gardiner's mid-nineteenth century prosperity was reflected in the fine homes which lined its streets. Notable among these is this Greek Revival mansion on Pleasant Street, which businessman John S. Mitchell purchased in 1855 from the local builders John T. and Seth G. Moore. Mitchell's daughter Susan inherited the house and resided there with her husband, Freeman Patten, who served as president of the board of trade and Gardiner's mayor (1899–1900). Photographed in 1903, the house retains its stately classical appearance to this day.

Built in 1828, the Highland Avenue Methodist Church assumed its present appearance with the addition of its clock tower and belfry in 1854, and its spire in 1867. After much debate in 1892 about constructing a new church, the congregation decided to retain this historic building, which remains in use to this day.

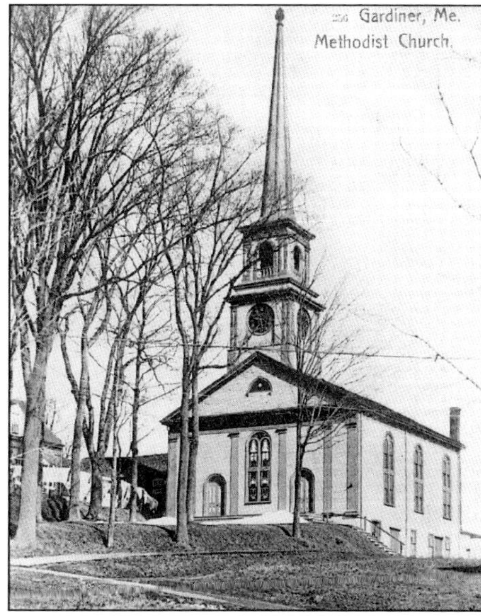

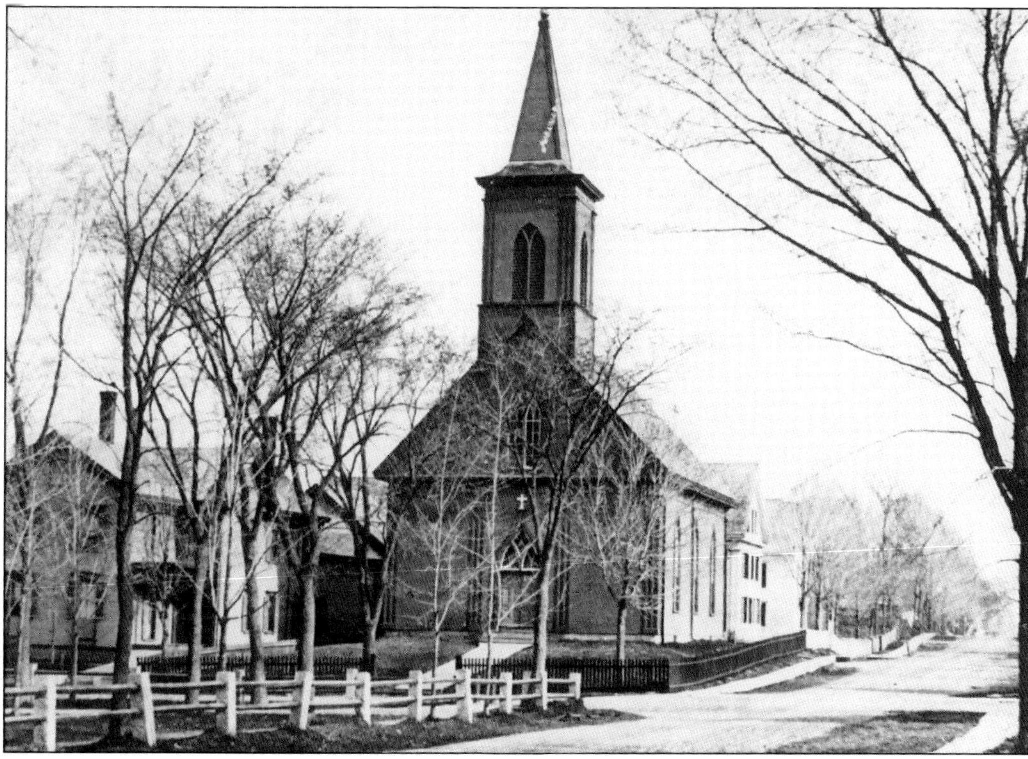

This 1877 photograph shows the original St. Joseph's Catholic Church which was built at the corner of School Street and Lincoln Avenue in 1858. The first mass was celebrated there in October 1858, and the building was dedicated in June 1863. In 1890, the belfry and spire were replaced by a large corner tower as part of a remodeling project designed by Gardiner architect Edwin E. Lewis. In 1914, the building was moved back to face on Lincoln Street in order to make way for the present St. Joseph's church. After the new church was dedicated in 1916, the old one served as a parish hall until its demolition about 1933.

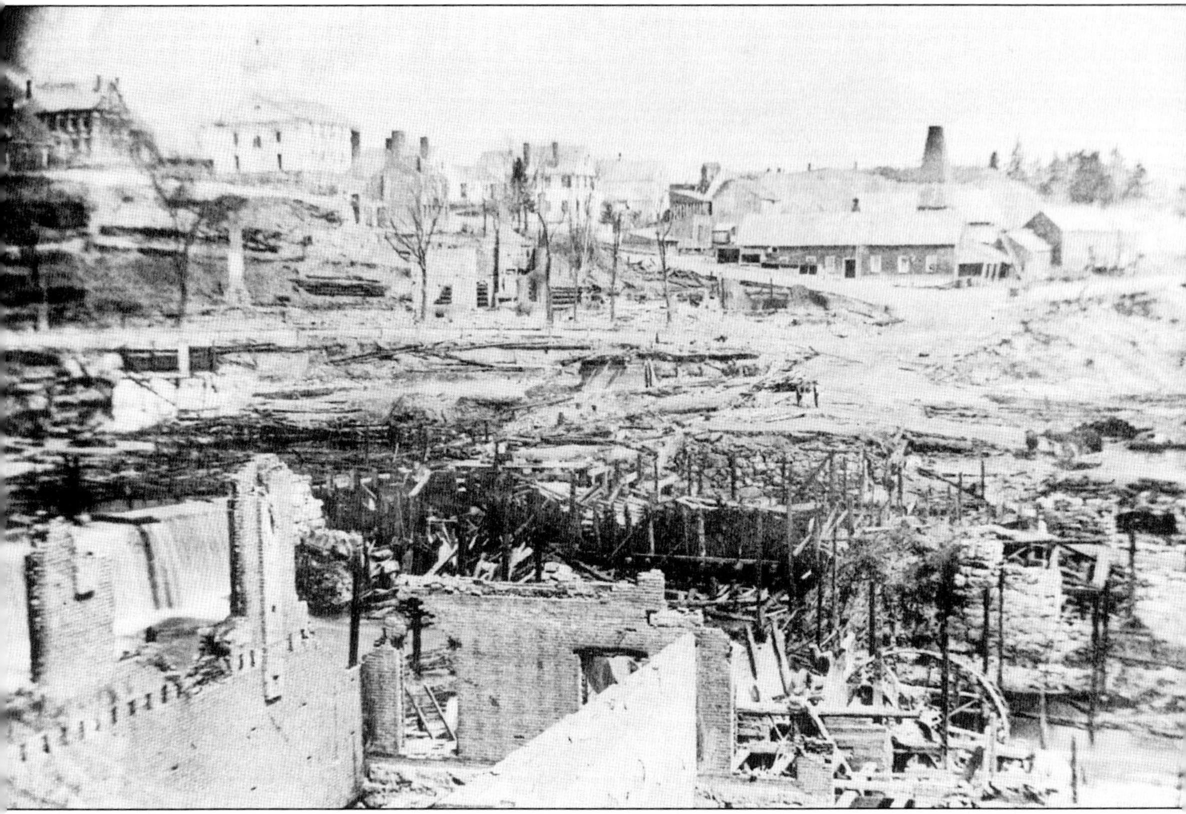

The great fire started at 10 pm on the night of April 25, 1860, and by midnight it had leveled the entire area from approximately the present sites of MacDonald's Bakery on Water Street to MacDonald's restaurant on Bridge Street. The fire completely destroyed four stores on Water Street, the bridge, the gristmill, two shops below it, five sawmills, about a dozen shops on Bridge Street, two residences on Highland Avenue, five houses on Summer Street, flumes from the dam, and the railroad tracks by the dam: a total of thirty buildings. Seventeen families were left homeless and one hundred fifty workers without employment. The destruction was appraised at $72,000, of which only $27,000 was insured. Ætna paid out half of the insured claims. The fire started in the old gristmill at the corner of Bridge Street, but its cause was never determined.

Four

The Golden Age 1861–1896

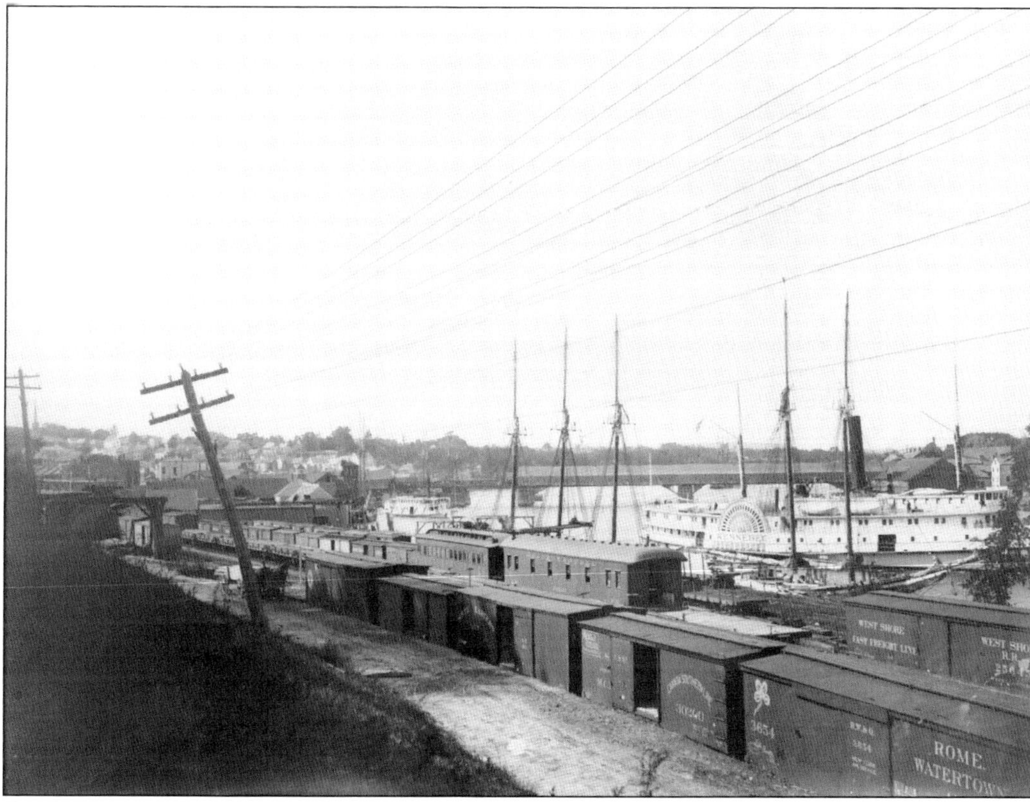

Gardiner's nineteenth-century economic vitality depended upon the transportation systems symbolized in this 1890s view south of the business district along the Kennebec River. Taken from Water Street, the photograph shows the Maine Central Railroad yard filled with freight cars. Docked at the railroad wharf are two coastal schooners, while the steamer *Kennebec* heads for Boston. Through the masts of the schooners, the covered bridge linking Gardiner with Randolph can be seen.

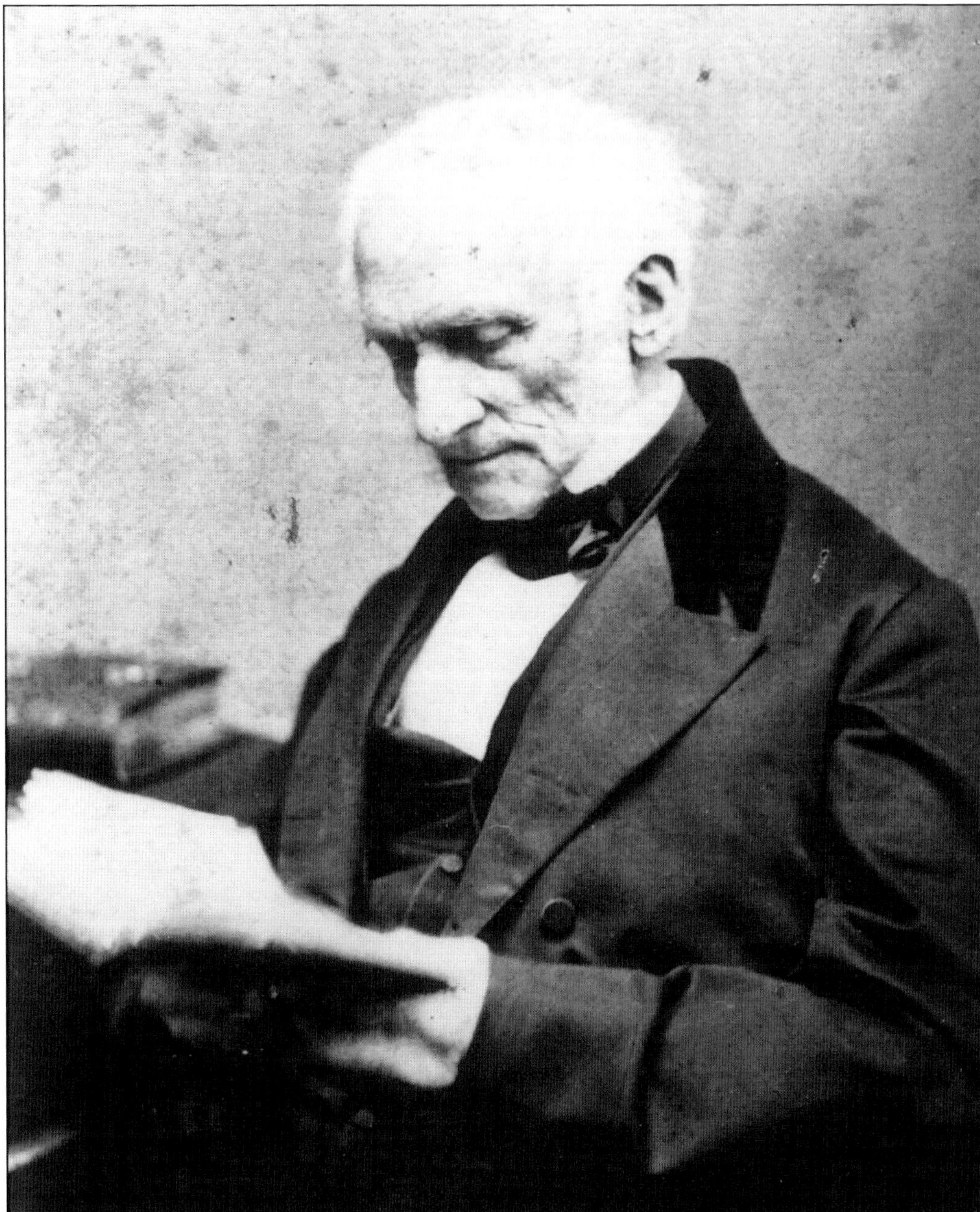

Remarkable lines characterize the face of Robert Hallowell Gardiner I (1782–1864), shown here in 1860. This is the man who struggled for six decades to raise the community from a frontier outpost to a thriving industrial center with transportation links to the outside world. His keen insight into human personality and his fine fine literary ability are evident in his autobiography, *Early Recollections*, published by his great-grandchildren in 1936. The first of six generations of gentlemen, all named Robert Hallowell Gardiner, his progeny now includes eighth-generation descendants. His current namesake is Robert Hallowell Gardiner VI, born in 1944, president of Maine Public Broadcasting.

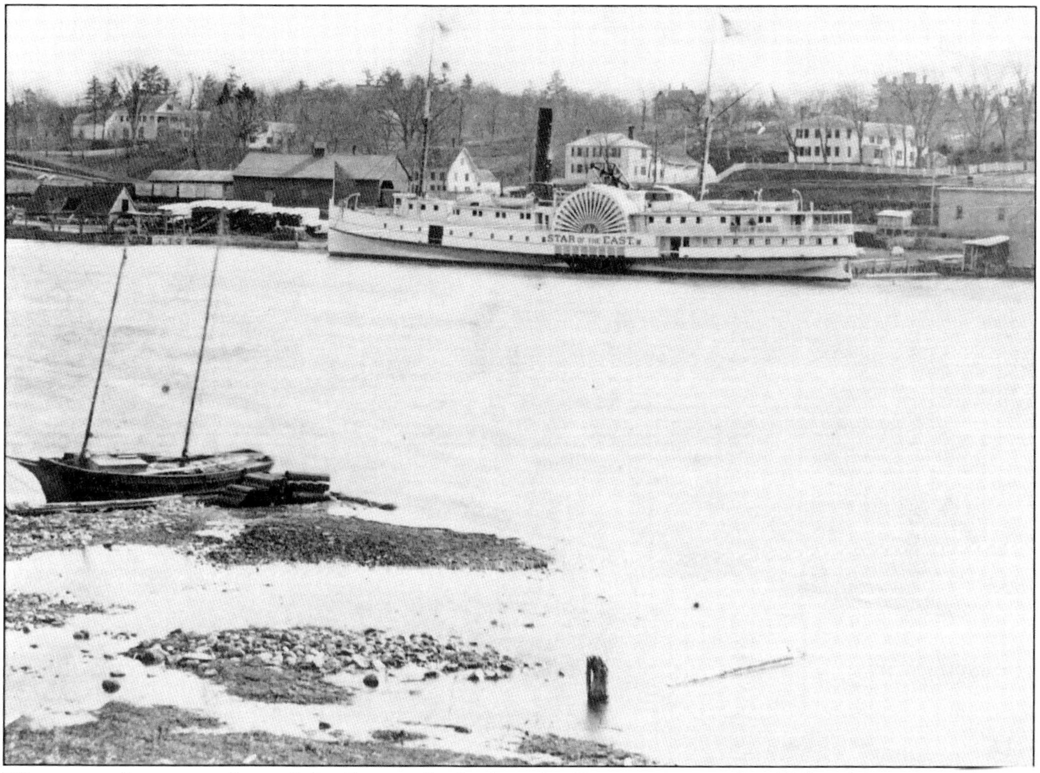

The coastal steamer *Star of the East* is docked at the Boston Steamship Wharf on Water Street opposite Vine Street in this *c.* 1875 photograph. Constructed in New York City in 1866, the vessel provided passenger and freight service between Boston and Gardiner for many years. Her first captain was Jason Collins, who owned a share of the steamer along with Peter G. Bradstreet and Massachusetts parties. After an 1890–91 rebuilding, the *Star of the East* continued to sail under the new name of *Sagadahoc*.

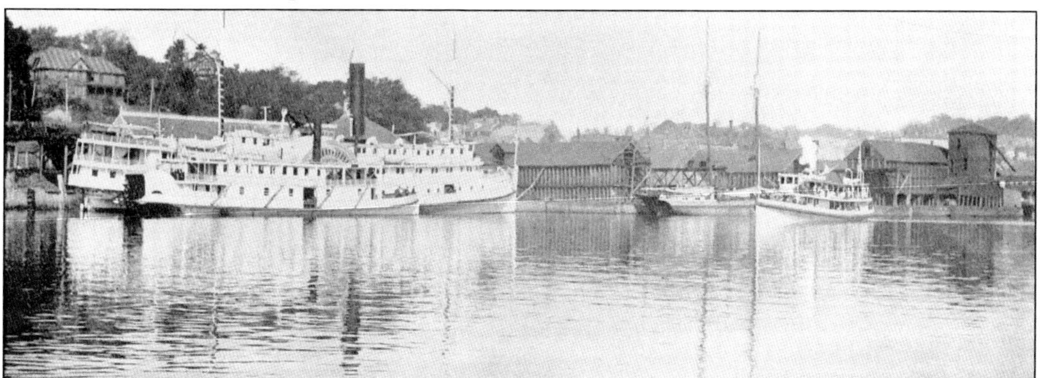

In 1896, the book *Picturesque Gardiner* published this photograph of three of the vessels owned by the Kennebec & Boston Steamboat Company lying at anchor south of the Gardiner-Randolph bridge. The largest, the *Sagadahoc* (left), made regular runs between Gardiner and Boston in tandem with her sister ship the *Kennebec* (not shown). Alongside the *Sagadahoc* is the *Della Collins*, the transfer boat which took passengers and freight up river to Hallowell and Augusta. At the right is the first *Islander*, a steamer built at Bath in 1883 to provide service to the summer resorts of the Boothbay Harbor area.

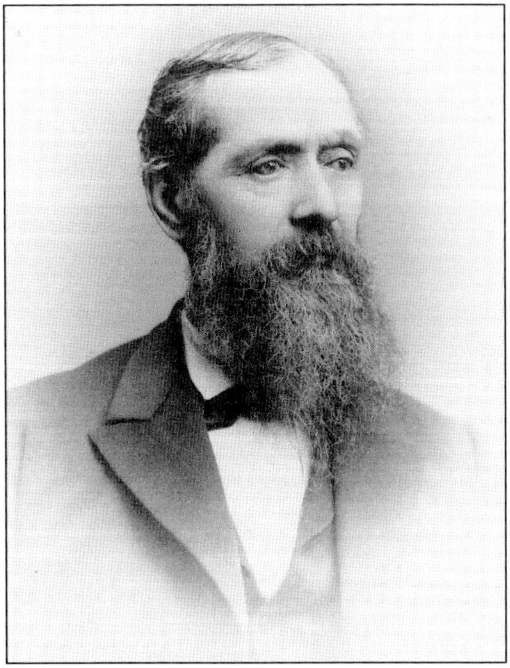

The legendary steamboat captain Jason Collins (1817–1907), born to a long line of seafaring kin, piloted vessels for almost the entire steamboat era, when that mode of transportation was one of the principal routes to the outside world. Starting as a pilot on the *Eastern Queen*, the *State of Maine*, and the *Union*, he acquired fame with the new steamer *Star of the East* on the Boston route from 1866 to 1889, when he assumed command of the *Kennebec*. A major investor with the Bradstreets in the vessels on the Kennebec River, he named one for his daughter, Della Collins.

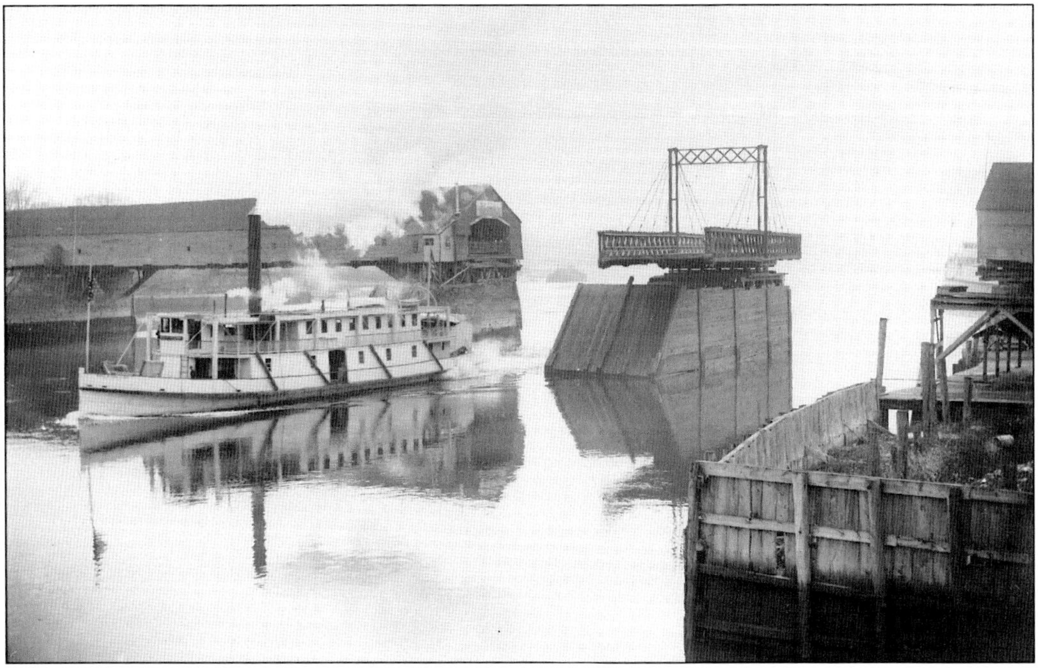

The *Della Collins* is shown passing through the swing section of the Gardiner-Randolph bridge on the Kennebec River about 1895. Built at East Boston in 1879, this stern wheeler served as a transfer boat, taking passengers and freight from the Boston steamers which docked at Gardiner up river to Hallowell and Augusta. The owner, Captain Jason Collins, named the vessel for his daughter. Toward the end of her twenty-six years on the river, the *Della Collins* ran between Bath and Augusta and was said to have needed "bit and blinders" to get across Merrymeeting Bay.

For Kennebec River,

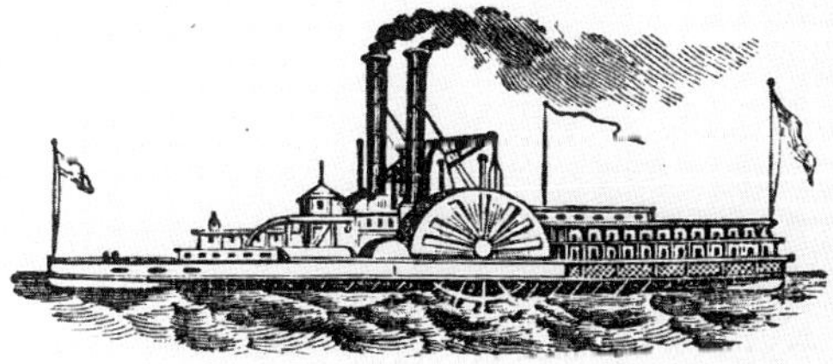

The Splendid Sea-going Steamer

STAR OF THE EAST,

CAPT. JASON COLLINS,

Will leave the End of Union Wharf, Boston,

EVERY TUESDAY & FRIDAY,

AT 6 O'CLOCK, P. M.,

Connecting at Gardiner with the Steamer Clarion, Capt. McLaughlin, for Hallowell and Augusta. Also, connecting with all stages running East and West from the River.

RETURNING,

Leave Augusta at 12 M.; Hallowell at 1.45 P. M.; Gardiner at 3; Richmond at 4; Bath at 6;

EVERY MONDAY AND THURSDAY.

FREIGHT TAKEN AT VERY LOW RATES.

AGENTS.

H. H. HYDE, Boston. ***BLANCHARD & REED, Gardiner.***

A period account described the *Star of the East*'s trip between Boston and Gardiner: "Leaving Boston at 6 p.m., passengers are at the Gardiner wharf early the following morning, having enjoyed not only the beauties of the evening sail along the Massachusetts coast, but a never-to-be-forgotten view of the picturesque Kennebec River. Passing at daylight by the famous Sequin and Pond Island Lights, by Fort Popham and its long beach, hotels, summer cottages, and government life-saving station, thence up the river and by the great shipbuilding city of Bath, with its long line of shipyards, filled with craft of all kinds from the mammoth government warship to mercantile steamers, ships, and barges, we then come to our great industry, the scores of ice houses."

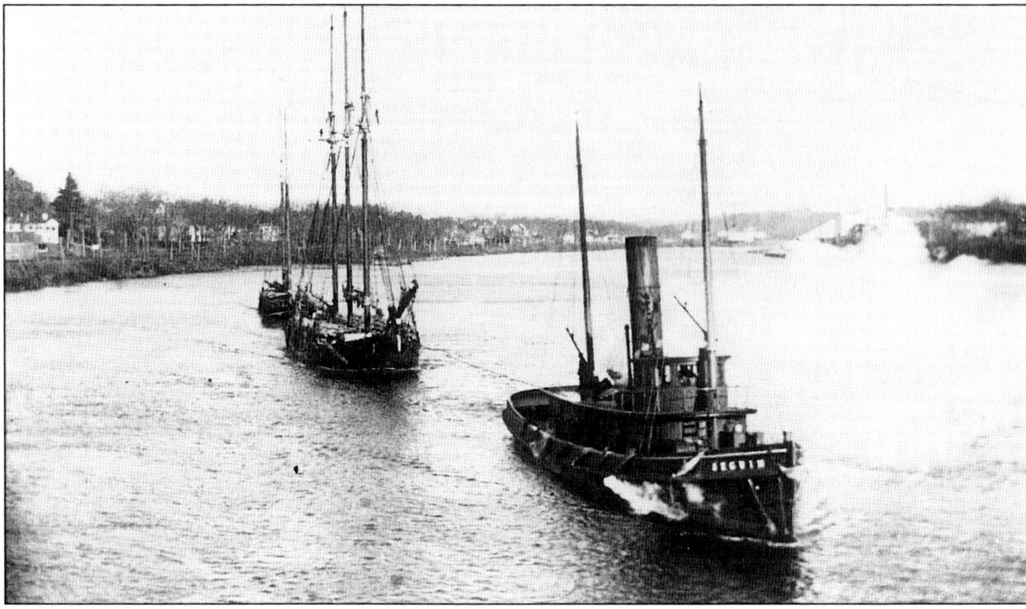

A fixture for decades on the Kennebec River, the tugboat *Seguin* was photographed by E.W. Cunningham on December 18, 1897, as she approached the swing section of the Gardiner-Randolph bridge from the north with two schooners in tow. Built in 1884 at the Morse Shipyard in Bath, the *Seguin* was the ninth tug of the Knickerbocker Steam Towage Company fleet. In May of that year, 892 vessels passed in and out of the Kennebec, many of which required the assistance of hard-working tugs like the *Seguin*.

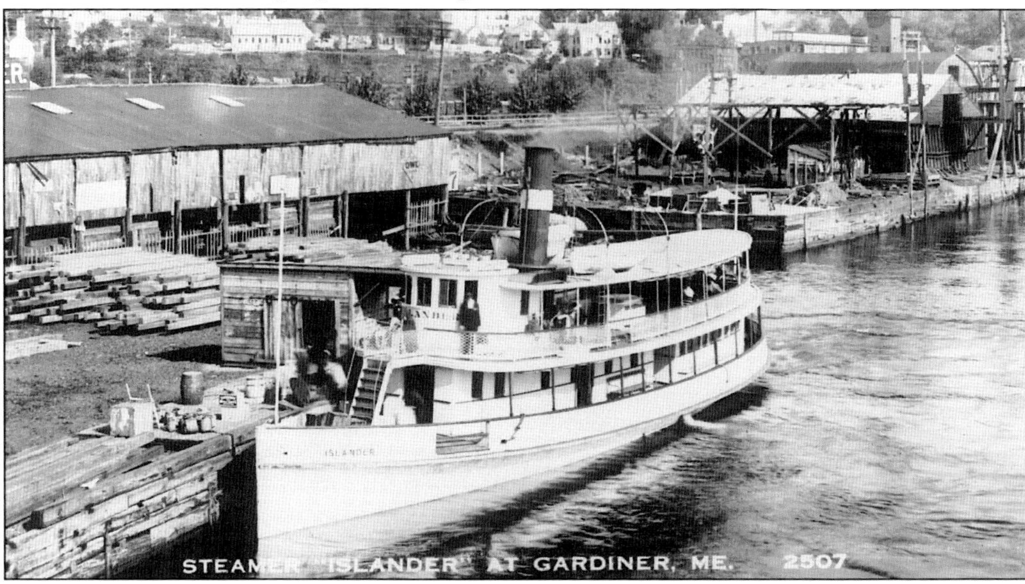

The second *Islander* was put in service in 1908 to replace the *Gardiner*. Built by W.I. Adams and Son in East Boothbay, the new *Islander* continued the tradition of its namesake vessel in linking Augusta, Hallowell, and Gardiner with the summer resorts of Boothbay Harbor. Many residents of these central Maine cities depended on steamers such as the *Islander* to transport them to the coastal cottages, boarding houses, and hotels which provided an escape from the summer heat of the Kennebec River Valley.

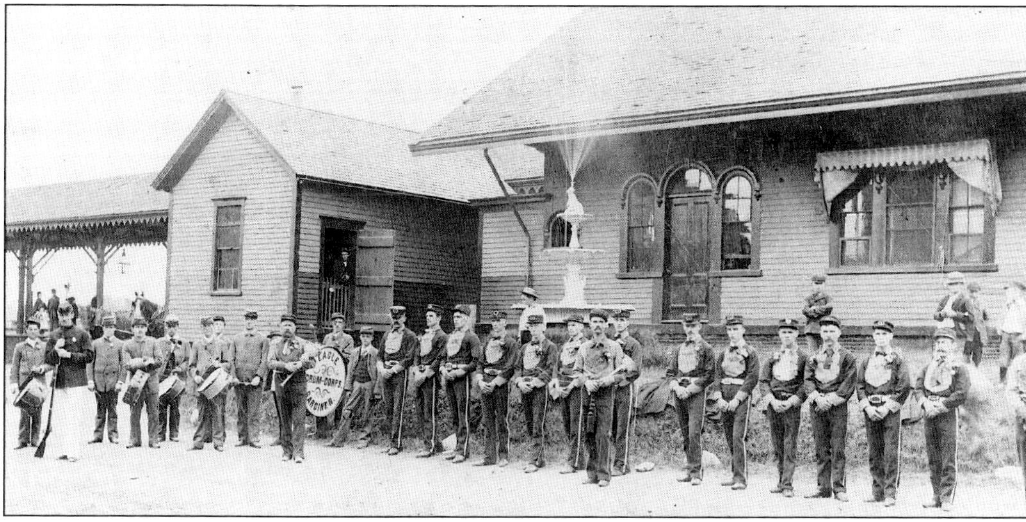

The Maine Central Railroad station on Depot Square was the scene of numerous late-nineteenth-century events such as this performance by the local Eagle Drum Corps. Between 1847 and 1852 the Kennebec and Portland Railroad was constructed to link Portland with Augusta. This line reached Gardiner in 1851.The first, modest station in Gardiner gave way in 1866 to the more stylish Italianate one shown in the photograph. By then, the Kennebec and Portland Railroad was known as the Portland and Kennebec Railroad, which became part of the Maine Central Railroad in 1870. The Maine Central replaced the 1866 station with the present brick and stone one on Maine Avenue in 1911.

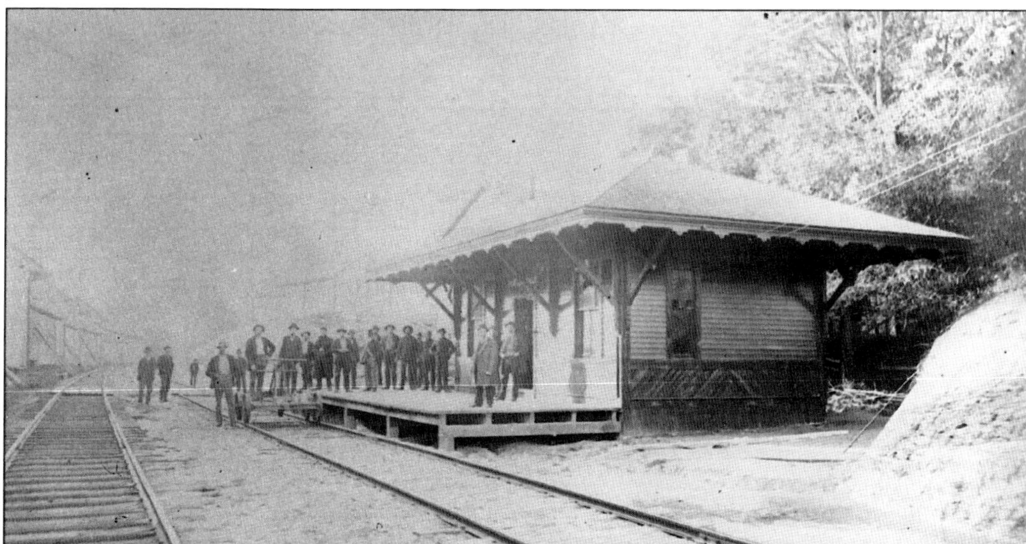

The Kennebec and Portland Railroad was completing its line to Augusta in 1852 when Farmingdale was incorporated as a town from parts of Gardiner, Hallowell, and West Gardiner. By 1879, the Maine Central Railroad had built a riverside station off Maine Avenue between Grant and Bowman Streets to serve Farmingdale's growing industries. As George J. Varney observed of the town in his 1881 *Gazetteer of the State of Maine:* "The nearness of good markets makes farming and gardening profitable. Along the river are several ice-houses. There are manufacturers of stoneware, drain-tile, and brick, and sandpaper and glue."

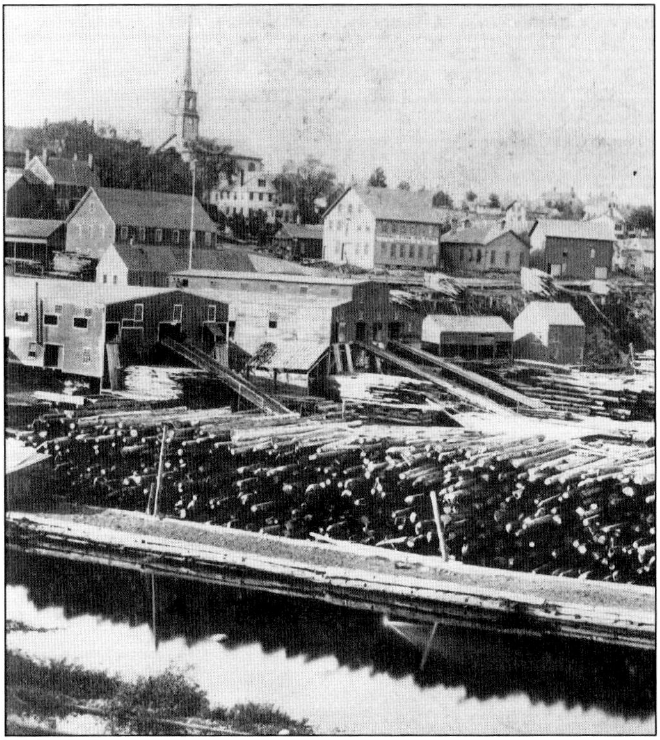

Dam No.1 near Bridge Street flourished from about 1754 until the 1917 flood washed it out, and it was never rebuilt. As shown in this 1870s view, logs cut on the headwaters of the Kennebec were floated downriver and diverted to the mill pond at the mouth of Cobbossee Stream. By the late 1840s, a causeway, now the stretch of Maine Avenue opposite Shop and Save, was in place for the railroad, and a system of locks held water here to transport logs to the thirty-odd factories on Bridge Street which manufactured them into diverse products.

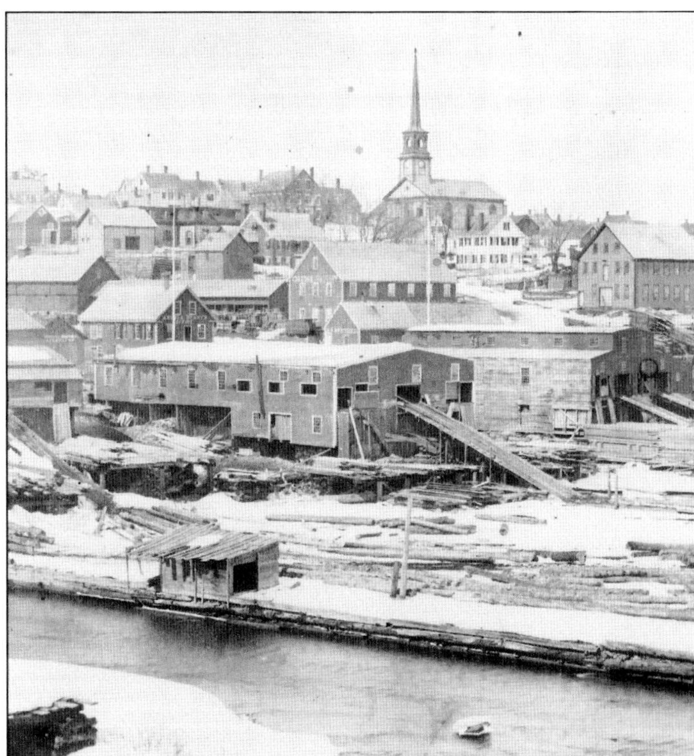

This 1870s view of the mill pond reveals the booms diverting logs to the sawmills. To make operations more efficient, earth, ashes, and rubbish were dumped here to bring the channel of Cobbossee Stream through the section in back of Water Street. This process converted the mill pond into man-made land. In 1898, the Commonwealth Shoe Factory built at one corner, and in 1957, the building of a new A & P supermarket completed the process. The shopping center came in 1967, and its owners are often reminded in flood season that Mother Nature is still trying to reclaim its ancient water course.

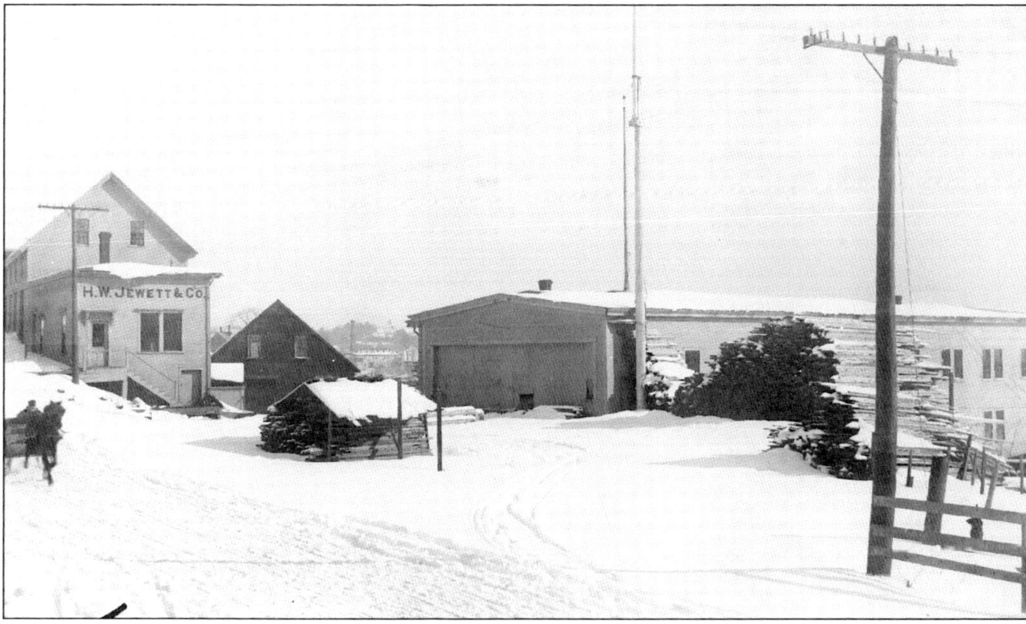

By the turn of the century Hartley W. Jewett (1826–1912) vied with Joshua Gray to be the city's largest employer. Jewett started work on the river as soon as he was large enough to raft logs. A bright young man eager for the main chance, he bought logs in the woods for resale, and by 1863 started the manufacture of lumber himself at Dam No. 1. Despite almost total losses in the great fire of August 1882, his creditors trusted him, and he rebuilt and expanded his operations. The retail office appears next to the mill, shown in full below.

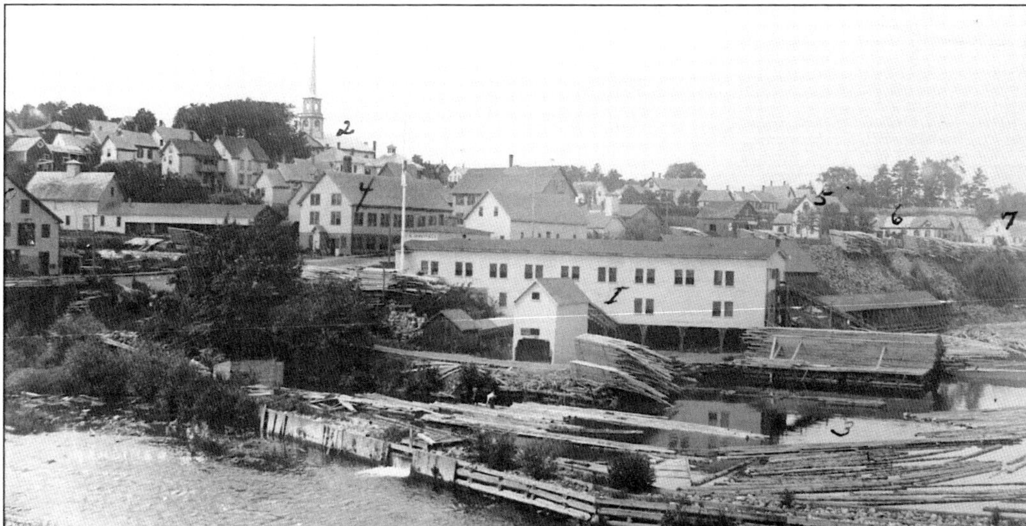

This photograph reveals the full length of Jewett's sawmill, one end of which appears next to the retail office at the top of this page. H.W. Jewett & Co. advertisements in the 1890s identified the company as manufacturers and dealers in all kinds of lumber, clapboards, shingles, and laths, and promised to saw all dimensions to order. In 1896, Jewett and his competitor Gray were the principal lumber dealers in the city, together producing sixty million board feet a year.

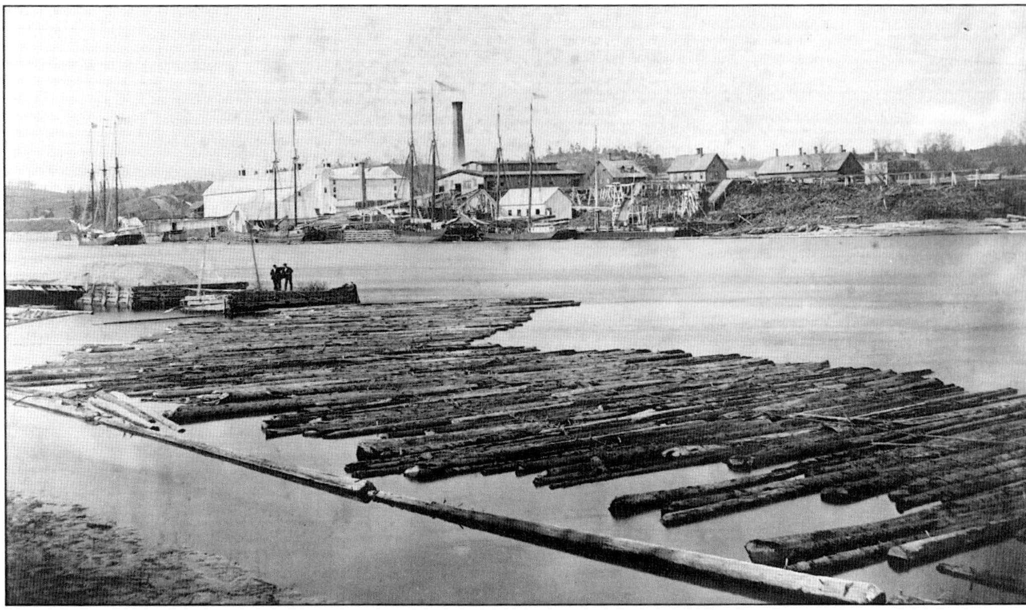

Lumber and ice, two of the great Kennebec River industries, came together in the Kennebec Land and Lumber Company, established at Pittston by Ira D. Sturgis in partnership with William Sprague of Rhode Island. Born in Vassalboro in 1814, Sturgis was an experienced shipbuilder, lumberman, and sawmill operator. In 1867, he built this large sawmill with its towering brick chimney on the Pittston side of the Kennebec opposite Grant Street in Farmingdale. Immediately north of the mill, Sturgis constructed a huge ice house, from which he marketed the river's ice to southern cities.

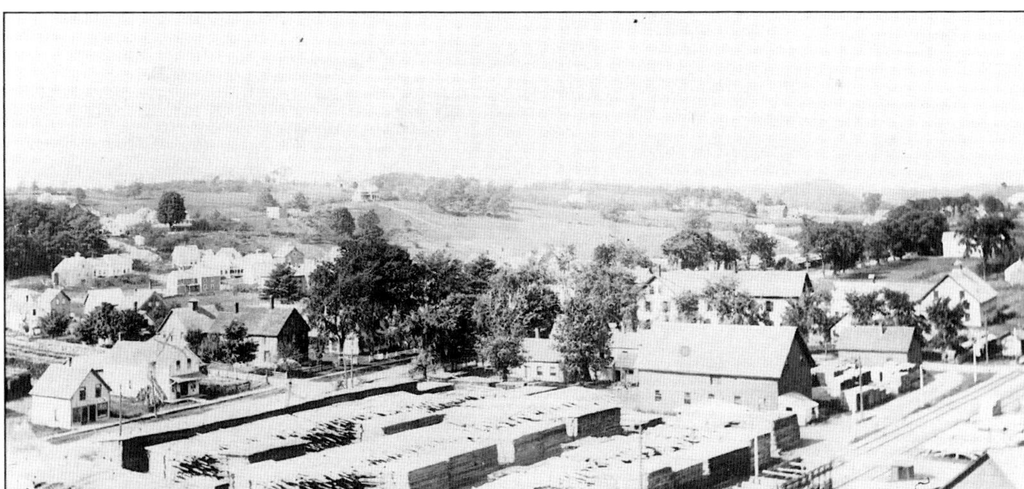

Two families, the Lawrences and the Bradstreets, operated large sawmills in South Gardiner during the late nineteenth century. This view shows the Bradstreet lumber yard. In 1876, Joseph S. and Frederick T. Bradstreet started their mill under the name of Bradstreet Brothers, which became the Bradstreet Lumber Company in 1881, with $100,000 in capital. By the 1890s, the firm employed 110 men, cutting fifteen million feet of spruce for the New York market each year. The source of these logs was the Bradstreets' timber lands on the Roach, Moose, and Dead Rivers in northern Maine.

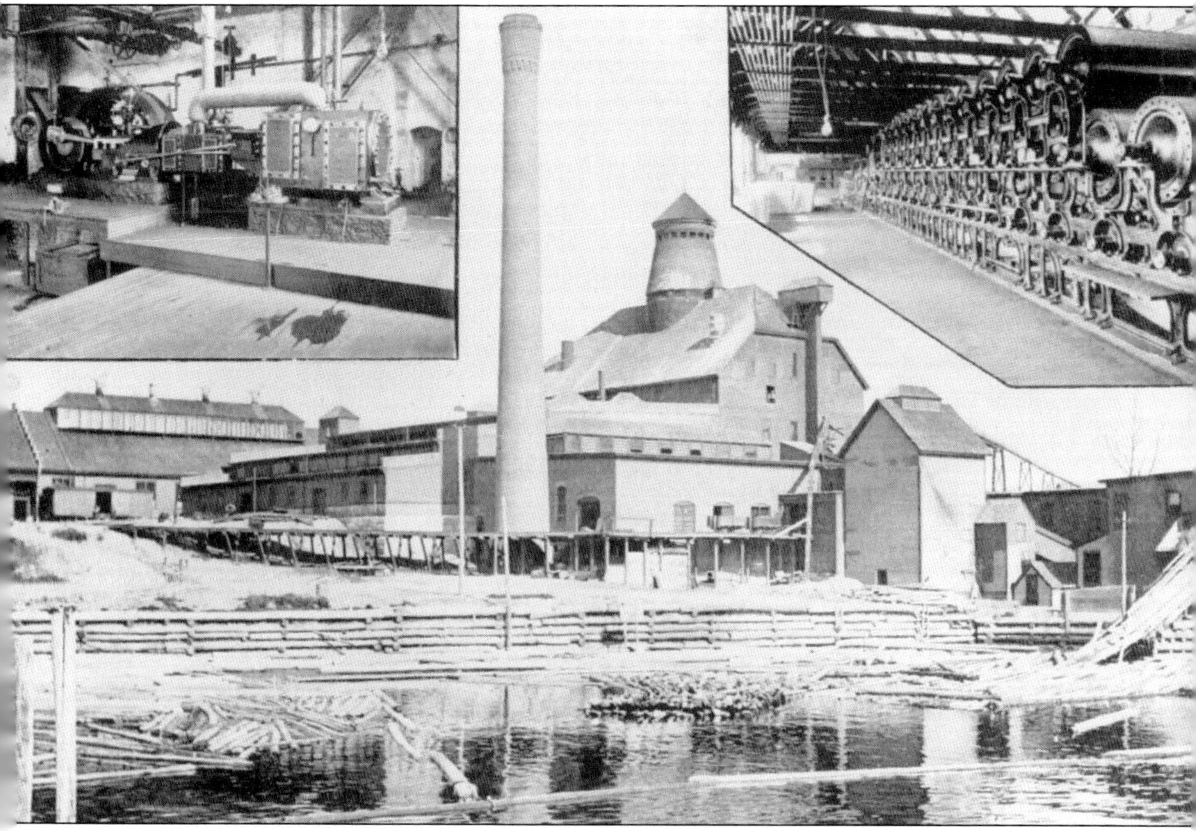

In 1889, Henry Richards moved the family paper mill from Dam No. 7 on the Cobbossee to South Gardiner, where he designed and built a pulp mill which used the latest technology from Europe. The market demanded cheap newsprint, and the Boston investors concluded that a new mill in South Gardiner would return better profits rather than retooling the obsolete mill at No. 7. The successful manufacture of 10 tons of sulfite pulp each day by eighty workers attracted a forced buyout from the International Paper Company in 1899, thereby freeing Mr. Richards to enter the most creative phase of his life when he returned to practice architecture and open Camp Merryweather.

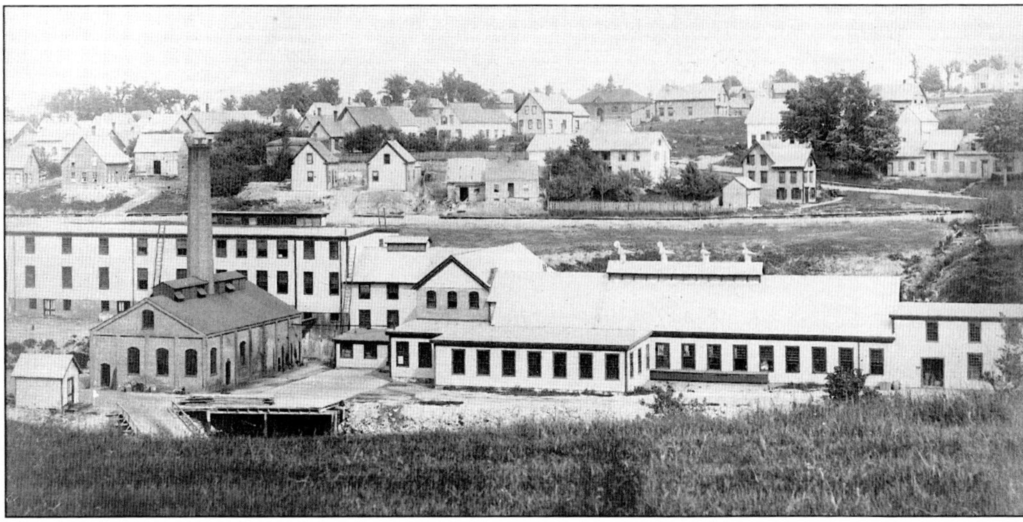

In 1876 and 1877, Ellis A. Hollingsworth and Leonard Whitney bought Dams No. 4 and 5. They erected a pulp mill at No. 4 called Aroostook Mill (shown here) and a manila paper mill at No. 5 called Cobbossee Mill, where the company introduced their newly invented satchel-bottom paper bags which made the older meal-bag style obsolete. The company closed its Gardiner plant in 1939. This photograph shows Hollingsworth and Whitney in relation to Central Street, where mill workers' houses were built.

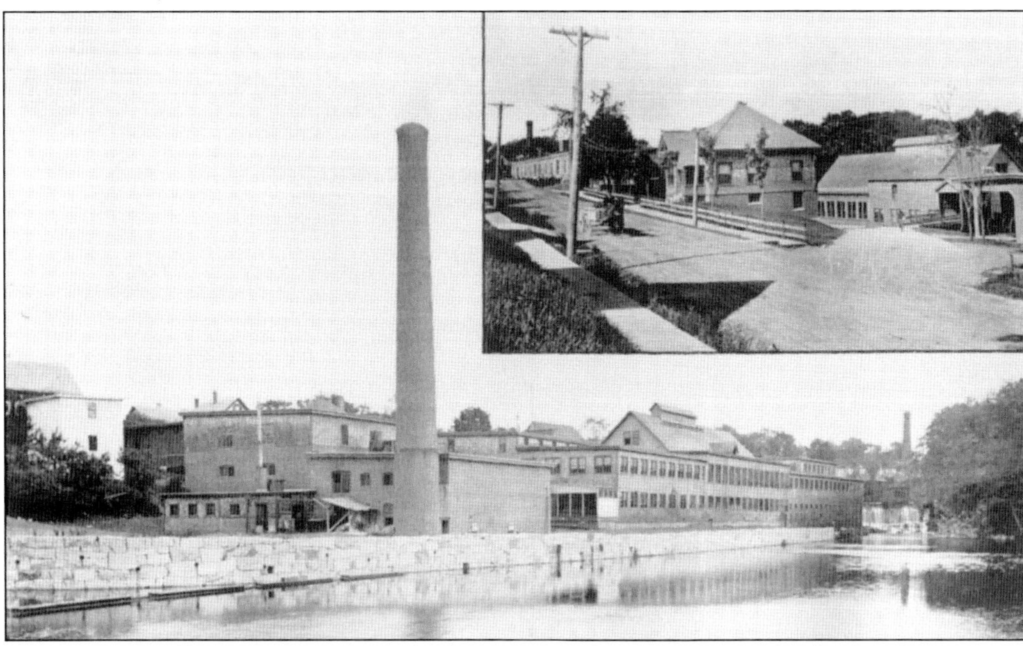

The original mill at Dam No. 6 was built in 1852. This view shows the final enlargement of the S.D. Warren Copsecook mill, when the Richards Paper Company moved out. In 1912, the mill was refitted to manufacture the product that would bring international attention to Gardiner: Bible paper. S.D. Warren closed in June 1969 when it could not meet the reduced pollution mandates of new environmental laws. The American Tissue Company reopened the plant in September 1969, but in November 1970 fire leveled the mill, forever ending paper manufacturing at Dams No. 6 and 7.

Joshua Gray (1814–1901) came to Gardiner in 1844 and became a leading capitalist in the city by buying all the mills at Dam No. 2, and buying the dam itself in 1870. In 1869 and 1870, he was both mayor and state senator. As president of the Oakland National Bank, he signed federal money from 1871. As director of the Kennebec Log Driving Company and owner of three townships on the headwaters of the Kennebec, he was one of the principal lumbermen in the state.

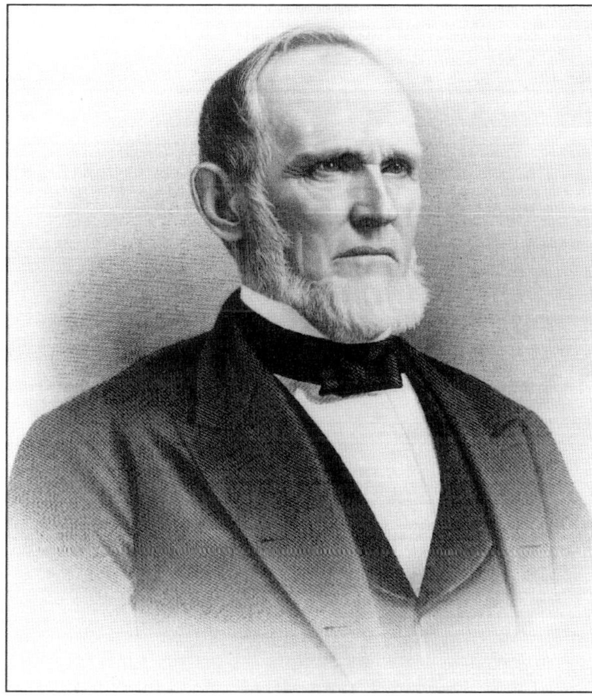

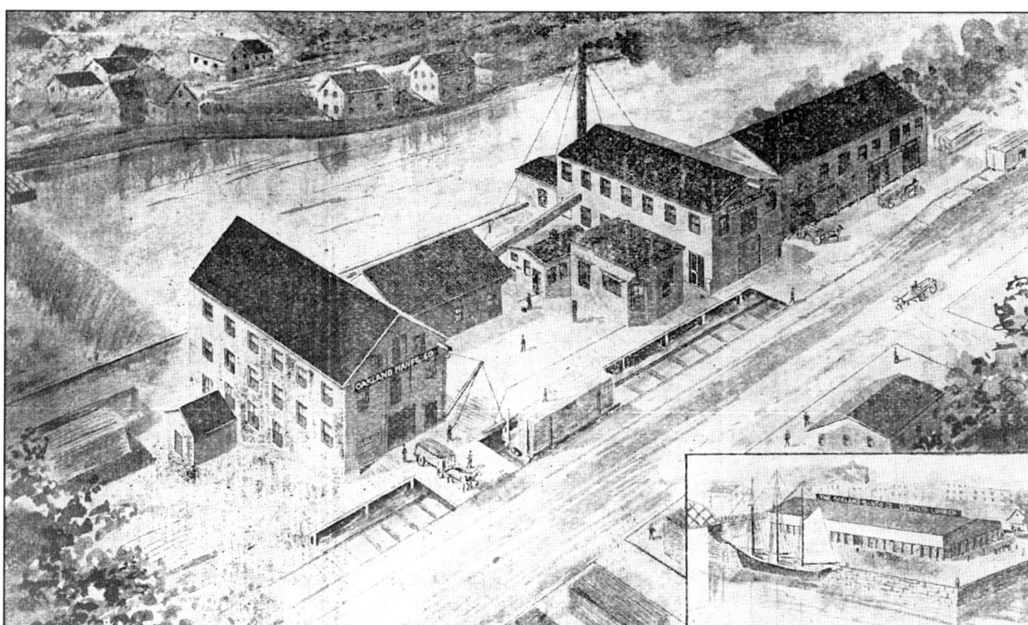

Joshua Gray organized the Oakland Manufacturing Company in 1871 to produce broom handles. By 1892, twenty-five workers were producing eight million broom handles annually, mostly for export to Europe. The factory occupied five buildings on 2 acres and used water power from Dam No. 2. In addition to handles, the company produced gutters, moldings, bed slats, and bed-spring stock. The mill burned about 1903 after which the Gray family directed their interests to the wholesale grocery business near this site known as the Gray-Hildreth Company.

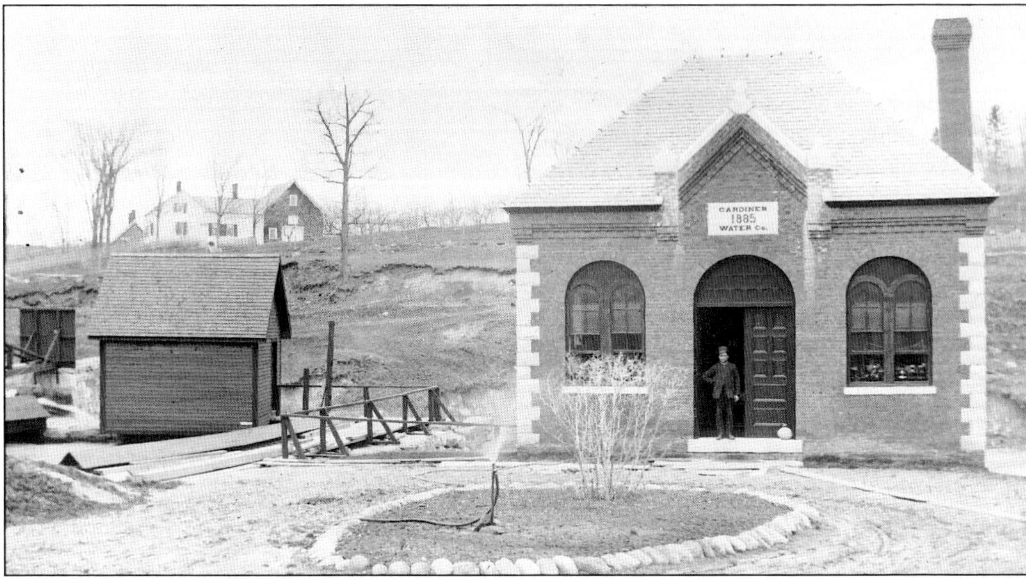

Chartered by the Maine Legislature in 1885, the Gardiner Water Company provided the city and surrounding towns with an efficient water system for fire protection and drinking water. Pumping equipment was housed in this brick Romanesque Revival-style building located at Dam No. 8 in New Mills. Designed in 1885 by Gardiner architect Edwin E. Lewis, the pumping station was later expanded by the addition of a bay at either side. The building remains in use today by the Gardiner Water District.

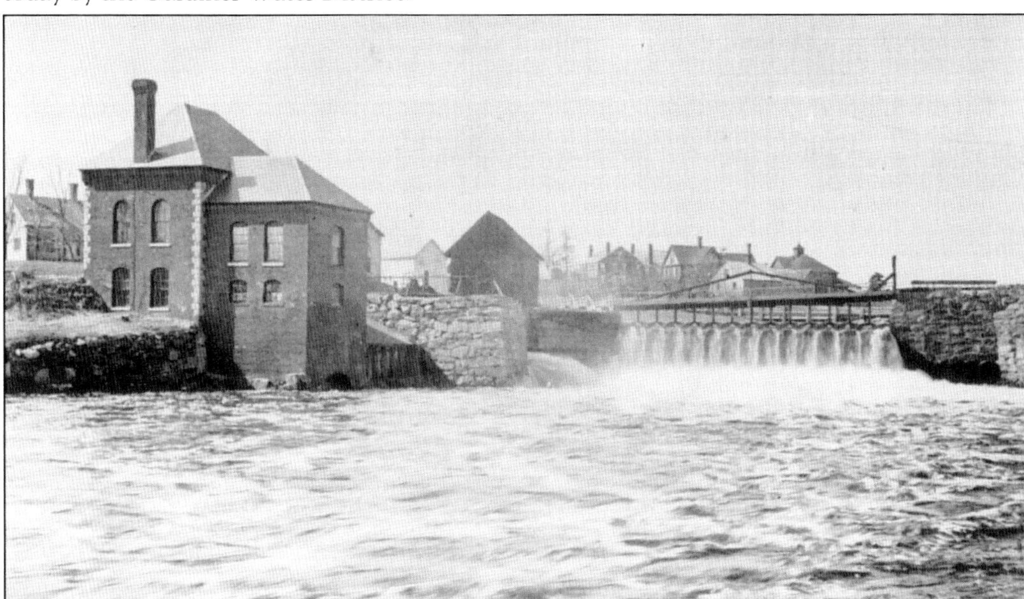

The Gardiner Water Company acquired Dam No. 8, the uppermost dam on Cobbossee Stream, in 1885 and used its water power to operate the brick pumping station on the left in this 1896 photograph. Above the mills and factories, the Cobbossee provided a pure source of water from which a nearby reservoir was filled for distribution to the community through cast-iron pipes. Gardiner's water system was one of the first in the state and served as a model for other municipalities.

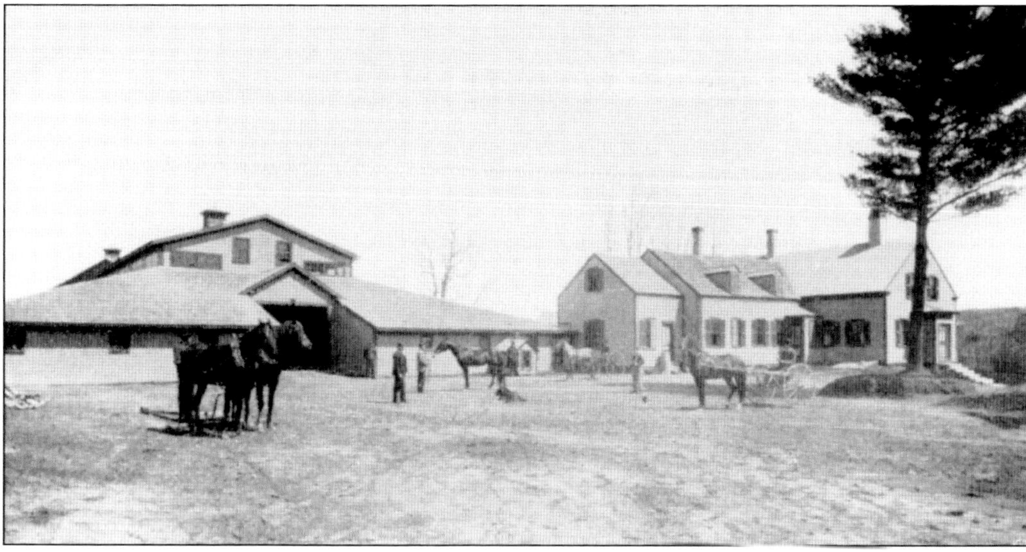

A.C. Stilphen described the Pine Tree Stock Farm as "one of the finest horse breeding farms in the state" in his 1892 history of Farmingdale. A.J. Libby managed this farm at 260 Maine Avenue in Farmingdale until the close of World War I. Under "Skipper" Bartlett, the farm became the Pine Tree Riding School in the 1940s and '50s. The Kennebec Heights Country Club now occupies the site, and Donaghy's Coastal garage, once known as Pine Tree Filling Station, is on a lot carved from the old farm.

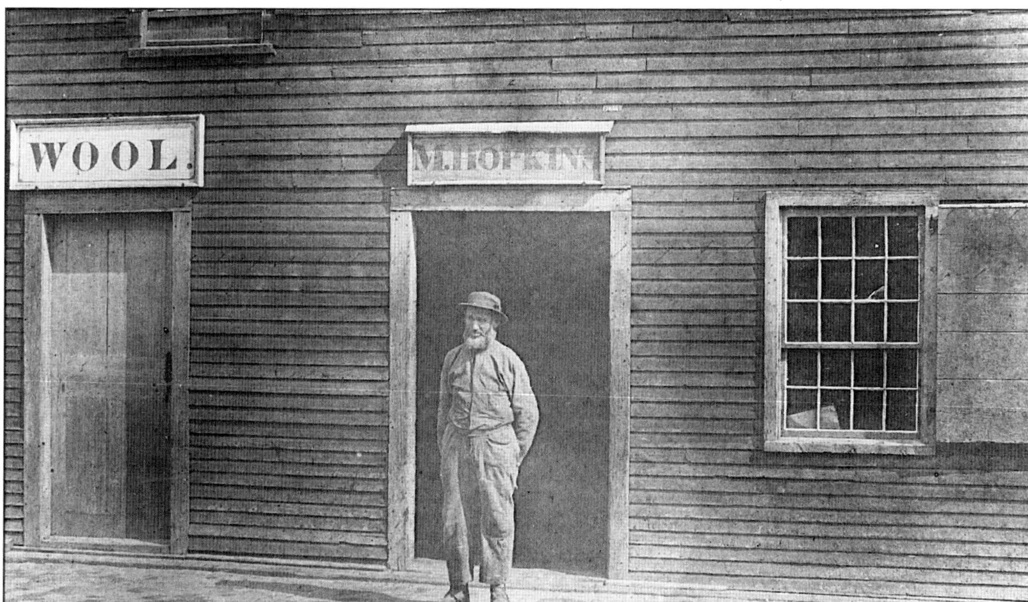

Pell Clason (1821–1892), standing in front of the Wool Shop on Water Street near the old gristmill, returned to Gardiner after the Civil War and worked here until his death. Under Myrick Hopkins's management, the Wool Shop prospered, and when he retired in 1885 he turned the business over to his son Augustus, who later sold it to Thomas Dick (owner of the local blacksmith shop from which T.W. Dick & Co. traces its organization). Clason was the father of Oliver B. Clason, attorney, mayor of Gardiner, and state representative and senator.

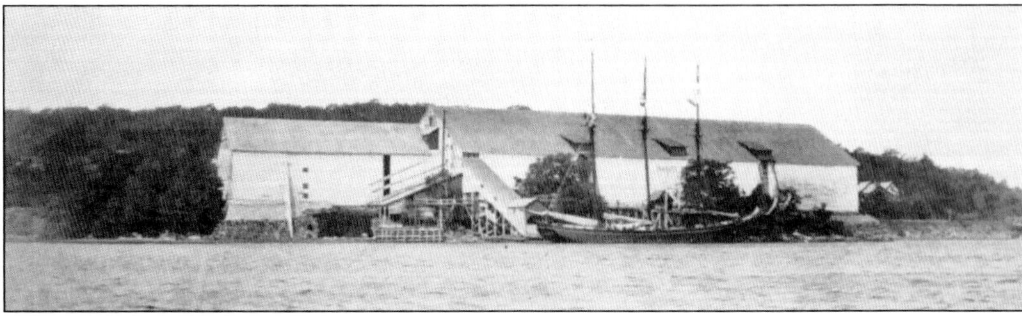

In the days before electric refrigeration, ice stored in the Eben D. Haley Ice House in South Gardiner was shipped to the major cities on the Atlantic seaboard, the West Indies, and beyond. At the turn of the century, twenty-five thousand men "harvested" ice valued annually at two million dollars, leading one historian to call it "frozen gold." Haley's was one of the fifty-five ice houses with total storage capacity of 1.5 million tons on the Kennebec. This one, which held 16,000 tons, was considered mid-range in a scale of structures which could store more than 70,000 tons.

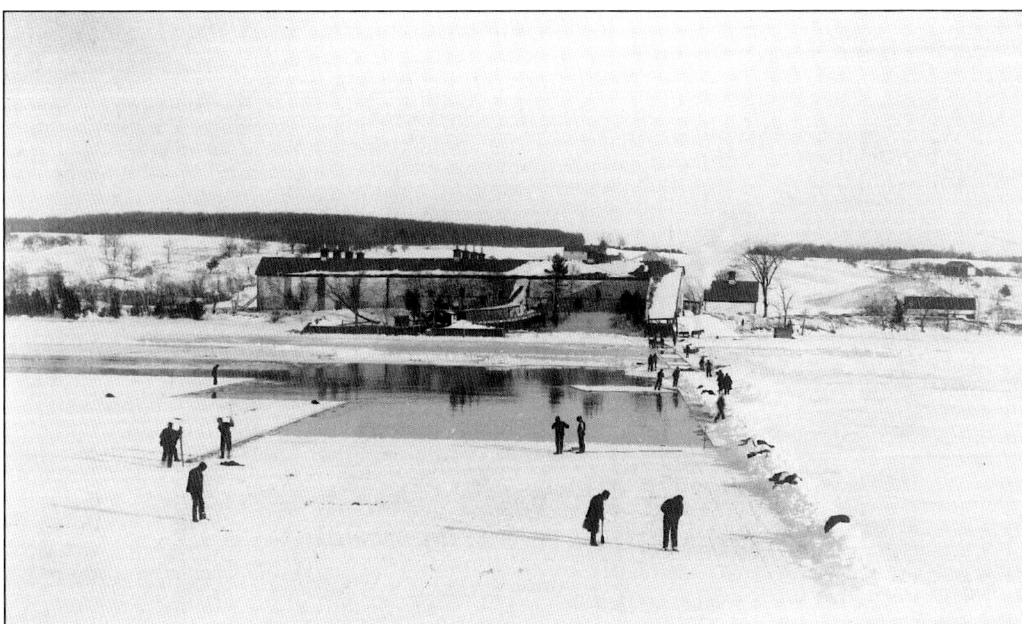

Two phases of ice harvesting appear in this photograph taken at the Independent Ice House in Pittston. Men in the foreground break open grooves in the ice to segregate sheets, and in the background, ice that has already been harvested is split into smaller pieces which will fit onto the elevator belt.

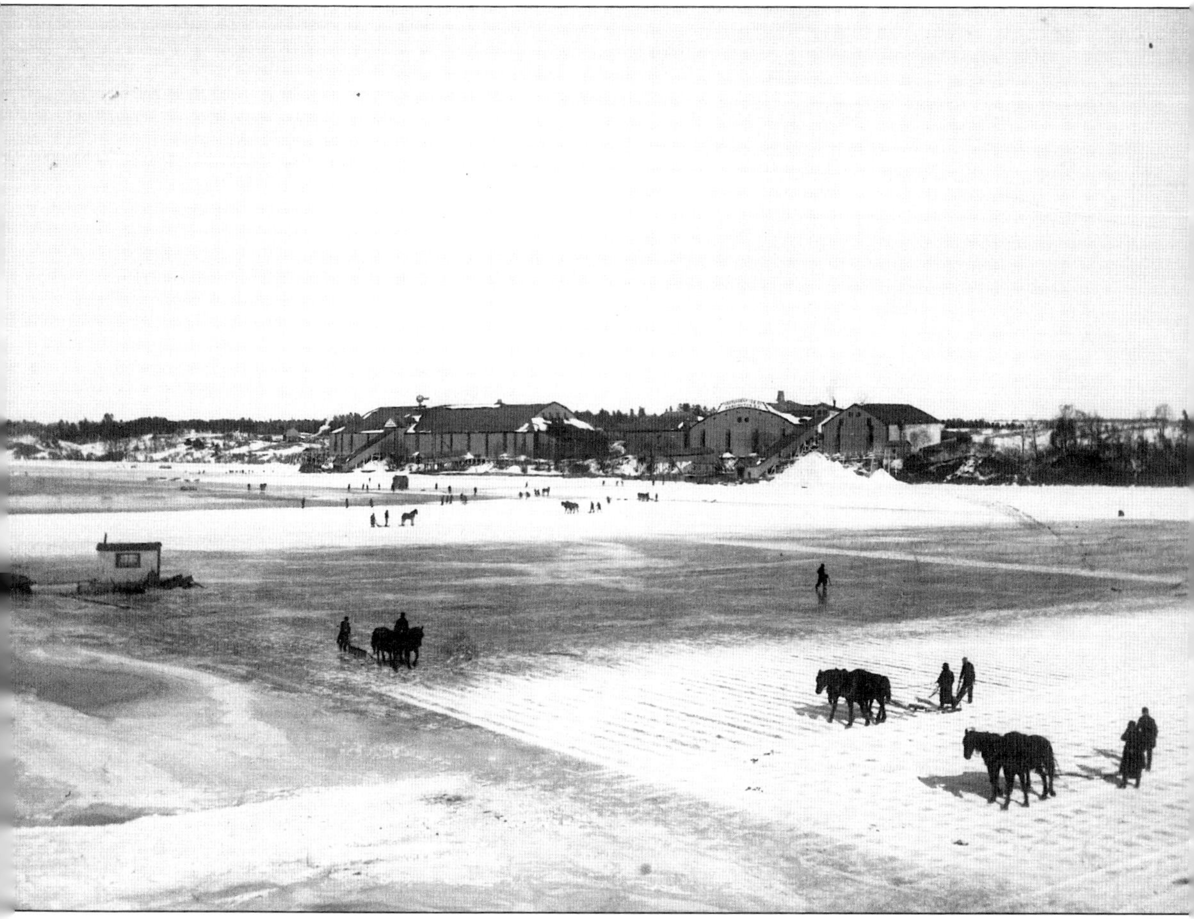

Also at the Independent Ice Company, horse-drawn markers lay out the ice field in a grid. These lines were essential for the men who were to follow with chisels, saws, busting bars, and picks so they could break the ice off at right angles for transport through canals and up the elevator to the ice house.

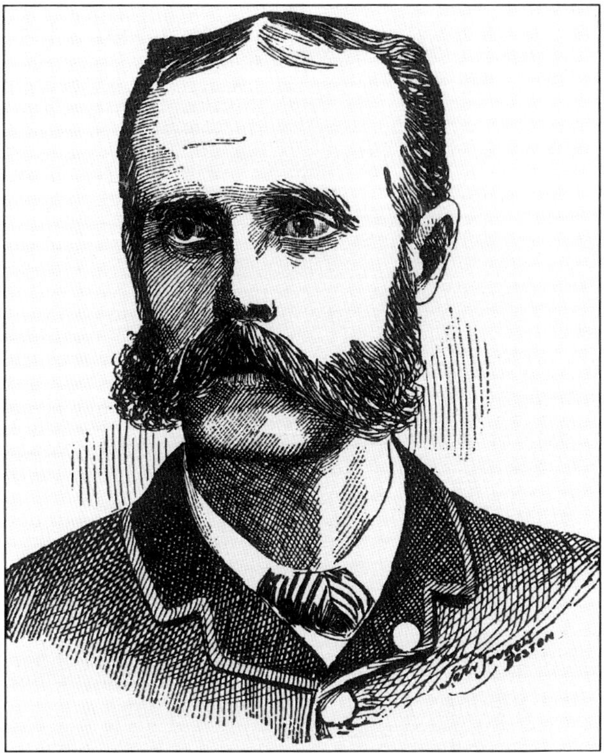

During the 1880s and '90s, many of Gardiner's homes, churches, and commercial buildings were designed by Edwin E. Lewis (1846–1928). A native of Cornish, New Hampshire, Lewis served in Vermont's 8th Infantry Regiment during the Civil War. From 1884 to 1897, he practiced architecture in Gardiner and received commissions for work throughout central Maine. In 1897, he was appointed chief engineer of the Soldiers Home at Togus, and for the next twenty years he either designed or supervised the construction of new buildings at the military hospital.

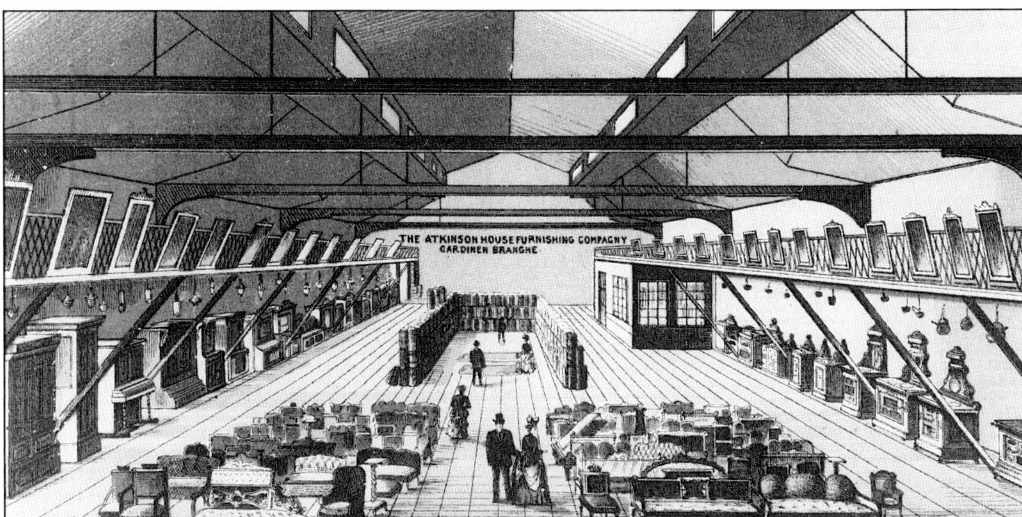

The novelty of the Gardiner Coliseum was short-lived. By 1889, the state's largest convention hall was sold to the Atkinson House Furnishing Company. However, the great hall had a moment of glory when the furniture was removed for the carnival week of May 20–25, 1895. The carnival's sponsor, the Gardiner Board of Trade, held several events in the elaborately-decorated auditorium, including a fair, band concerts, and "Our Baby Congress," which brought together 119 of the city's youngest citizens. A fire claimed the Coliseum in 1904, bringing an end to what the press had described only twenty years before as "Gardiner's grand amphitheater."

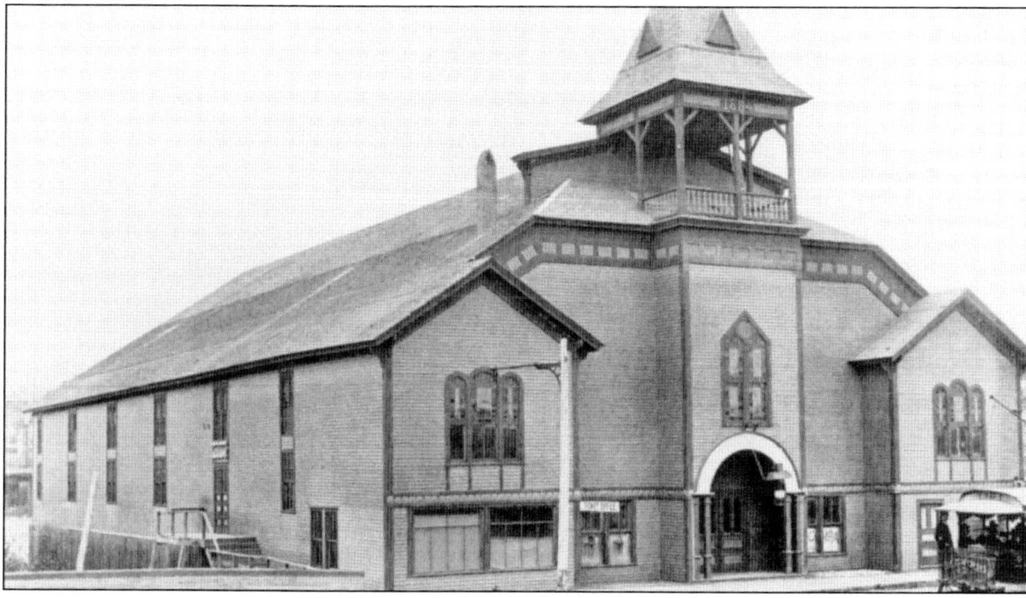

In 1884, the Gardiner Coliseum Company built the state's largest convention hall on Maine Avenue just north of the Cobbossee Stream. Designed by Gardiner architect Edwin E. Lewis, this 81-by-155-foot Queen Anne-style frame structure housed an auditorium which featured a stage, galleries, and a roller skating rink. The hall could seat 2,500 people, or 1,000 if the skating surface was in use.

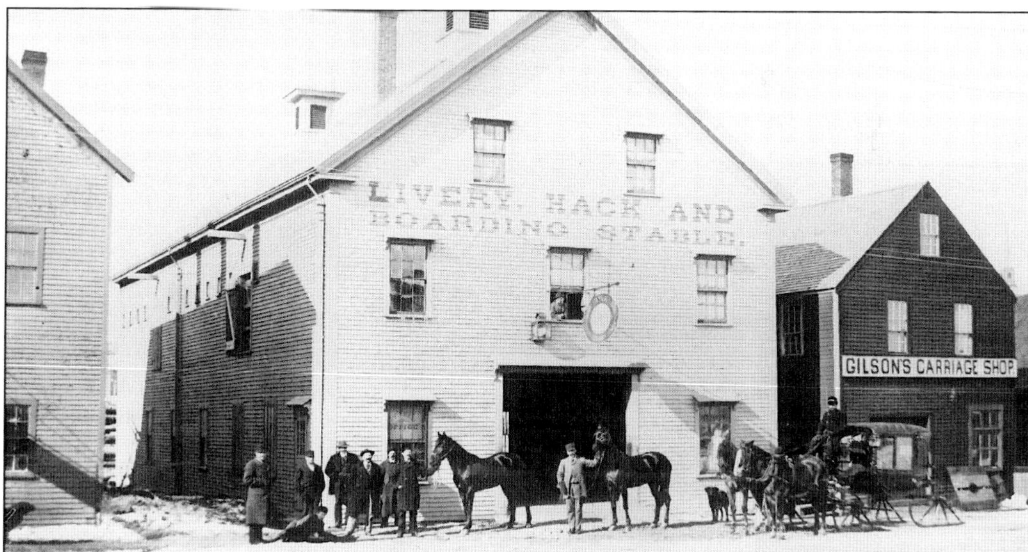

The livery station, established in 1879 by E.D. Tasker & Co., opposite the depot in this building, boarded horses for passengers departing on the train and rented teams to people arriving in town. In 1889, they advertised that their horses "will be supplied for Funerals, Parties, Weddings or other occasions at short notice, and careful expert drivers are invariably placed in charge of such conveyances." By 1911, when the depot moved to the north side of the stream, automobiles were rapidly replacing horse and buggies. The sagging walls of Harvey's Hardware, which occupies the building today, resulted from the tremendous weight of the stalls on the second story.

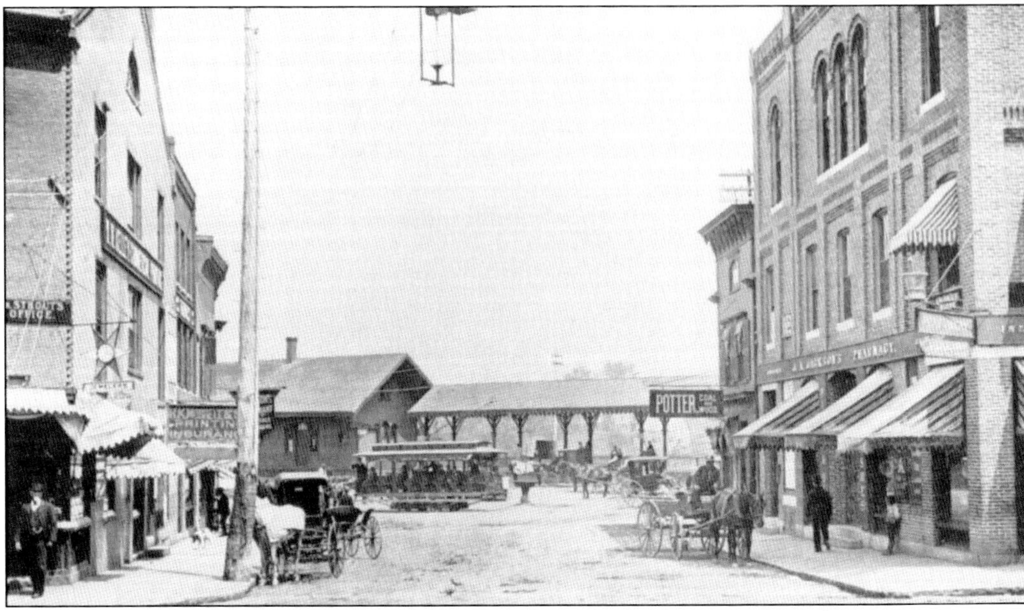

During the second half of the nineteenth century, Depot Square was the nerve center of transportation. Between 1851 and 1911 passengers debarked here where several hotels and restaurants were within a few minutes walking distance. Opposite the depot from 1884 to 1904, the coliseum drew crowds from around the state. A brief trip across the Gardiner-Randolph bridge at the right gave travelers access to the train to Togus which operated until 1926. Nearby, the steamboat landing provided the link to the water route to Boston. Between 1889 and 1932 trolley cars from Augusta also arrived here.

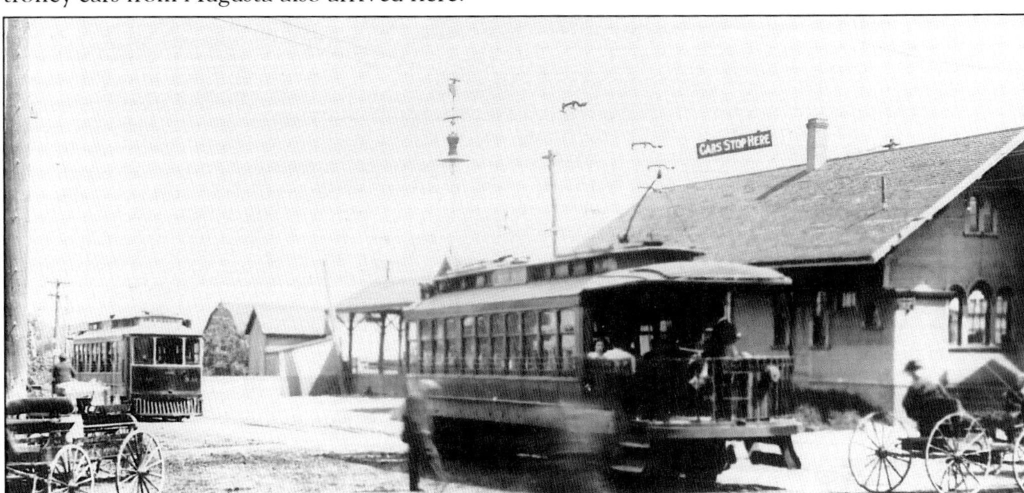

This photograph shows two of the 320–334 class cars at the turnout at Depot Square. As the second trolley company in the state, the Augusta, Winthrop and Gardiner Railroad ran its first car from Augusta to Gardiner on March 6, 1889. The company recorded its first deficit in 1930 during the Great Depression, when it could not rebuild its aging tracks. At the same time, the state made the first major improvements to Route 201 for automobiles. The last trolley came to Gardiner on July 31, 1932, and by the end of that year the tracks and overhead lines were removed.

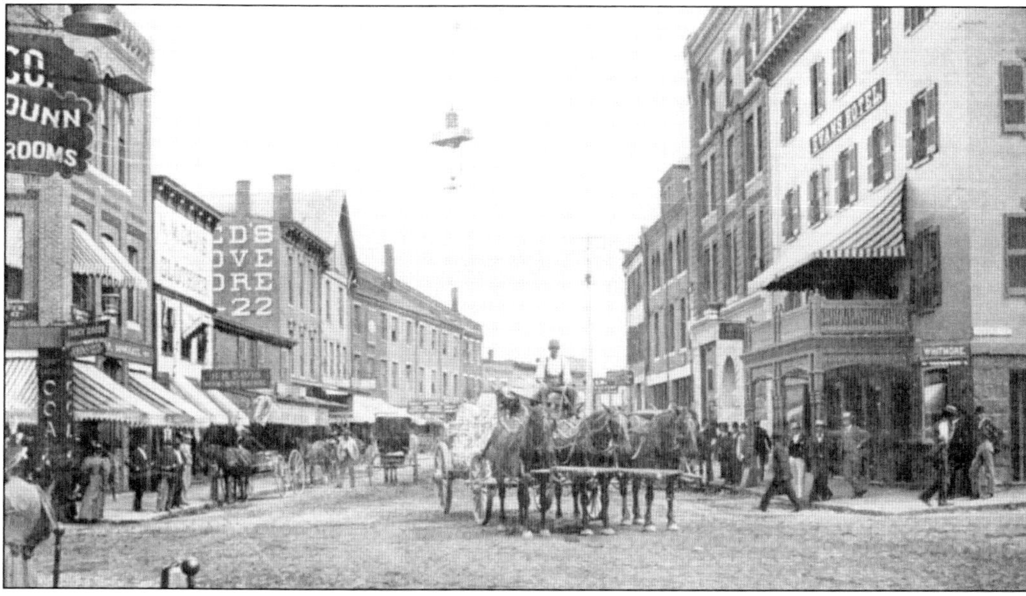

This photograph, featured in *Picturesque Gardiner* (1896), shows the south end of the business district looking from the corner of Water and Church Streets. At the left is a newly completed building now used by Gardiner Oil, while at the right stands the Evans Hotel and the Gardiner Savings Institution.

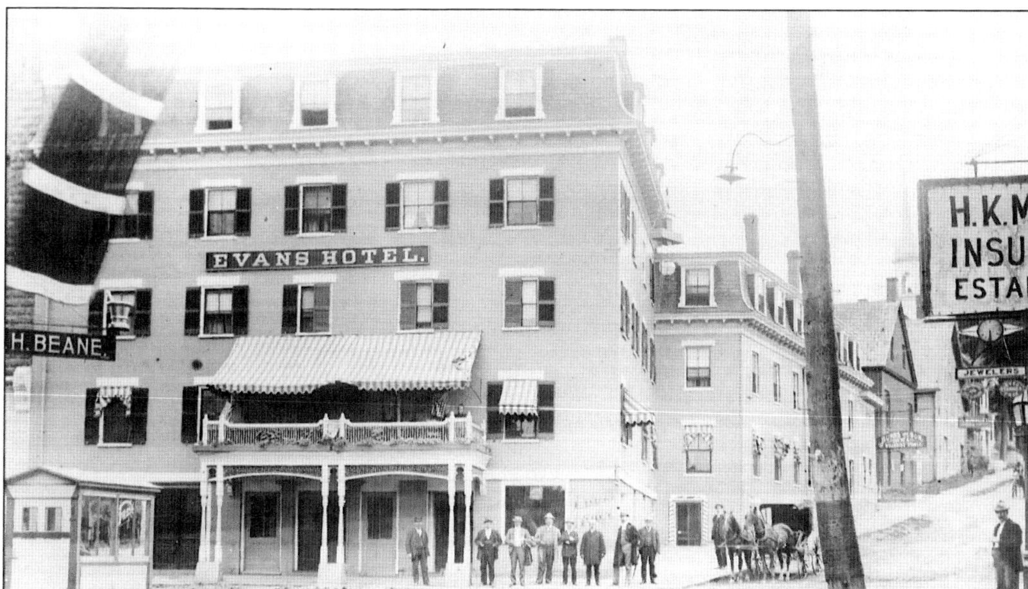

On August 14, 1900, these Gardiner citizens paused for a moment at Water and Church Streets to be captured by the camera in front of the Evans Hotel. The photographer included the portable lunch cart (at the left) and a horse-drawn carriage (at the right). Built as the Gardiner Hotel in 1837, the Evans was enlarged to its four-story appearance in 1870. An 1879 advertisement described the establishment as being "pleasantly located within two minutes walk from the depot" and having a billiard room, a barber shop, and a livery stable. Rates were $2 per night.

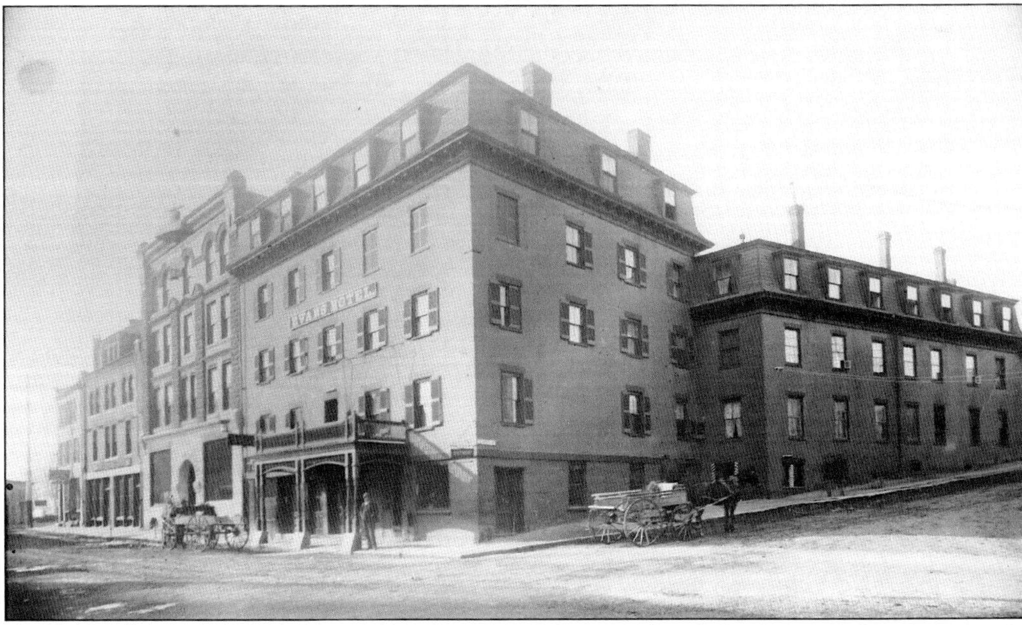

This panoramic view of the west side of Water Street at Church Street was taken prior to the fire which destroyed the Evans Hotel on March 22, 1901. From left to right are the Sawyer-Foy Building, a commercial block, the Gardiner Savings Institution, the Evans Hotel, and its three-story wing. Today only the Sawyer-Foy Building remains; the commercial block and the adjacent bank were replaced in 1954 by the present Gardiner Savings Bank, and Fleet Bank occupies the hotel site.

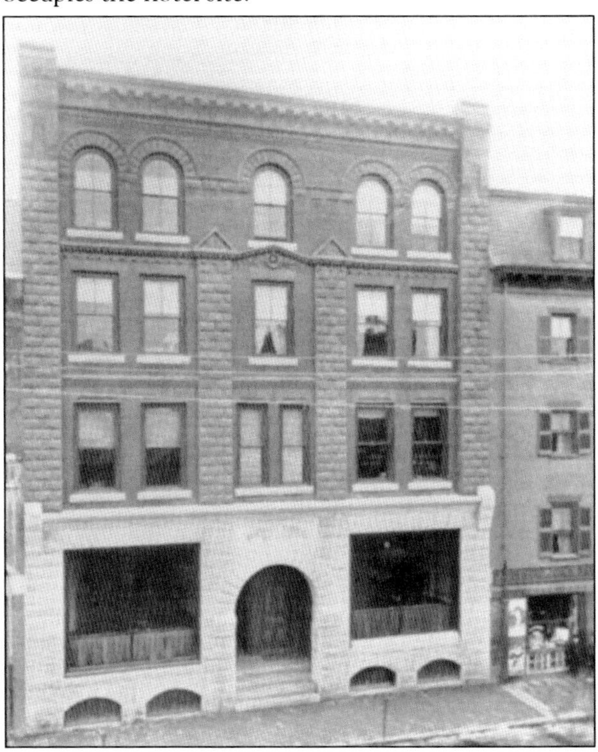

The Gardiner Savings Institution was founded in 1834 as Maine's third savings bank. In 1891, the bank built this four-story headquarters on Water Street, adjacent to the Evans Hotel. Designed by Gardiner architect Edwin E. Lewis, the Gardiner Savings Institution was a handsome brick and stone block in the Romanesque Revival style. It was torn down in 1954 to make way for the present Gardiner Savings Bank.

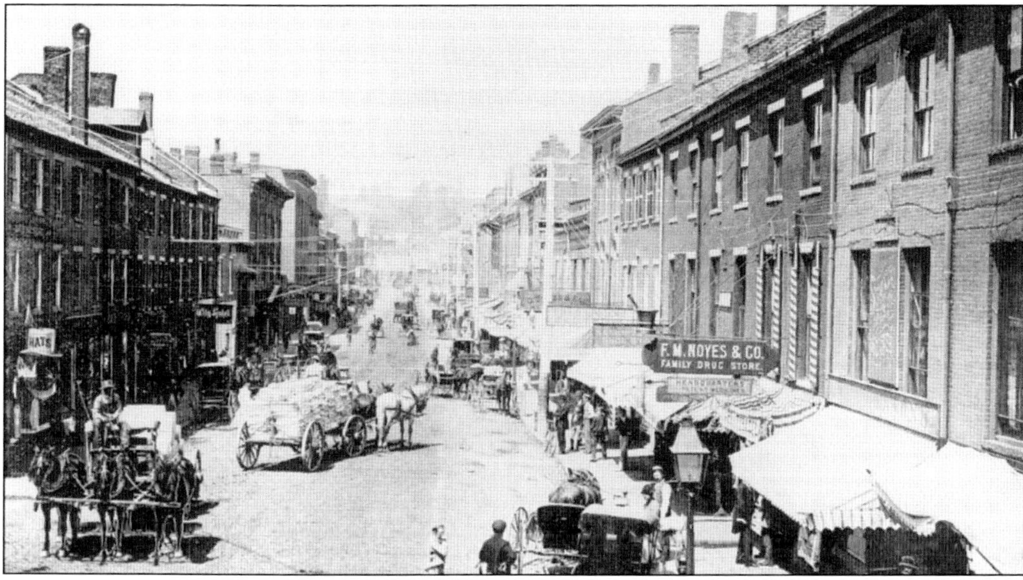

This scene of Water Street from the corner of Maine Avenue captures the activity of downtown Gardiner in the 1890s. Henry Richards described late-nineteenth-century Water Street in his 1940 memoir, *Ninety Years On*: "Shopping trips in the village were like neighborly calls, because all of the stores in those days were kept by Gardiner men and women . . . One could feel the pulse of the town, as it were, by such shopping trips and neighborly calls up and down the main street."

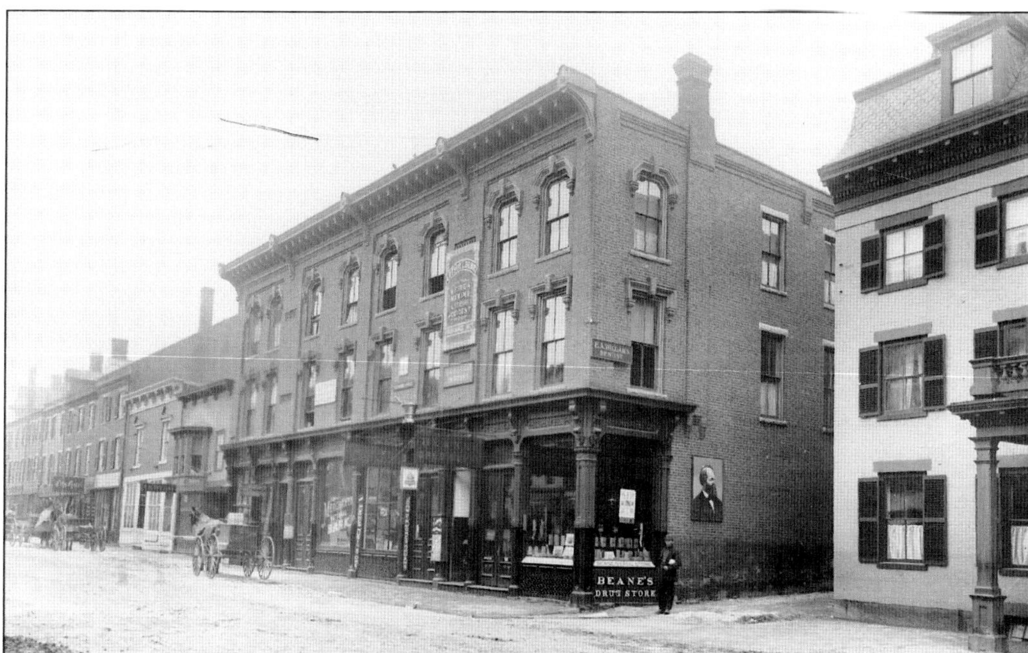

The Milliken Block was Water Street's largest Victorian commercial block. Three structures were removed in the spring of 1876 to provide the site for this three-story Italianate brick building. Completed that September, the Milliken Block featured a cast-iron storefront and window caps. The Johnson House appears at the right in this turn-of-the-century photograph.

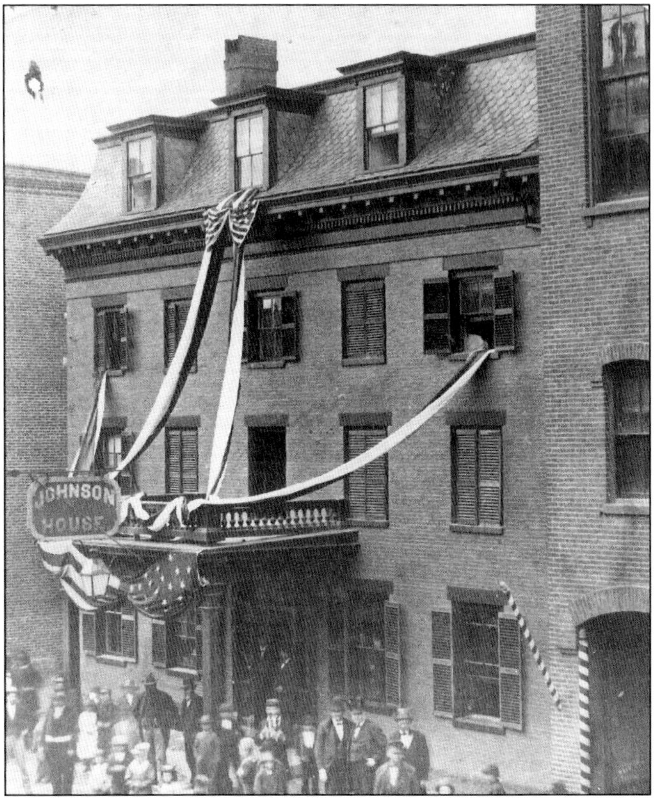

A crowd stands in front of the flag-draped Johnson House on Water Street in 1877 for a patriotic or a political event. Under Benjamin Johnson's management from the 1850s to the 1890s, the hotel became a focal point for gatherings, with speakers delivering addresses from atop the front portico. Johnson remodeled the Cobbossee House of 1827 into a fashionable mansard-roofed hotel in 1863 and added the popular Johnson Hall next door in 1864, a corner of which shows at the right of this period photograph.

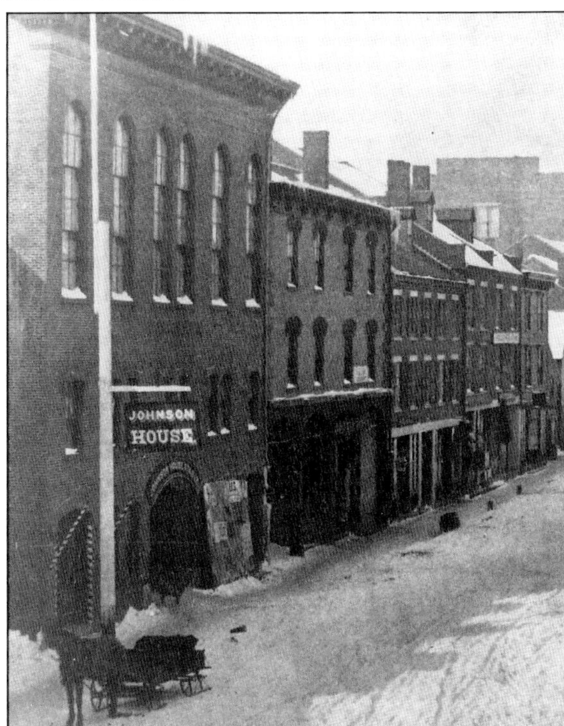

This winter scene of Water Street in the 1870s shows Johnson Hall with the Johnson House sign in the foreground. In 1864, Benjamin Johnson replaced his wooden stable with a four-story Italianate brick building. While the first and second stories contained a new hotel stable, the third and fourth stories were devoted to a theater. From its opening late in 1864 until 1930, Johnson Hall was the scene of countless plays, operas, concerts, lectures by famous personalities (such as Kit Carson), panoramas, church and society fairs, and GAR and fire department balls.

The opulence of Gardiner's golden age is best expressed in the elaborate Italianate architecture of the Charles A. White House of 1875 on Church Street. After nearly two decades as a druggist on Water Street, White became a successful stock broker in the 1870s, enabling him to build this a fine home. The White House has seen so little change since its completion that it is easily recognized today.

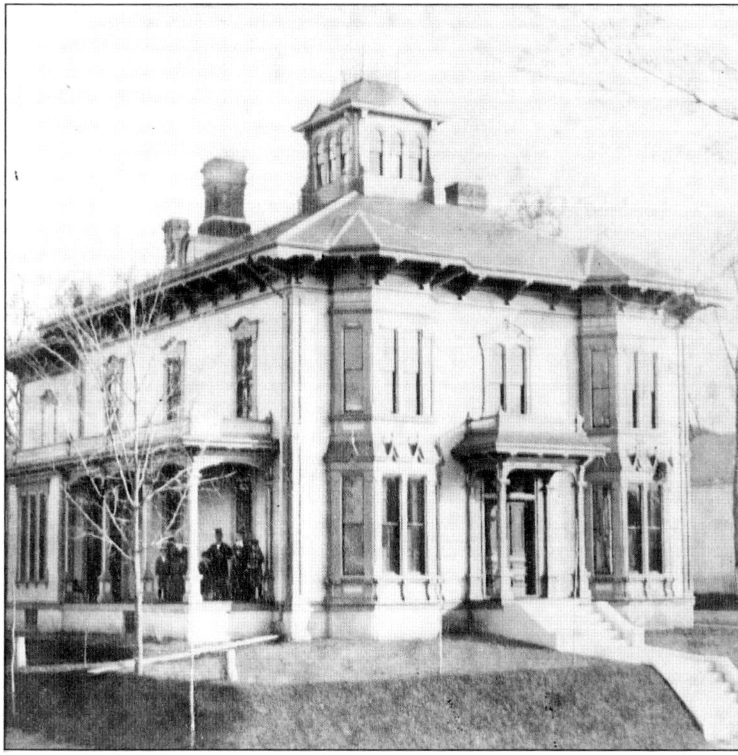

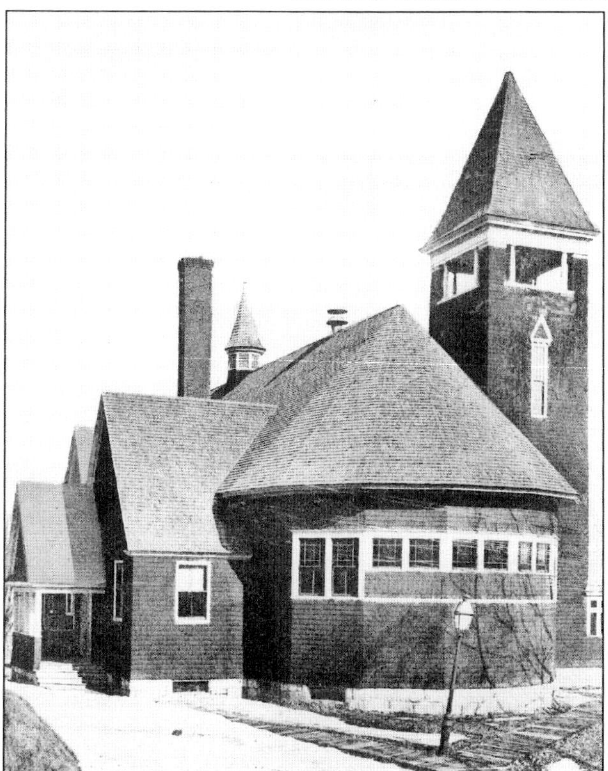

The First Baptist Church originated as the Gardiner Village Baptist Church in 1843. The congregation held services in a church on Brunswick Avenue from 1855 until 1881, when the building became the GAR Hall. With the assistance of the State Baptist Convention, the present First Baptist Church was built on Church Street in 1889 at a cost of $10,000. Designed by noted Portland architect John Calvin Stevens, this fine example of Shingle-Style architecture is similar to Baptist churches planned by Stevens in Skowhegan, Yarmouth, Westbrook, and several other Maine communities.

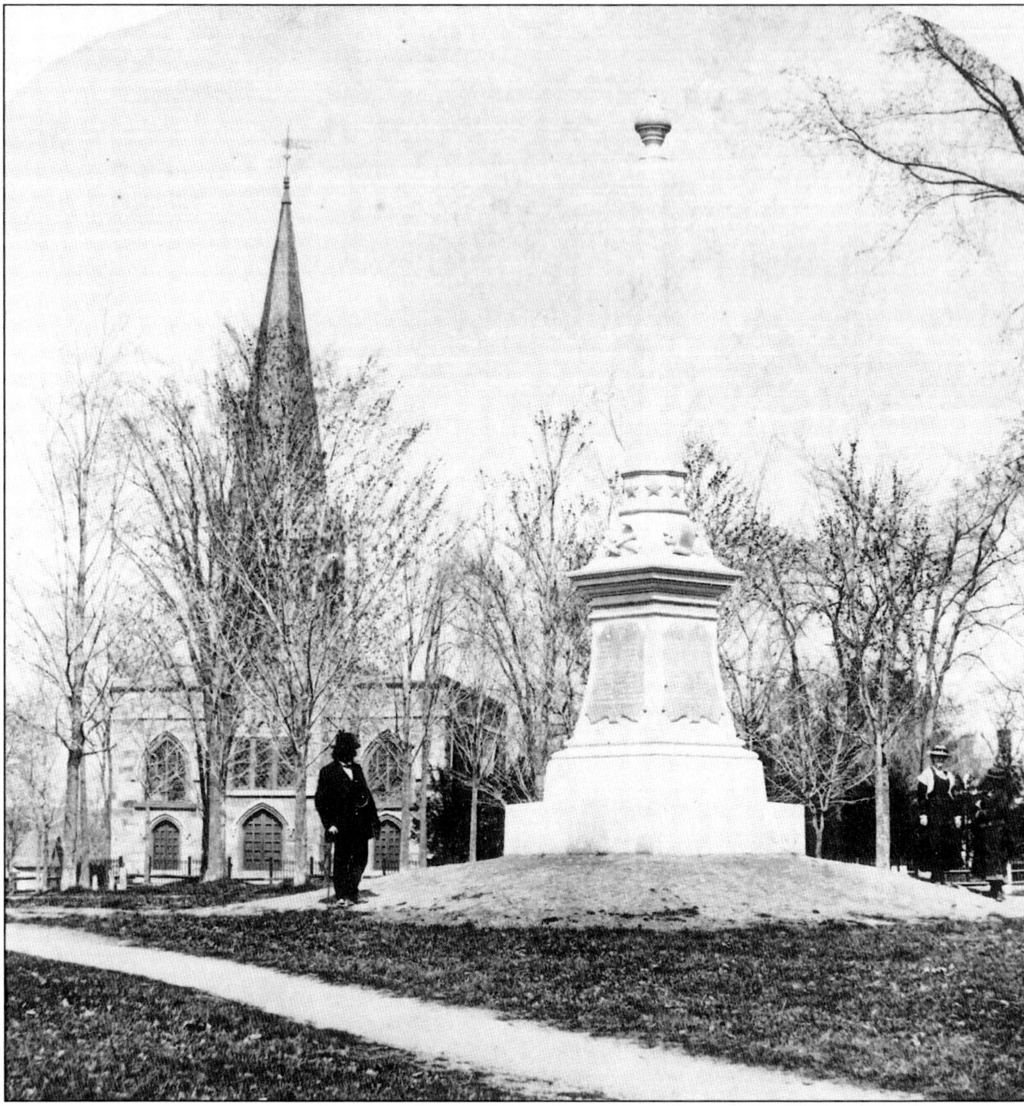

Of the 475 men from Gardiner who served in the Civil War, seventy-one were killed in battle or died from disease in the hospital—an extraordinary number compared to the sixty who fell in the next four wars. They are commemorated by this monument erected on the Common in 1875. Christ Church appears in the background. Shortly after this photograph was taken in 1877, an iron fence graced the monument, but its metal, considered essential for the allied armies of World War II, was sacrificed for another heroic effort.

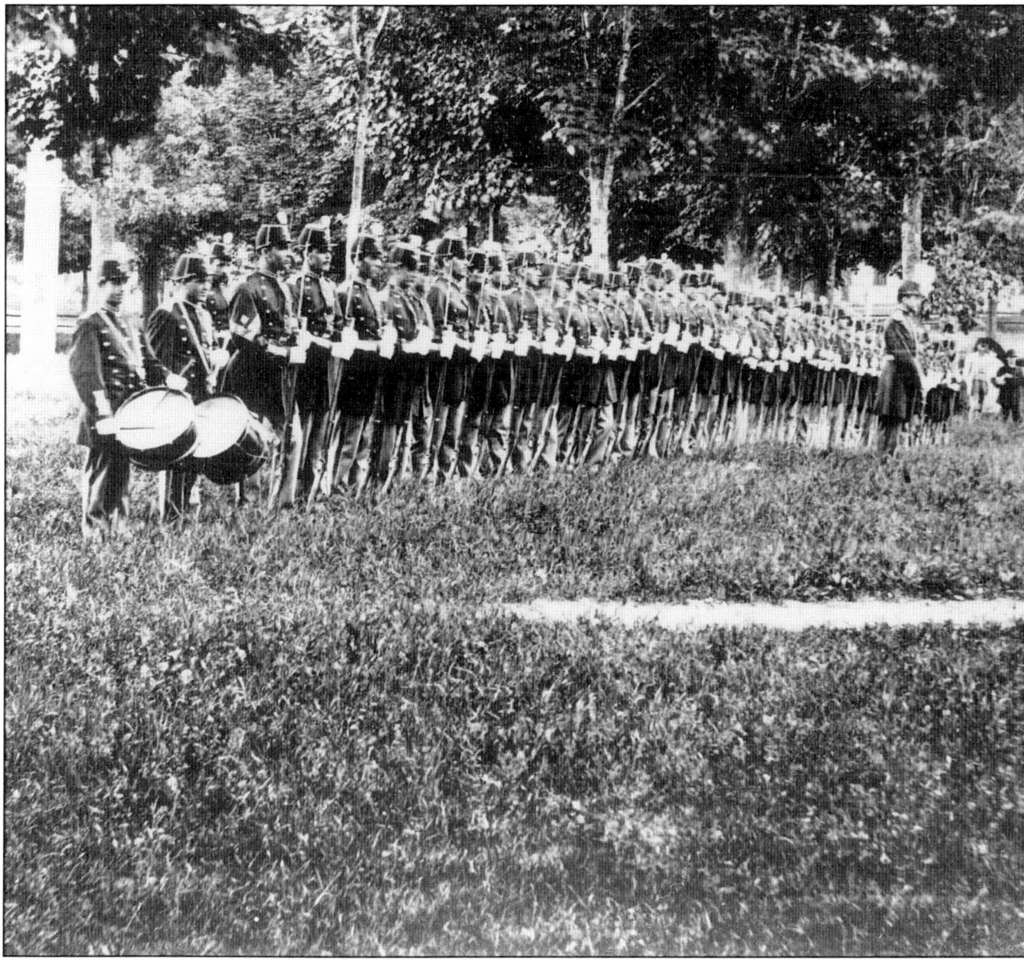

The local militia company convened on the Gardiner Common in the 1870s, when uniforms still resembled those from the Civil War. The practice of annual musters, or military training sessions, dates from the founding of New England. When Maine became a state in 1820, the constitution provided for the militia to enroll all males between eighteen and forty-five, exempting clergy, Quakers, and certain civil officials. After the Civil War, the militia was reorganized to drill males between eighteen and twenty-four on a regular basis, but, by the time of the Spanish-American War, a volunteer National Guard had replaced the old military organization.

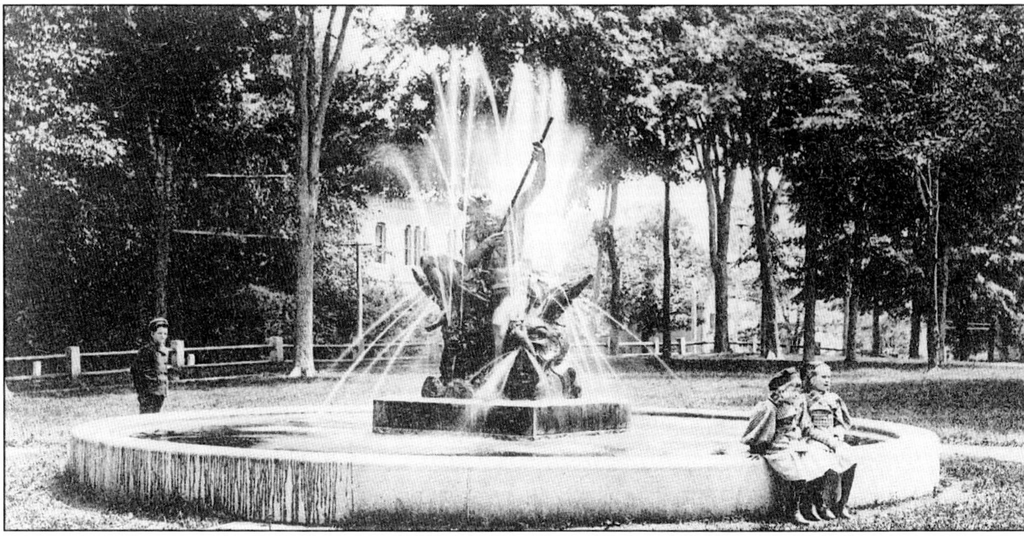

Susan Palmer presented this fountain to the city in 1894 to commemorate her late husband, Dr. Gideon S. Palmer, a Gardiner native who served as brigade surgeon in the Civil War and later as professor of physiology at Howard University. In her deed of gift she stipulated that it be 20 feet in diameter, surmounted by a bronze figure, and never be moved from the corner near Christ Church. The statue of Neptune seen in this 1896 view was sacrificed for its metal during World War II, but since 1977, Norman Therrien's statue *The Lady and the Birds* has graced the fountain.

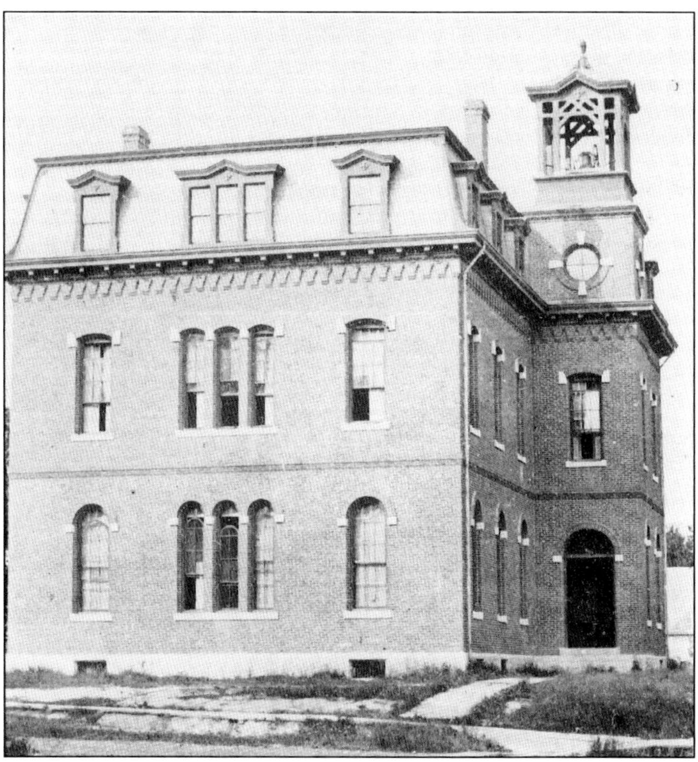

Gardiner High School was erected in 1870 at Dresden Avenue and School Streets to replace the 1822 Lyceum, which had served as the community's high school since the 1850s. Designed by Portland architect Francis H. Fassett, this brick mansard-roofed building was the city's high school until 1921, when a new facility was constructed on an adjacent lot. During the next four decades, the old high school was used as a junior high and for overflow high school classes. The building was torn down in 1969, just short of its centennial year. Its most famous graduate was poet Edwin Arlington Robinson, a member of the class of 1888.

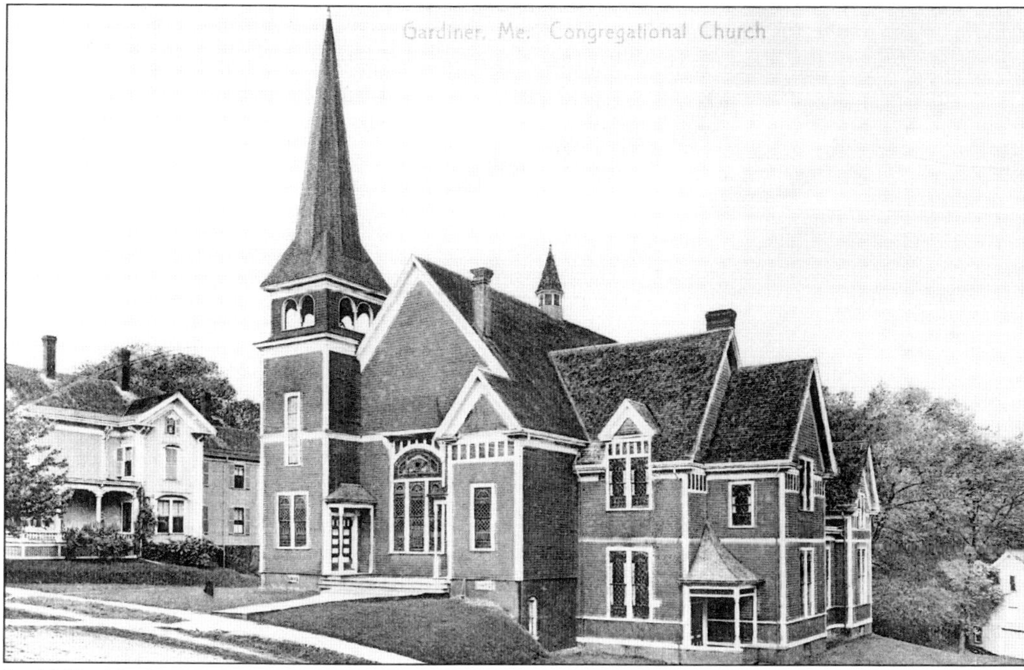

In 1889–90, the Congregationalists remodeled their 1836 meetinghouse on Brunswick Avenue into this picturesque Queen Anne-style church. Edwin E. Lewis of Gardiner served as the architect for the changes. The building was destroyed by fire in 1915, and its site is now occupied by Christy's Convenience Store.

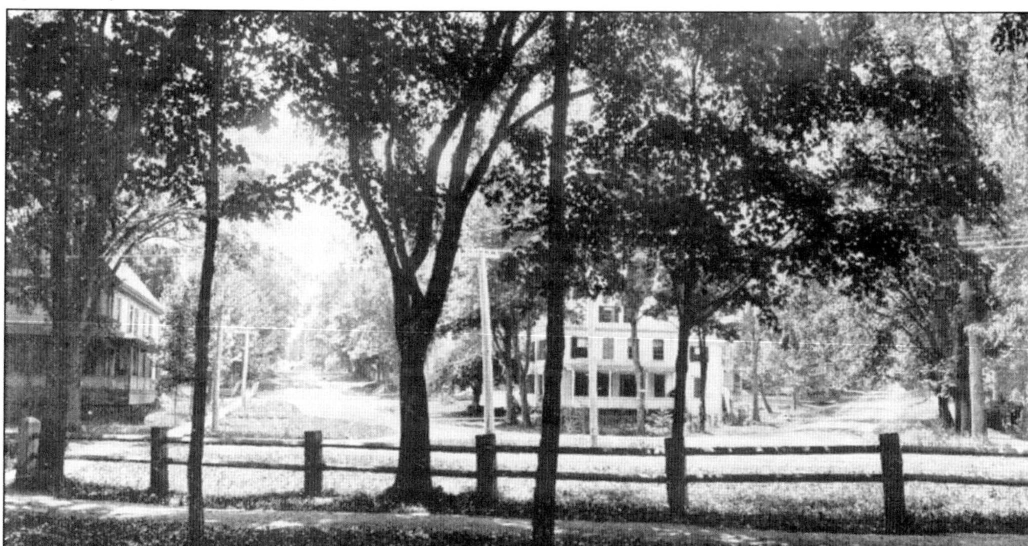

Robert Hallowell Gardiner I's establishment of a 5-acre Common in 1824 resulted in the development of a fine residential neighborhood on the surrounding streets. Along with constructing substantial homes, early residents planted graceful elm trees, which had attained a sizable growth by the time of this 1896 photograph. Here, the reader stands on the Common a century ago, looking up the lush, tree-lined thoroughfares of Brunswick Avenue at the left and Washington Avenue at the right.

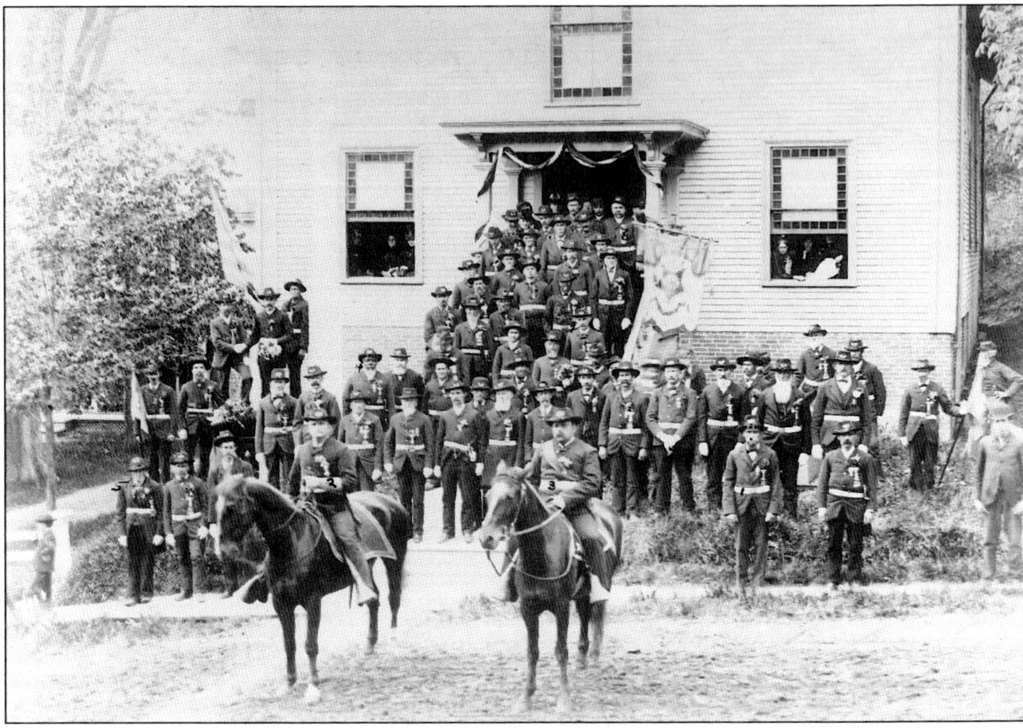

Members of the Heath Post of the Grand Army of the Republic (GAR) pose in front of their hall on Brunswick Avenue. After the Civil War, veterans formed posts across the nation in the same way that twentieth-century veterans have organized American Legion posts. Gardiner's GAR post honored the first soldier from this city to die in the Civil War: newspaper publisher Alvan M. C. Heath, who was killed in his first battle. He was the father of Dr. Gertrude E. Heath.

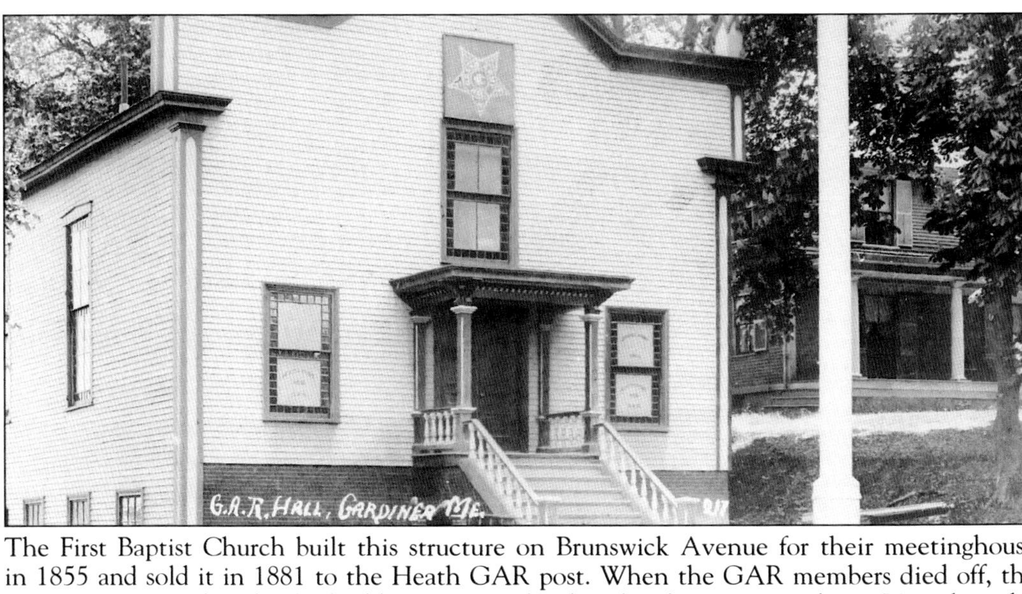

The First Baptist Church built this structure on Brunswick Avenue for their meetinghouse in 1855 and sold it in 1881 to the Heath GAR post. When the GAR members died off, the American Legion bought the building in 1922 for their headquarters. In the 1970s, when the Gardiner Legion built a new post on Griffin Street, this building was demolished.

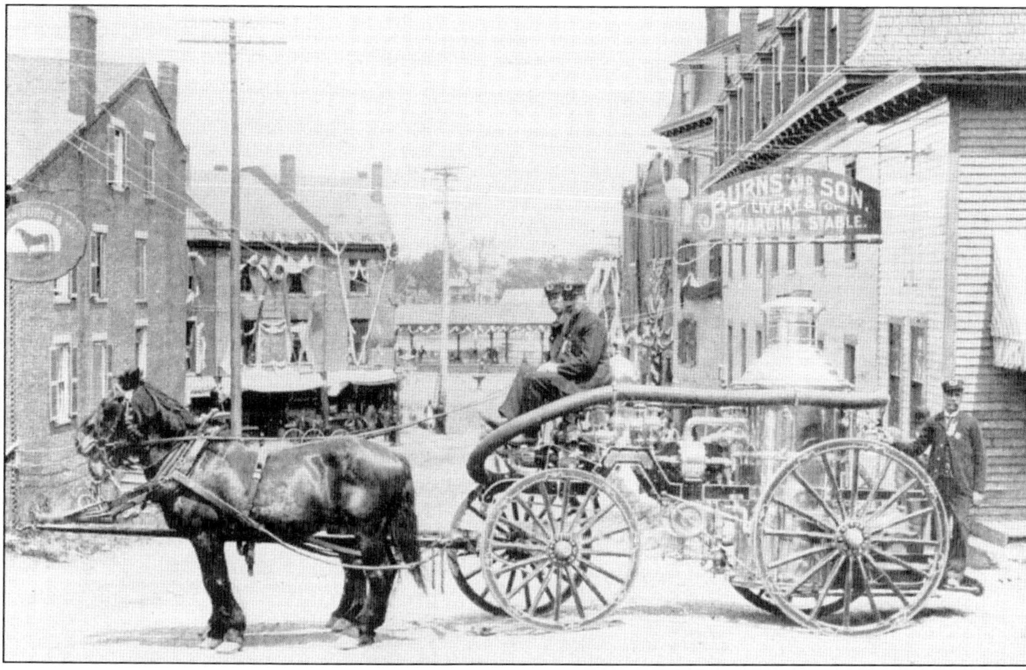

In 1860, a disastrous fire leveled thirty buildings in the center of Gardiner, a scene repeated in 1882 with a loss of sixty structures. In response to the second conflagration, the city purchased the steamer City of Gardiner from the Silsby Steam Engine Company of Seneca Falls, New York, in 1882. It is shown here about 1895 leaving the fire station on Church Street, with Water Street commercial buildings and Depot Square in the background.

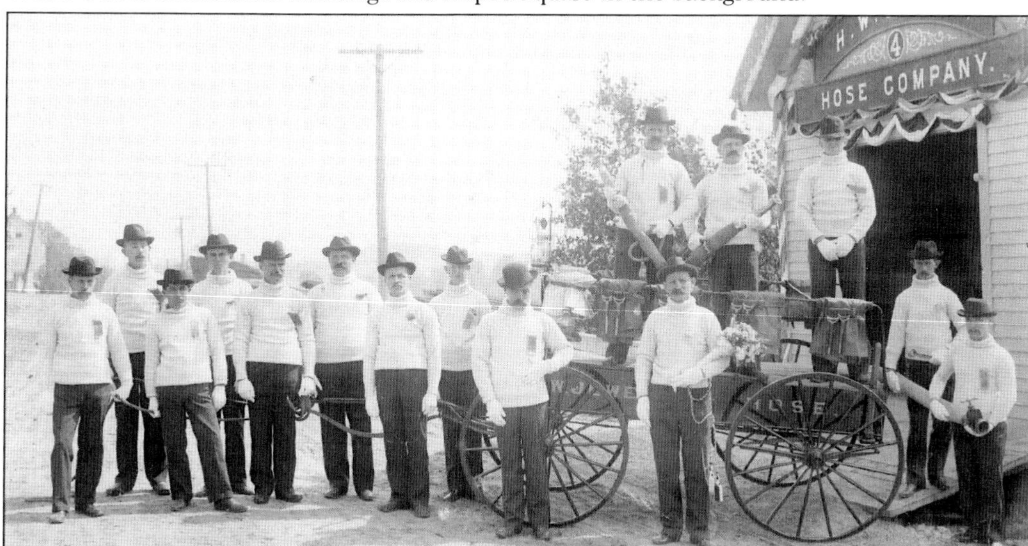

So great was the risk of fire at the sawmills on the mill pond that lumberman Hartley W. Jewett sponsored Hose Company No. 4, which bore his name. Shown here about 1898 are company members stylishly dressed in matching pants, turtleneck sweaters, and hats. Their hose wagon was kept in the wooden firehouse at the right, which stood on Bridge Street across from the present T.W. Dick Company.

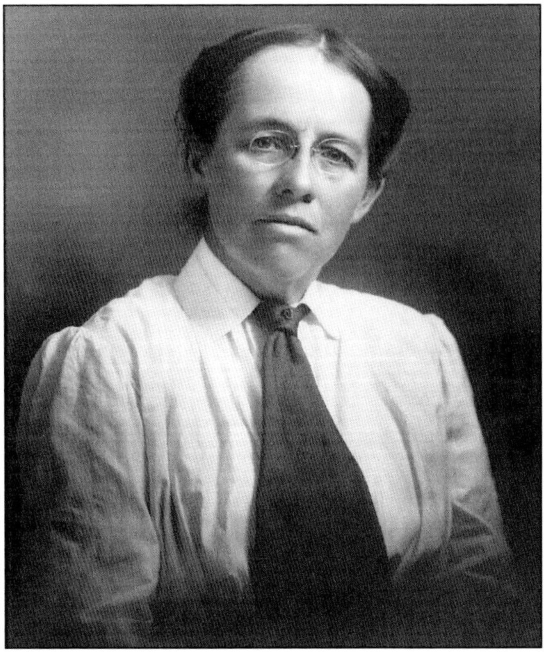

Alice M. Richards (1872–1922), eldest child of Henry and Laura E. Richards, graduated from Smith College in 1895 and became head of the English department and assistant principal at Gardiner High School until her untimely death from pneumonia. All stores in the city closed during her funeral, and her epitaph at Christ Church reads: "For twenty-seven years beloved teacher, leader, and comrade of the pupils of Gardiner High School." She is honored at the high school by the library and the annual cup given to the athlete who upholds "the spirit of true sportsmanship." Her personal motto was "To strive, to seek, to find, and not to yield."

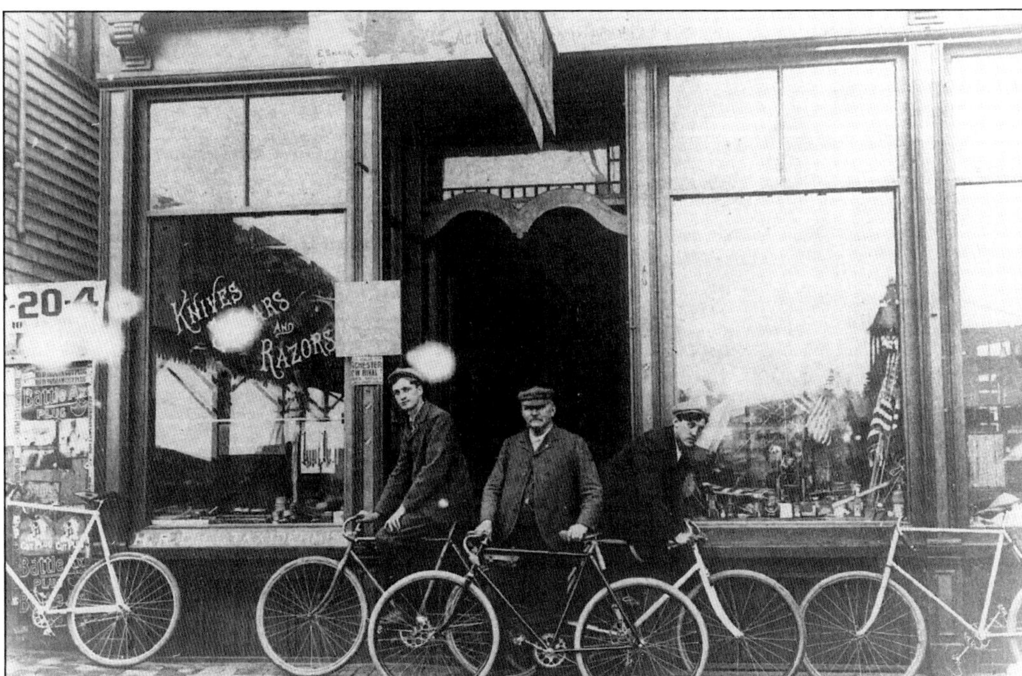

One of many nineteenth-century businesses on Water Street was Cross and Robinson's sporting goods store. After the Civil War, increasing leisure time resulted in many sporting activities, which ranged from hunting to bicycling, both of which are represented in this *c.* 1898 photograph. Hunters could have their trophies mounted at Cross and Robinson's by taxidermist H.R. Dill, while cycling enthusiasts could purchase a new bicycle from George Cross (center), his partner Arthur Robinson (right), or their assistant, Arthur L. Currier (left).

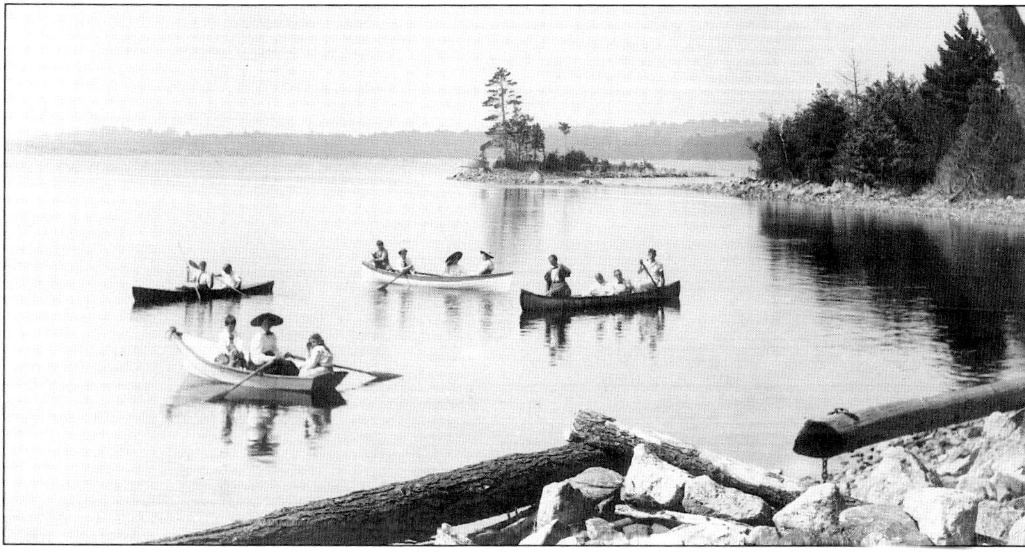

Here the Richards family enjoys an outing on Cobbossee Lake in, clockwise beginning in the foreground: the *Wobler*, the *Rob Roy*, *the Skiff*, and *the Birch*. This last one was a canoe which Henry Richards bought in 1869 from a Penobscot Indian in Bar Harbor and lovingly described in his autobiography, *Ninety Years On*. Later the family established two very competitive canoe races at Camp Merryweather known as "Around the Horn," a 27-mile circuit, and the much more strenuous 56-mile race known as "Around the World."

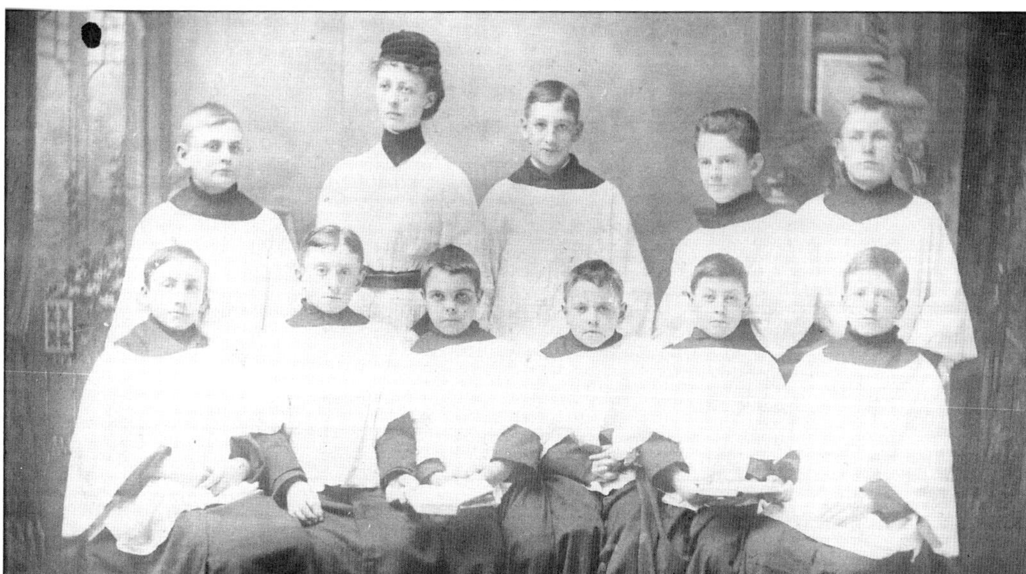

In January 1890, the choir at Christ Church wore vestments for the first time and hired Miss Pauline Johnson of Augusta as organist. The paid members, mostly drawn from the parish, acquired a high reputation throughout the state. From left to right are: (front row) Paul Berry, Joe Woodward, Frank Wadsworth, F. Dill, Charles Gay, and Ray Dennis; (back row) James Barstow, Miss Johnson, Arthur Strout, Arthur Grant, and Peter Berry. Dennis later became an investment banker in New York City and a partner of J.P. Morgan in an international shipping company.

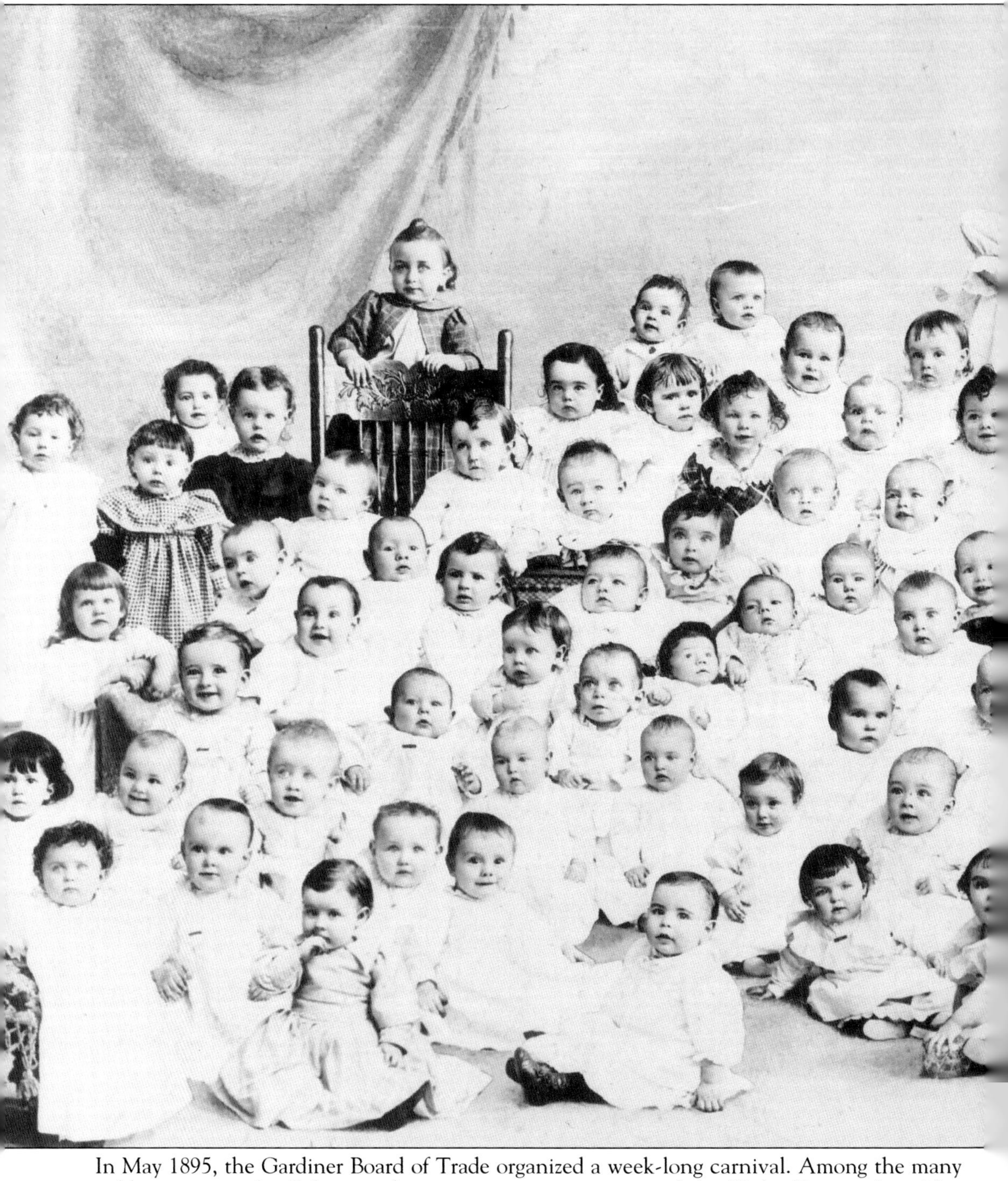

In May 1895, the Gardiner Board of Trade organized a week-long carnival. Among the many public events at the Coliseum, the executive committee staged the "Baby Congress" on May 22 which filled the building to record capacity by 2:30 pm. The next day, the *Gardiner Reporter Journal* remarked, "But what a sight, babies big, babies little, babies fat, babies lean, babies cross, babies good, BABIES." First prize of a baby carriage went to the most handsome baby, Thelma Lord of Randolph; second prize of a silver cup went to the largest, Eugene Collins, 38

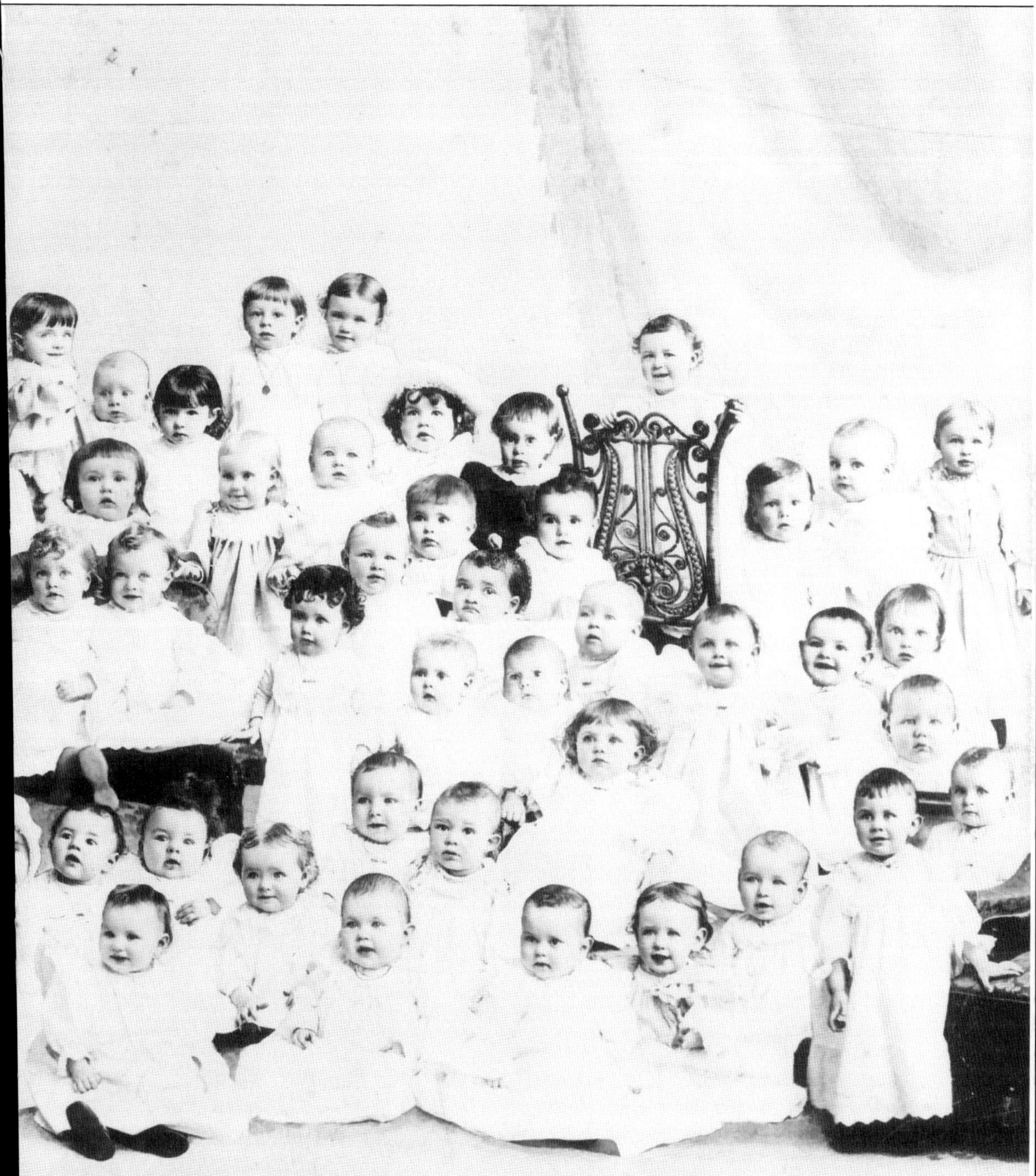

pounds; third prize of a silver cup went to the smallest, Chester Keen, 6.5 pounds; and fourth prize of a doll to each of the best pair of twins, Henry and Helen Smith. The 119 babies who entered the contest appear in this cut-and-paste composite published by the photographer A.T. Reynolds on May 28, 1895. In researching this photograph, co-author Danny Smith discovered his grandfather, Fred Linwood Smith (1894–1959), the boy with bangs, second left from the lyre-back chair, immediately below the baby in the black gown.

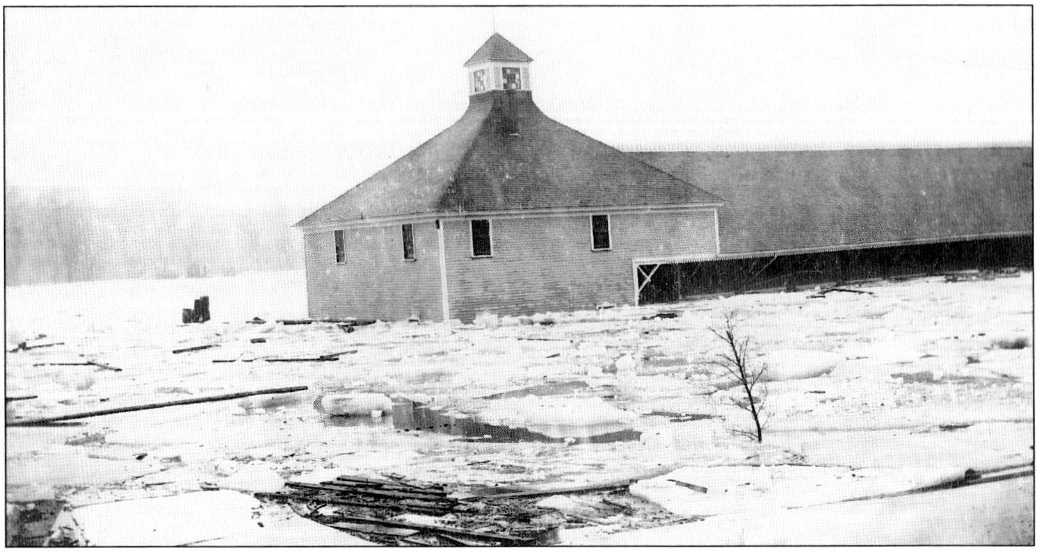

The descriptions of the flood of March 2, 1896, in this and the following captions come from an unpublished manuscript by Laura E. Richards written that very day. At 2 pm she wrote: "The river ran ice all morning but is now comparatively free—water still rising, this owing to a jam at Swan Island. The ice broke up this morning. The church bells rang the alarm. We woke and listened, and above the wind and rain heard crashing, grinding noises, with much roaring."

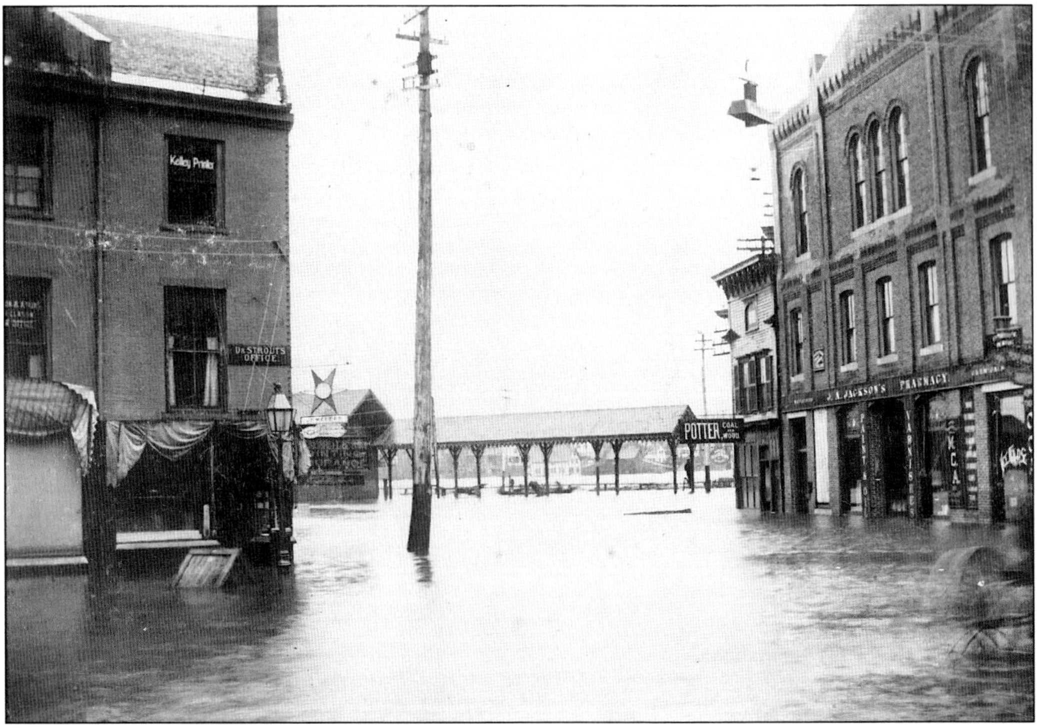

Of this scene at Depot Square, Mrs. Richards wrote: "Last night's west-bound Pullman went through this morning, and there have been no other trains either way. Henry Richards and Daniel Longfellow drove down to South Gardiner by the back (trotting-park) way early this morning, the river road being impassable."

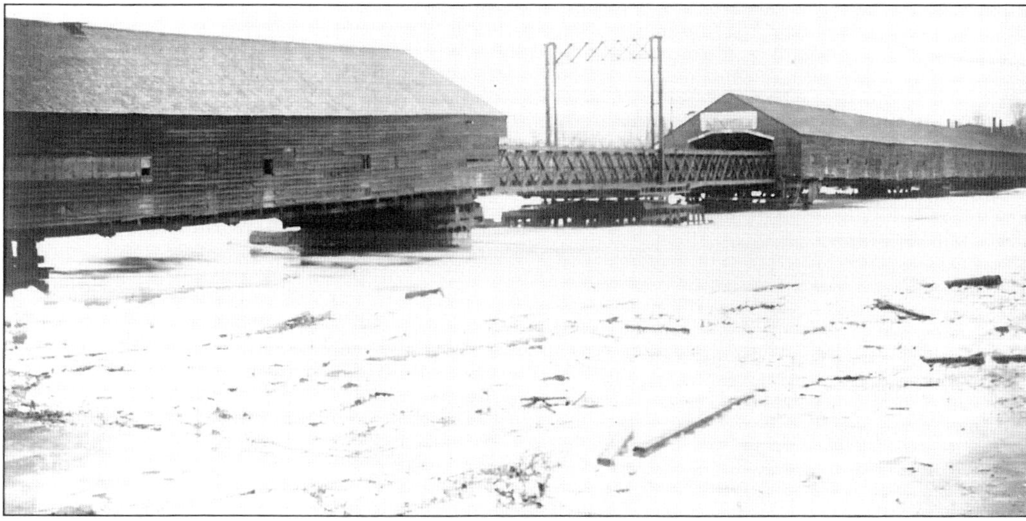

At 2 pm Mrs. Richards wrote: "The bridge still holds, and there is good hope of saving it. Going down about half-past seven a.m. we found a wild scene. The river was a white mass of rushing ice, heaving and grinding. The great ice-cakes flung themselves at the bridge piers and seemed like live things climbing up against them, trying to get over the top." At 5 pm she wrote: ". . . the bridge seemed to cling desperately to its piers. But now logs came drifting down, not singly as heretofore, but in great bristling rafts and tumbled masses. A huge mass of logs struck the wreck of the bridge; it shook, rose for a moment, then fell with a crash; the draw swung free; the roof, as the timbers dropped like a child's jackstraws, turned round, and floated quietly away down river."

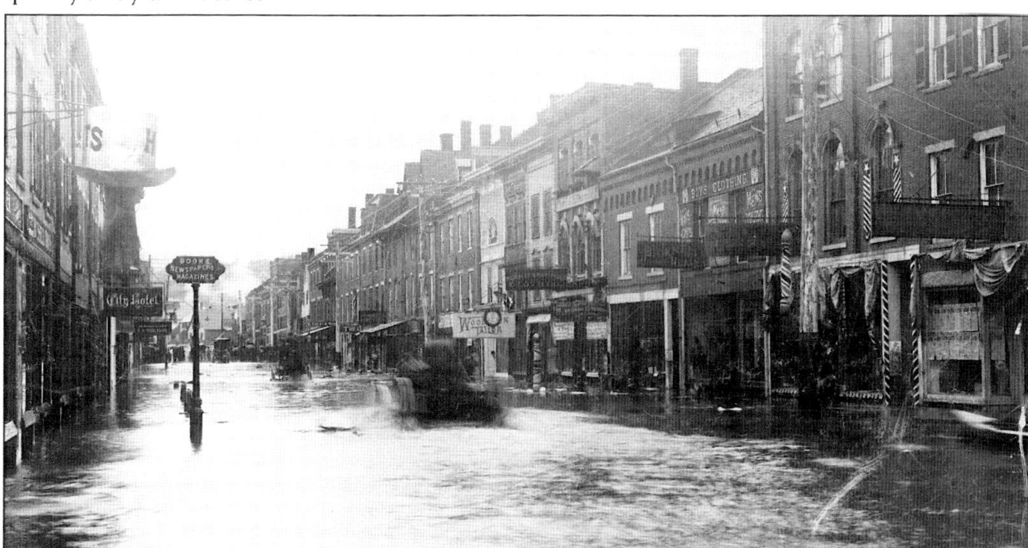

At 2 pm, Mrs. Richards found that "the water is three feet deep in Water Street, the causeway much deeper. The Water Street merchants are moving their goods as rapidly as possible, to upper stories, the first story being flooded. Horses are up to their bellies, and cabs at a premium. Boys (including our John, in his father's long wading boots) are helping move goods, and enjoying themselves immensely." At 5 p.m. she returned to this scene to find that ". . . Water Street seen from Brunswick Street looked like a Venetian canal."

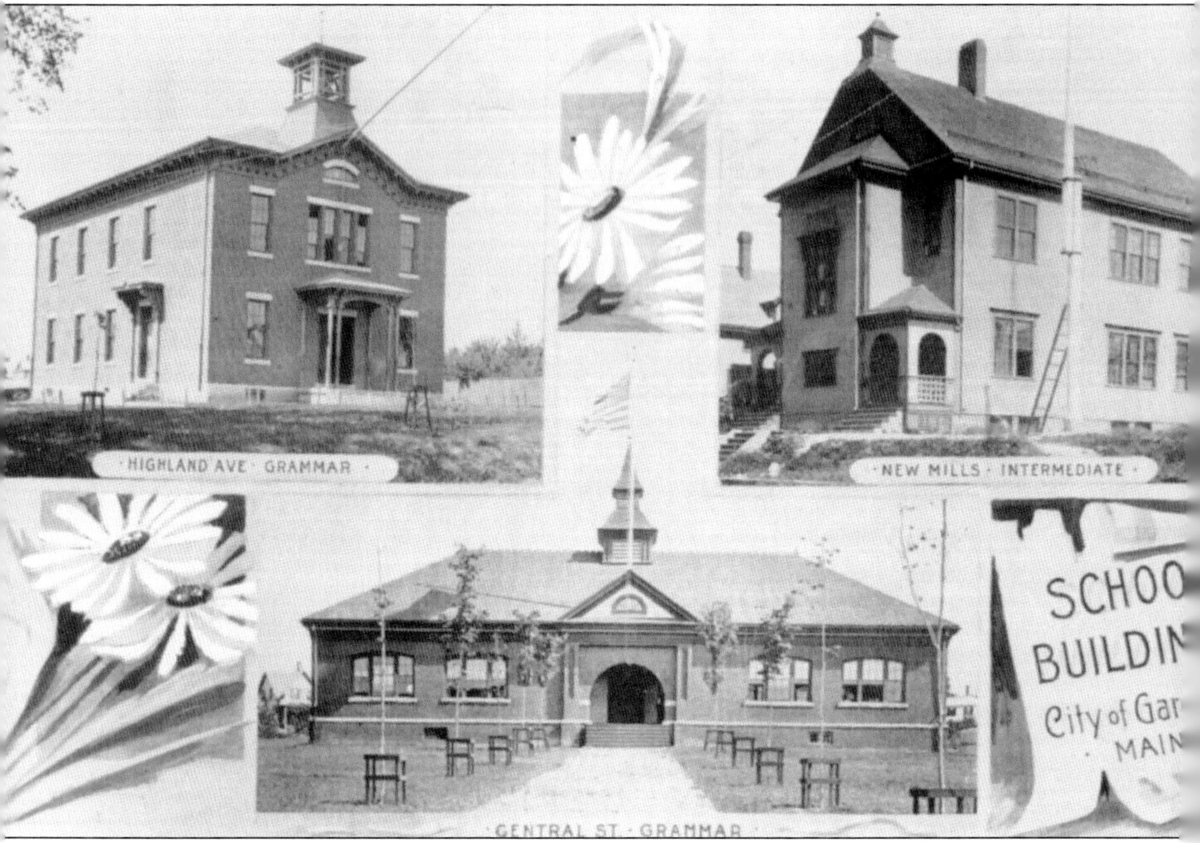

This page, from *Picturesque Gardiner* (1896), displays three of the city's late-nineteenth-century schools. Built in 1877–78 from designs by E.G. Snow, the Highland Avenue Grammar School now contains the offices of the superintendent of SAD 11. The Central Street Grammar School was designed in 1886 by Henry Richards, and the building is currently used by the Masons. In 1889, Edwin E. Lewis provided the plans for the New Mills Intermediate School, which is now an apartment house.

Five

Cultural and Literary Gardiner

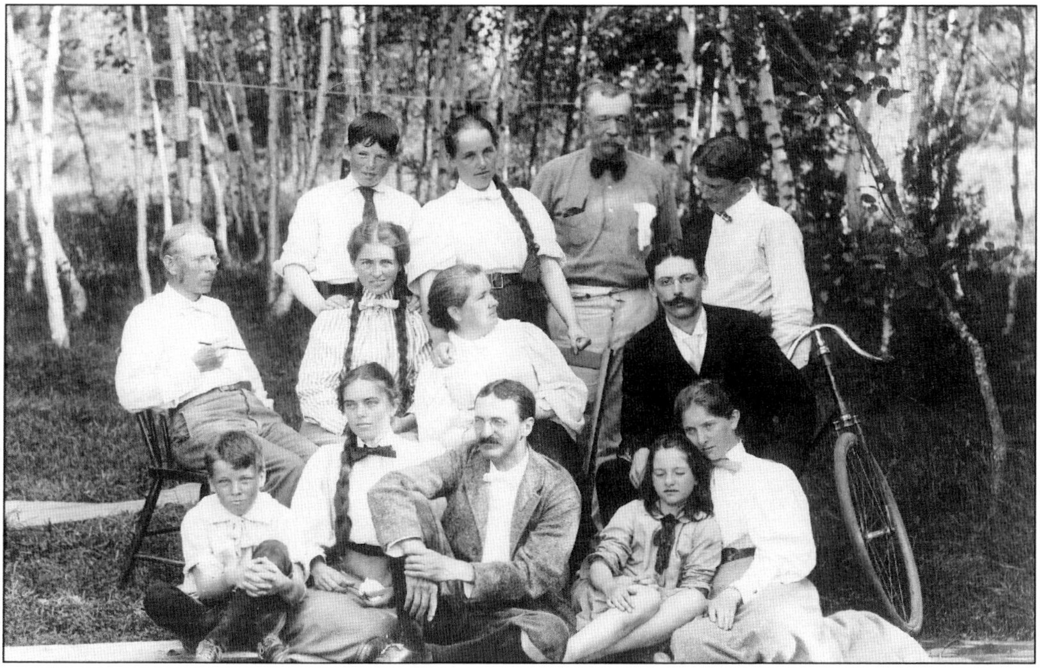

Gardiner's two Pulitzer Prize-winning authors, in the midst of Richards family kin, posed for this photograph in the late 1890s at Camp Cobbossee on Cram's Point in West Gardiner, the summer retreat for the family prior to 1900 when Camp Merryweather opened. The young Robinson, often tormented by doubt and depression, found much help in the ministrations of Laura E. Richards, who received him into the family circle. From left to right are: (front row) Charles Vaughan Ferguson (1885–1964); his sister Eleanor Ferguson (1876–1959); John Hays Gardiner (1863–1913); Laura Richards II (1886–1988); and Julia Ward Richards (1878–1977); (middle row) Reverend George Hodges, dean of the Episcopal Theological School in Cambridge; Rosalind Richards (1874–1964); Laura E. Richards; and Edwin Arlington Robinson; (back row) John Richards (1884–1975); Alice M. Richards (1872–1922); Robert H. Richards, professor at MIT, 1844–1945; and James S. Barstow, an early friend of the Richards children.

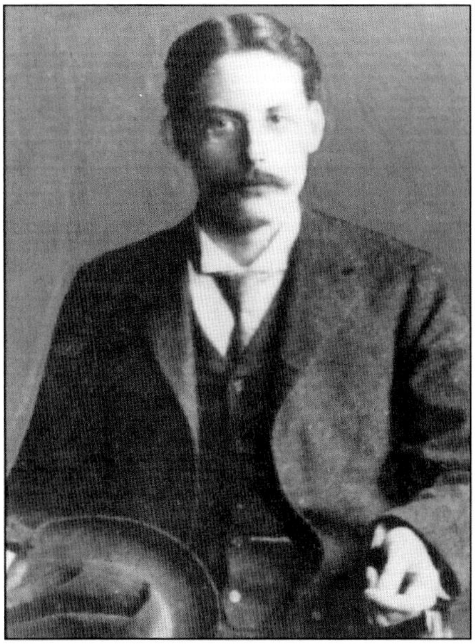

Edwin Arlington Robinson (1869–1935), usually described as "a poet's poet" of consummate artistry, spent his first twenty-eight years at the family residence on Lincoln Avenue in Gardiner. This city suggested many mythical characters to the Pulitzer Prize-winning poet, including "Richard Cory." Although Robinson self-published his first volume, *The Torrent and the Night Before*, he finally achieved recognition for his books, which received Pulitzer Prizes: *Collected Poems* (1925), *The Man Who Died Twice* (1925), and *Tristram* (1928).

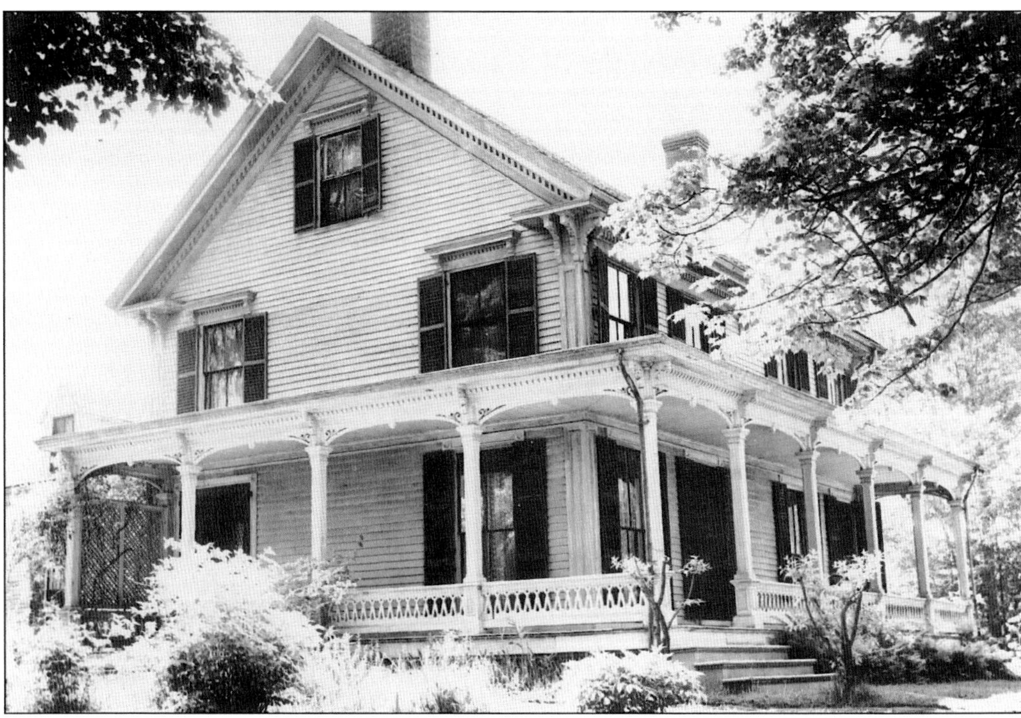

Edwin Arlington Robinson was born at Head Tide in Alna in 1869. When he was only six months old, his family moved to this house on Lincoln Avenue, which he considered his home until his departure for New York in 1897. Built prior to 1856 by S.W. Bates, the Robinson House was remodeled in the Italianate style by the poet's father in 1870. Here "E.A.R." began writing verse at the age of eleven. Laura E. Richards recalled that, "in the pleasant house on Lincoln Street, where Mr. Robinson established his family, the library grew with the children. It was a cheerful and cultivated home." In recognition of Robinson's literary achievements, the Department of the Interior has deemed the house a National Historic Landmark.

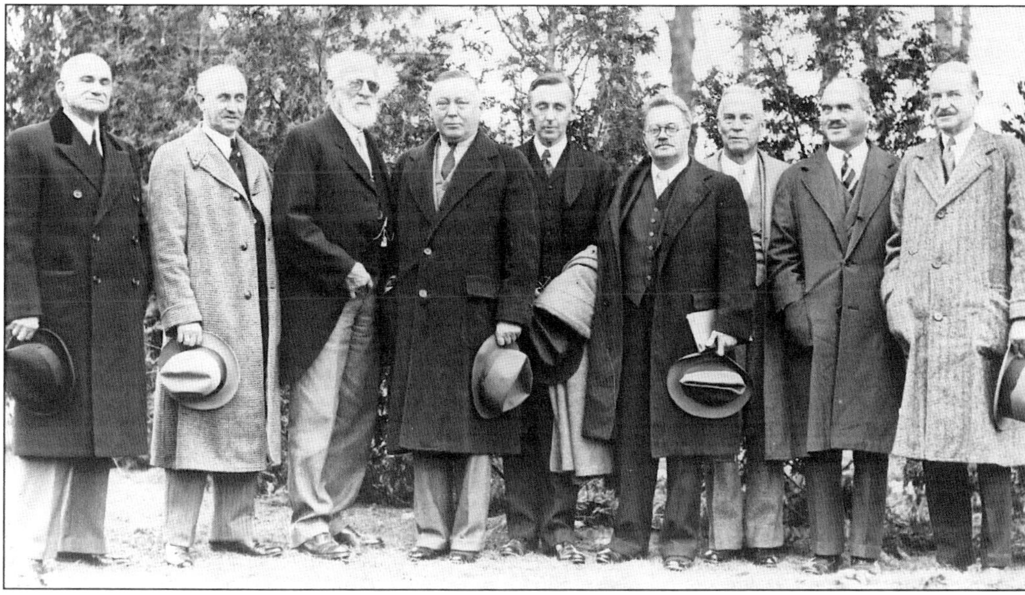

Participants in the dedication ceremony of October 18, 1936, pose in front of the Edwin Arlington Robinson memorial on the Common. From left to right are: Henry E. Dunnack, state librarian; Edwin P. Ladd, mayor of Gardiner; Henry Richards, whose wife Laura spearheaded the erection of the monument; Louis J. Brann, governor of Maine; Hermann Hagedorn, a biographer of Robinson who delivered the dedication address that day; the scholar-poet Harold T. Pulsifer; James M.L. Bates, the Gardiner resident who inventoried the Robinson papers at Colby College; William Tudor Gardiner, former governor of Maine; and Henry R. Shepley, Gardiner's brother-in-law and the monument's architect.

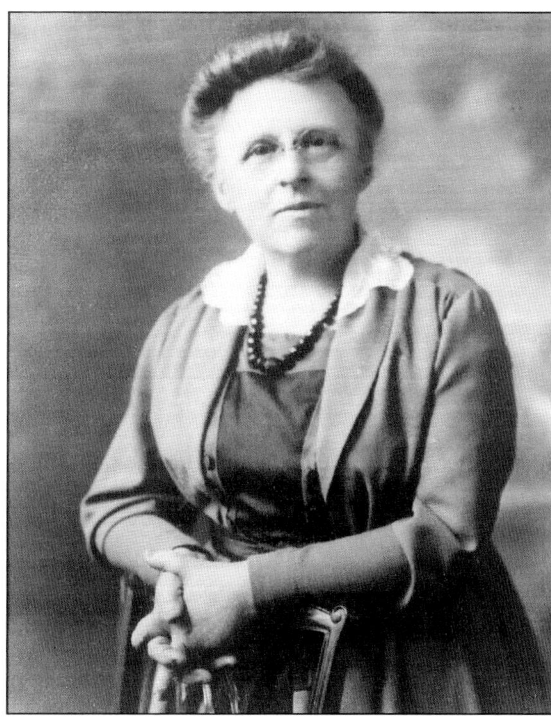

Dr. Gertrude E. Heath (1859–1935) was the daughter of Alvan M.C. Heath, for whom the GAR post was named. A graduate of Hahnemann College in Chicago, she returned to her native Gardiner to practice as a homeopathic physician from 1884 to 1918. Although regarded as a successful doctor, her real niche in Gardiner's history is that of poet and writer of the "Flag Song" in 1899, which was later set to music by Kate Vannah. It soon became one of the most popular songs sung by schoolchildren across the nation.

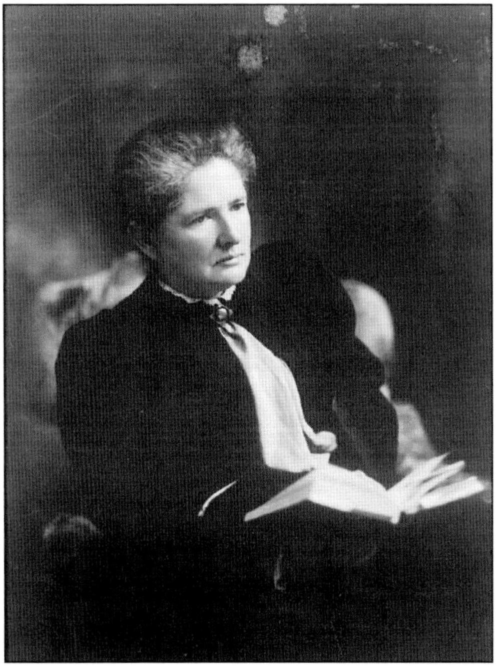

Laura E. Richards (1850–1943), Gardiner's grand lady of literature and civic leadership, was born in Boston, the daughter of Dr. Samuel Gridley Howe (founder of the Perkins School for the Blind) and Julia Ward Howe (who wrote the "Battle Hymn of the Republic"). In 1871, she married Henry Richards and moved to Yellow House in 1878, where she wrote ninety books, mostly for children, and several biographies, including one about her mother which received the first Pulitzer Prize in biography. Her most popular book was *Captain January* (1890), twice made into movies. In 1992, the city named the elementary school on Brunswick Avenue in her honor.

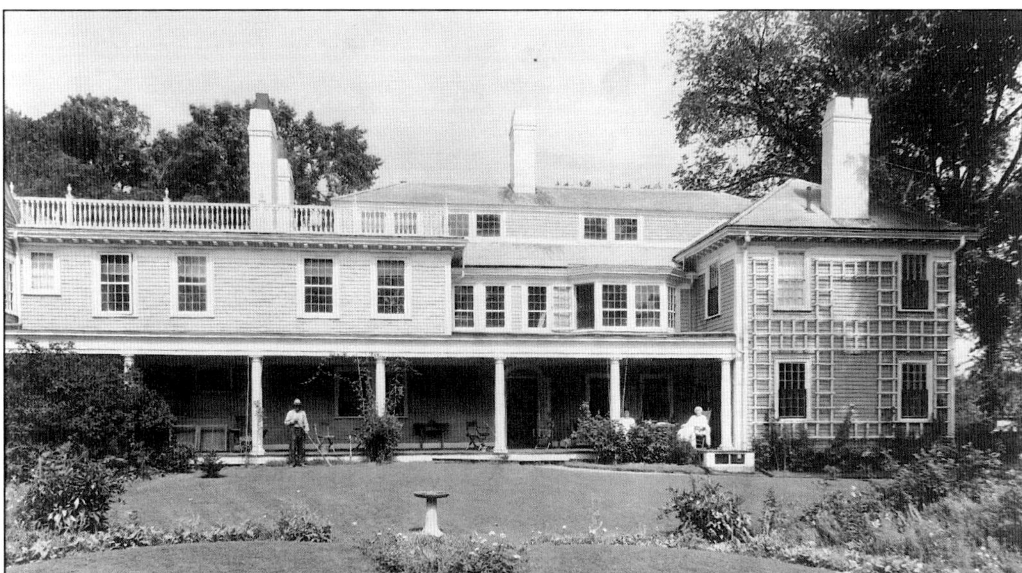

Henry and Laura E. Richards moved into this house at the corner of Dennis and School Streets in July 1878 and, soon after, painted it a new color. Since then, it has been known as Yellow House. This Federal-style house, built in 1814, is of frame construction, with a hipped roof, clapboard siding, denticulated cornice, and central facade reflecting the center hall plan of the building. This view shows the garden side with flower beds duplicating those at the Richards manor house in England which Henry Richards knew in his youth. At the turn of the century, Henry Richards, an accomplished architect, added the third story in the form of a monitor, the bay window, and the piazza featuring Etruscan columns, duplicating ones from another Richards manor in England.

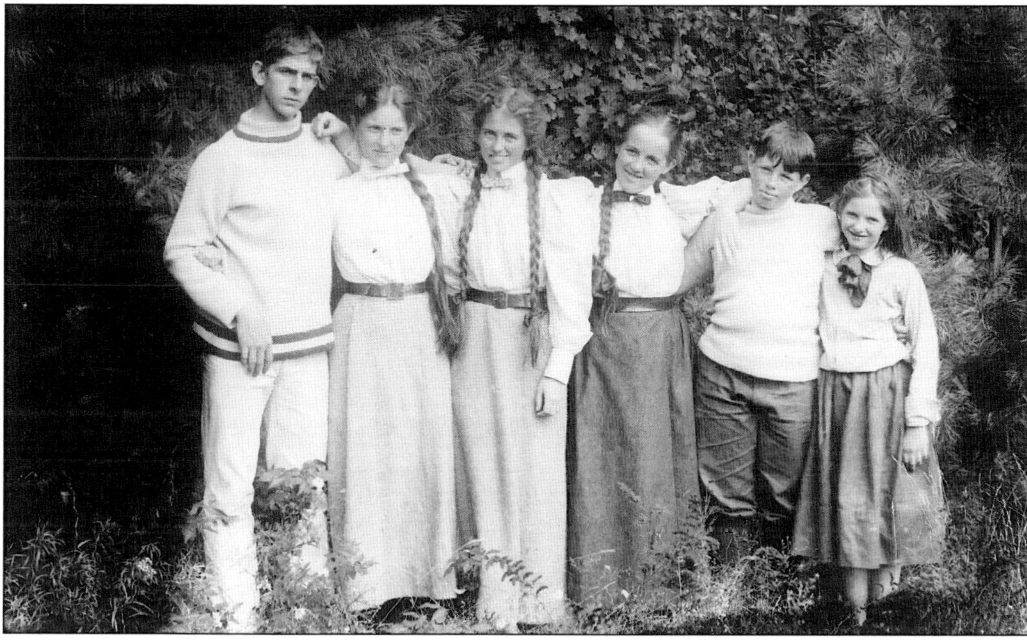

The Noble Six, as their mother called them, were the children of Henry and Laura E. Richards. They all became school masters or married school masters, and they attained a total group age of 524 years, or an 87.3 average. From left to right are: Henry Howe Richards (1876–1968), Julia Ward Richards (1878–1977), Rosalind Richards (1874–1964), Alice Maud Richards (1872–1922), John Richards (1884–1975), and Laura Elizabeth Richards II (1886–1988).

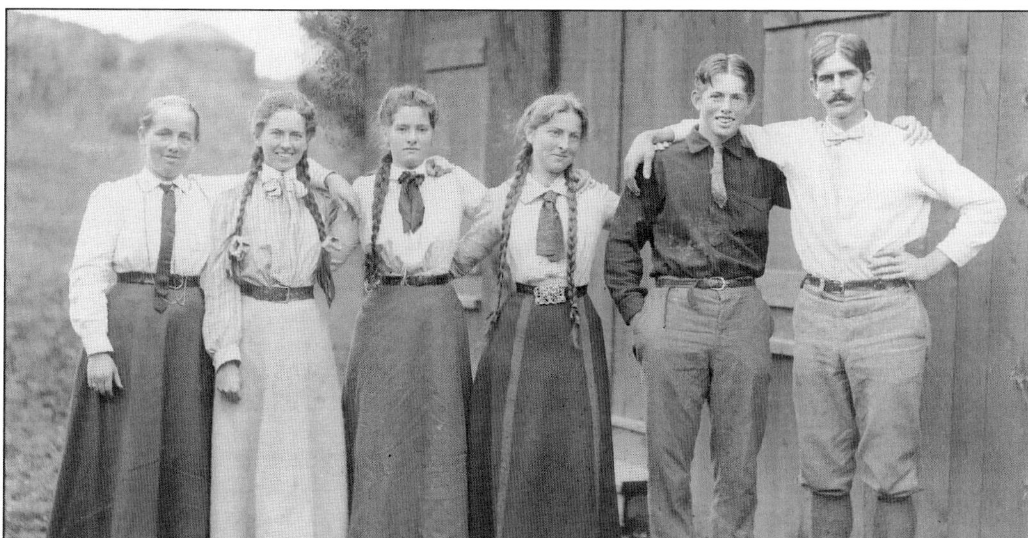

The Noble Six are shown here as young adults at Camp Merryweather in North Belgrade. From left to right are: Miss Alice, head of the English department at Gardiner High School for twenty-seven years; Miss Rosalind, who published three books and took care of Yellow House; Betty, later Mrs. Charles Wiggins of Noble and Greenough School in Dedham; Julia, later Mrs. Carleton Shaw of Red House School in Concord and the grandmother of John D. Shaw Jr., who has resided at Yellow house since 1989; John, who was head of the English department at St. Paul's School; and Henry Howe, head of the English department at Groton School.

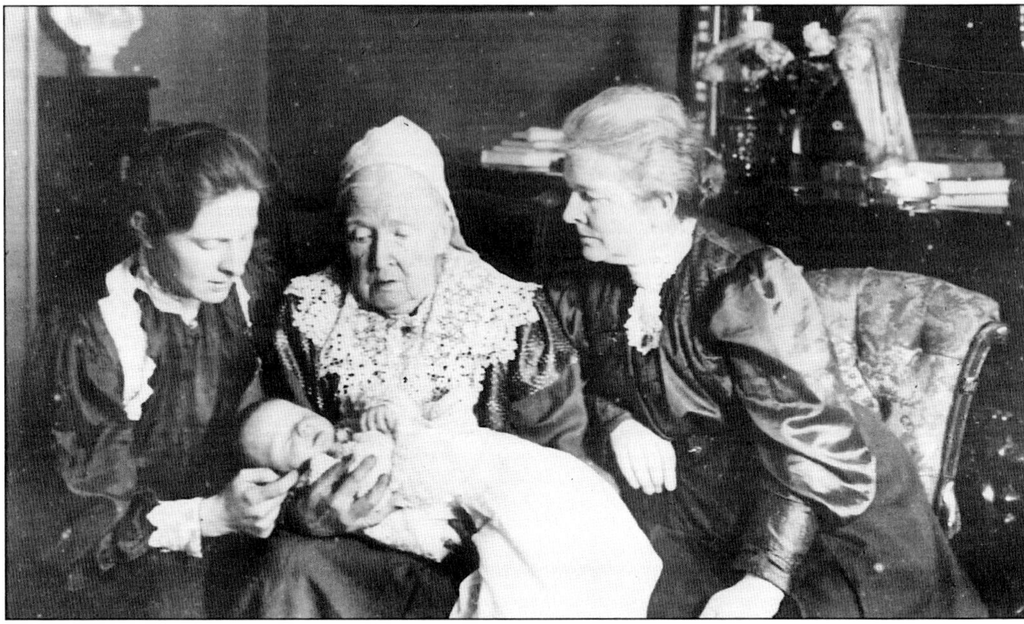

Four generations of the family of Julia Ward Howe (1819–1910) gathered in her drawing room at 241 Beacon Street in Boston, a site recently added to the Freedom Trail. From left to right are: Julia Ward (Richards) Shaw, her granddaughter (1878–1977); Julia Ward Howe, holding her great-grandson Henry Shaw, born in 1906 and still living in 1996; and Laura E. Richards, her daughter (1850–1943. Julia Ward Howe was a leader in the women's movement and the peace movement which led to the establishment of Mother's Day. A classical scholar, poet, and social reformer, she was widely published. During the last thirty years of her life, she visited her daughter Laura at least twice a year in Gardiner.

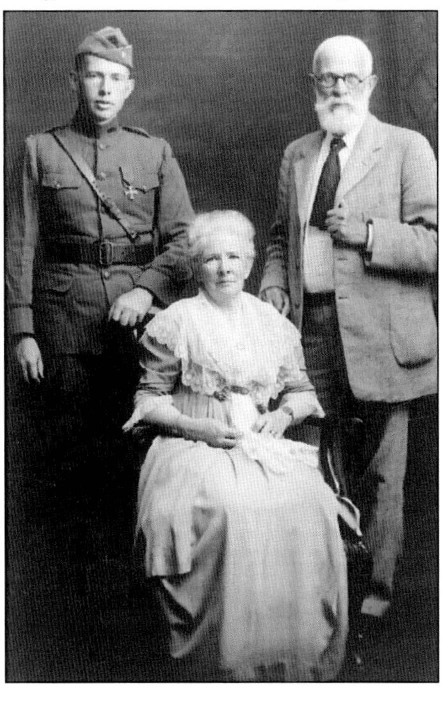

John Richards (1884–1975) attended Army Officers Candidates School in Plattsburg, New York, and was commissioned second lieutenant in the 369th Infantry in World War I. The scouting game his parents taught at Camp Merryweather saved him from gun fire at the battle front many times. He received the Croix de Guerre and the Purple Heart for severe wounds incurred at the Battle of Champagne. Here he appears with his parents, Henry and Laura Richards, when he returned from war in 1919.

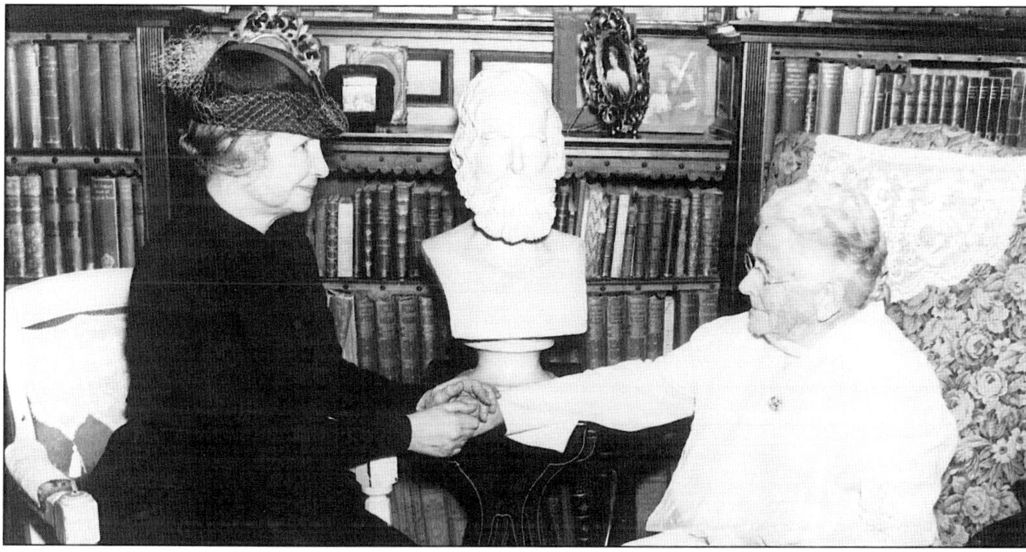

Helen Keller (1880–1968, on the left), who achieved fame by triumphing over blindness, was a frequent visitor to Yellow House when she helped Laura E. Richards (on the right) to raise money to support education for the blind. On March 9, 1939, Mrs. Richards wrote to her sister about the visit shown in the above photograph: "Helen Keller spoke in Augusta last night, to the Legislature, in behalf of the Adult Blind; is coming to lunch with us today. She came here as a child, to one of the little fairs we had for the Blind Kindergarten; spent the night, and Rosalind recited ballads to her half the night!"

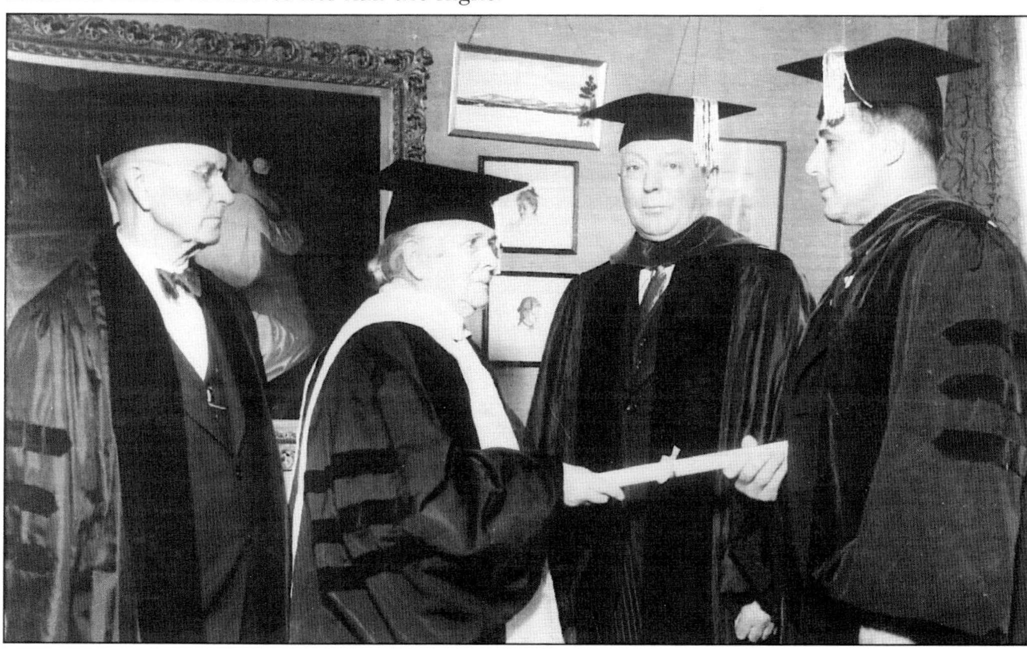

Dignitaries from Maine's colleges gathered at Yellow House on June 10, 1935, to honor Laura E. Richards as President Arthur A. Hauck of the University of Maine conferred upon her the degree of Doctor of Letters for "the fine ideals you have maintained in the field of literature." From left to right are: Harmon G. Allen, president of the board of trustees; Mrs. Richards; Governor Louis J. Brann; and President Hauck, tending the diploma.

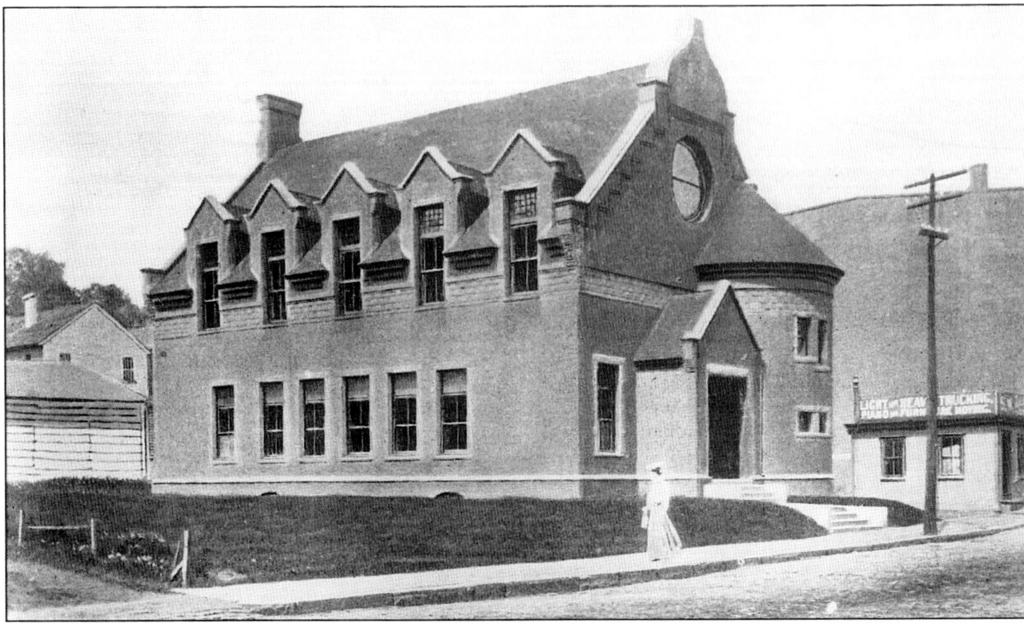

In January 1881, William W. and Peter G. Bradstreet offered to donate a lot on Water Street for a public library if a building could be completed debt-free by July 1, 1882. The Gardiner Library Association met this challenge by erecting Maine's second public library between July 1881 and April 1882 at a cost of $11,000. Designed by Henry Richards, this substantial brick and stone building reflects the English Jacobean style in its distinctive facade gable and side dormers.

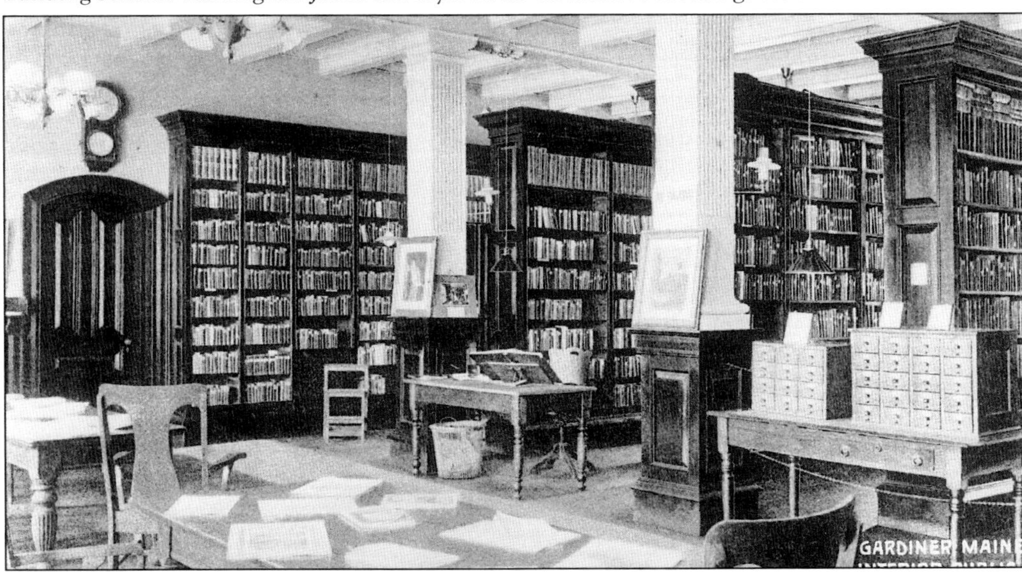

This 1909 view of the first floor reading room and book stacks of the Gardiner Public Library reflects the inviting atmosphere which remains the library's trademark to this day. In January 1881, the *Gardiner Home Journal* made the following case for a public library: "The public library supplements the school and college and does more to make a community cultured and happy than any other institution." With a weekly visitation of 1,800 in the 1990s and an annual circulation of 132,000 items, the Gardiner Public Library is actively fulfilling the vision of its founders.

Judge Henry Sewall Webster (1846–1917) published volumes of vital records, local history pamphlets, and lengthy columns on Gardiner history in the local newspapers which are central to any investigation of this community's past. A graduate of Bowdoin College, he practiced law here, later becoming judge of the Kennebec County Probate Court. With the Richards family, he helped to establish many philanthropic institutions throughout the city.

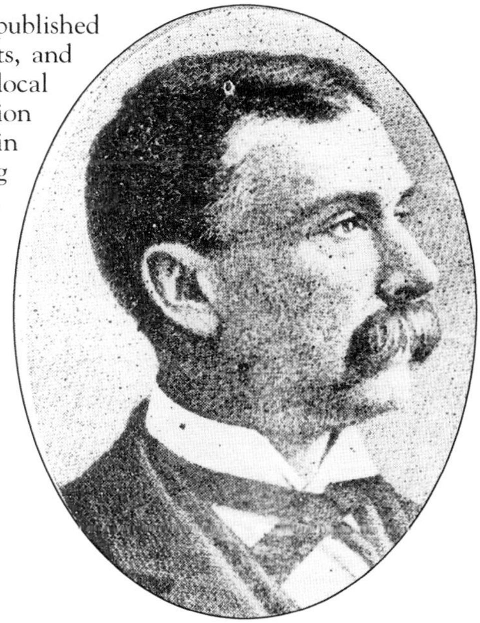

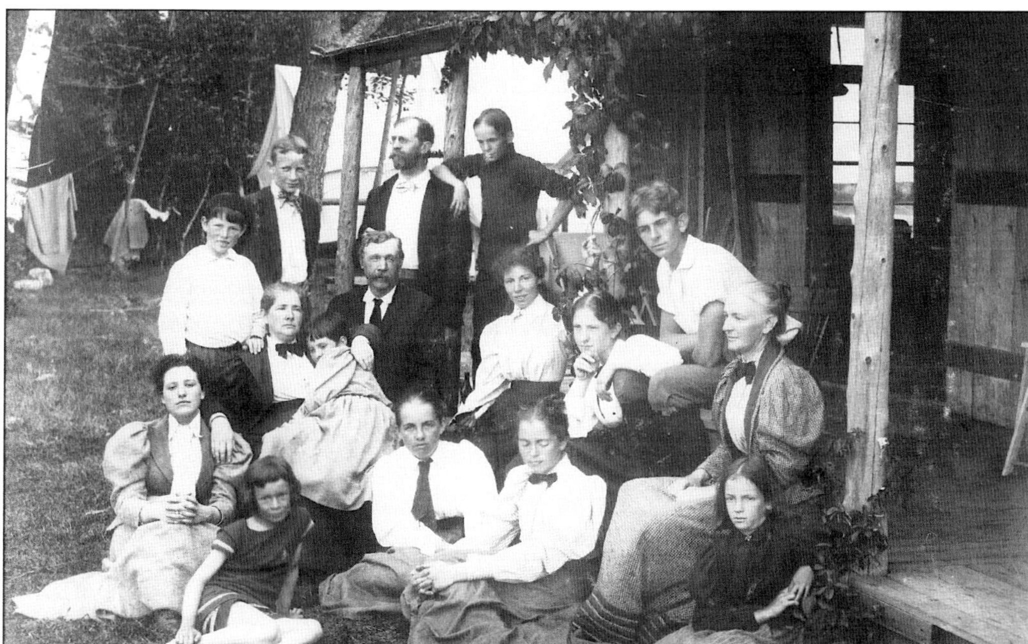

Shown here in the mid-1890s at Camp Cobbossee are the two founders of the Gardiner Library: Laura E. Richards and the talented fund-raiser Reverend Leverett Bradley (1846–1902), rector of Christ Church from 1879 to 1884. Pictured are, from left to right: (front row) Alice Chanler, Ralph Bradley, Alice Richards, Rosalind Richards, and an unidentified girl; (middle row) John Richards, Laura E. Richards (holding Betty), Professor Robert H. Richards, Peggy Bradley, Julia Richards, Henry Howe Richards, and Bradley's wife, Susan (Hinckley) Bradley; (back row) Leverett Bradley Jr. (with his father) and Walter Bradley (with his elbow on his father's shoulder).

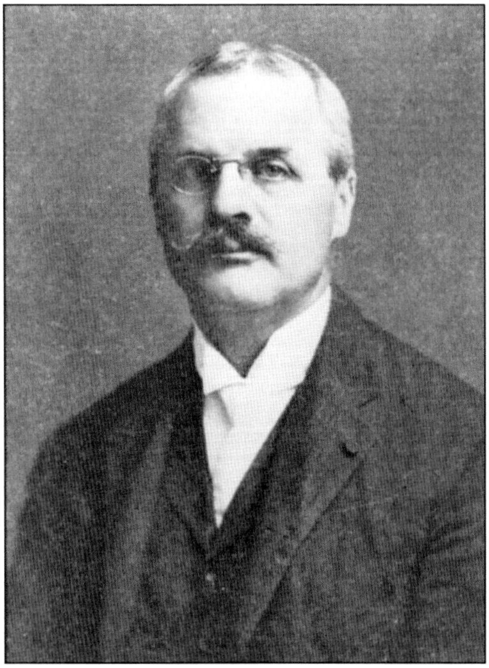

Robert Hallowell Gardiner III (1855–1924), grandson of Robert Hallowell Gardiner I, inherited Oaklands in 1886 from his uncle. A successful lawyer, investment banker, and trustee in Boston, he used his fortune to establish the World Conference on Faith and Order which is now the World Council of Churches. His life's work is commemorated on a marble tablet on the southwest wall of Christ Church.

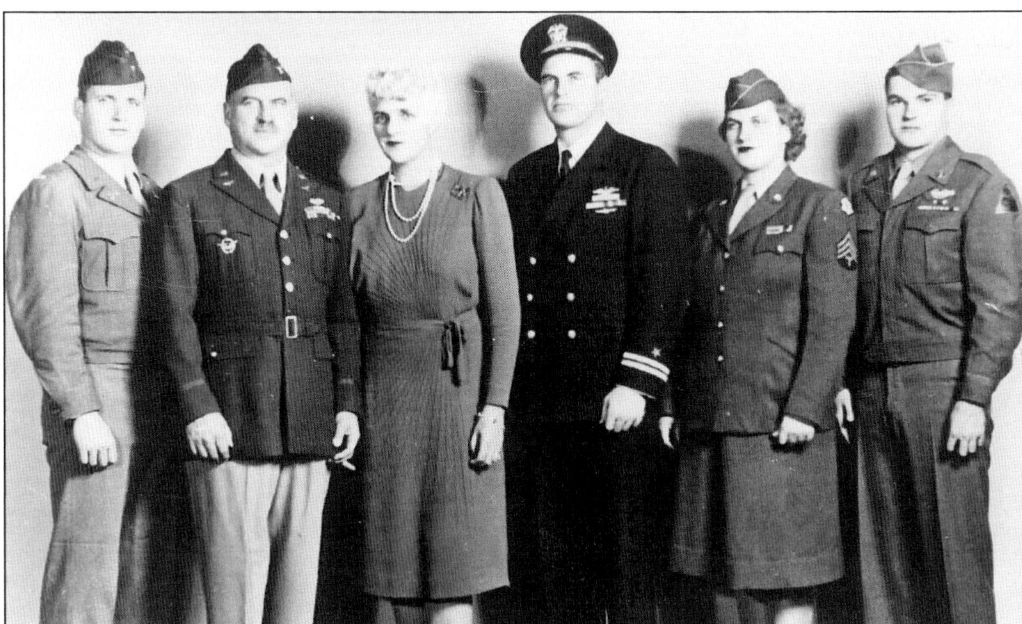

Governor William Tudor Gardiner (1892–1953) and his family donned military uniforms in defense of their country during World War II. William was a son of Robert Hallowell Gardiner III. As governor of Maine from 1929 to 1933, he enacted the Administrative Code, which established the modern organization of state government. During the World War II, he and General Maxwell Taylor secretly entered Rome while Italy was under German occupation to assure early surrender. From left to right are: Tudor (1918–1986); Governor Gardiner and his wife Margaret (1889–1981); Thomas (1920–1995); Margaret, the well-known breeder of Morgan horses and the sole survivor in 1996; and Sylvester (1924–1947).

John Frank Stevens (1853–1943) was born in West Gardiner and is considered one of the greatest railroad engineers of all time, laying out the Canadian Pacific Railroad and the transcontinental railroad, as well as discovering the Marias Pass at the Continental Divide. He concluded work on the Panama Canal when he departed from failed sea-level designs of his predecessors and established multi-leveling locks. He explained his success: "By working all day and studying half the night. Work and study is the secret of 90% of all achievement."

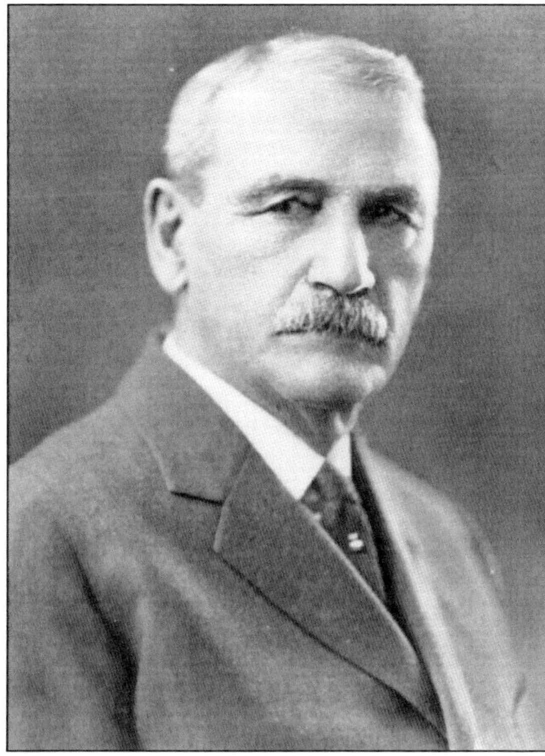

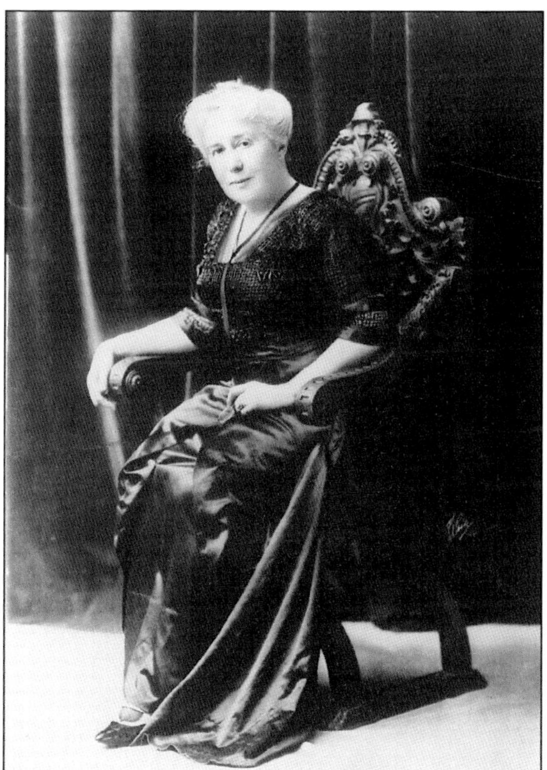

The talented musical composer and poet Kate Vannah was born in Gardiner in 1855. Her career as pianist started at age nine and took her to Boston and New York. She published two books of poetry, *Verses* (1883) and *From Heart to Heart* (1897), and composed over two hundred pieces, including music for Dr. Heath's "Flag Song" and the hymn for the International Eucharistic Congress in Chicago in 1926.

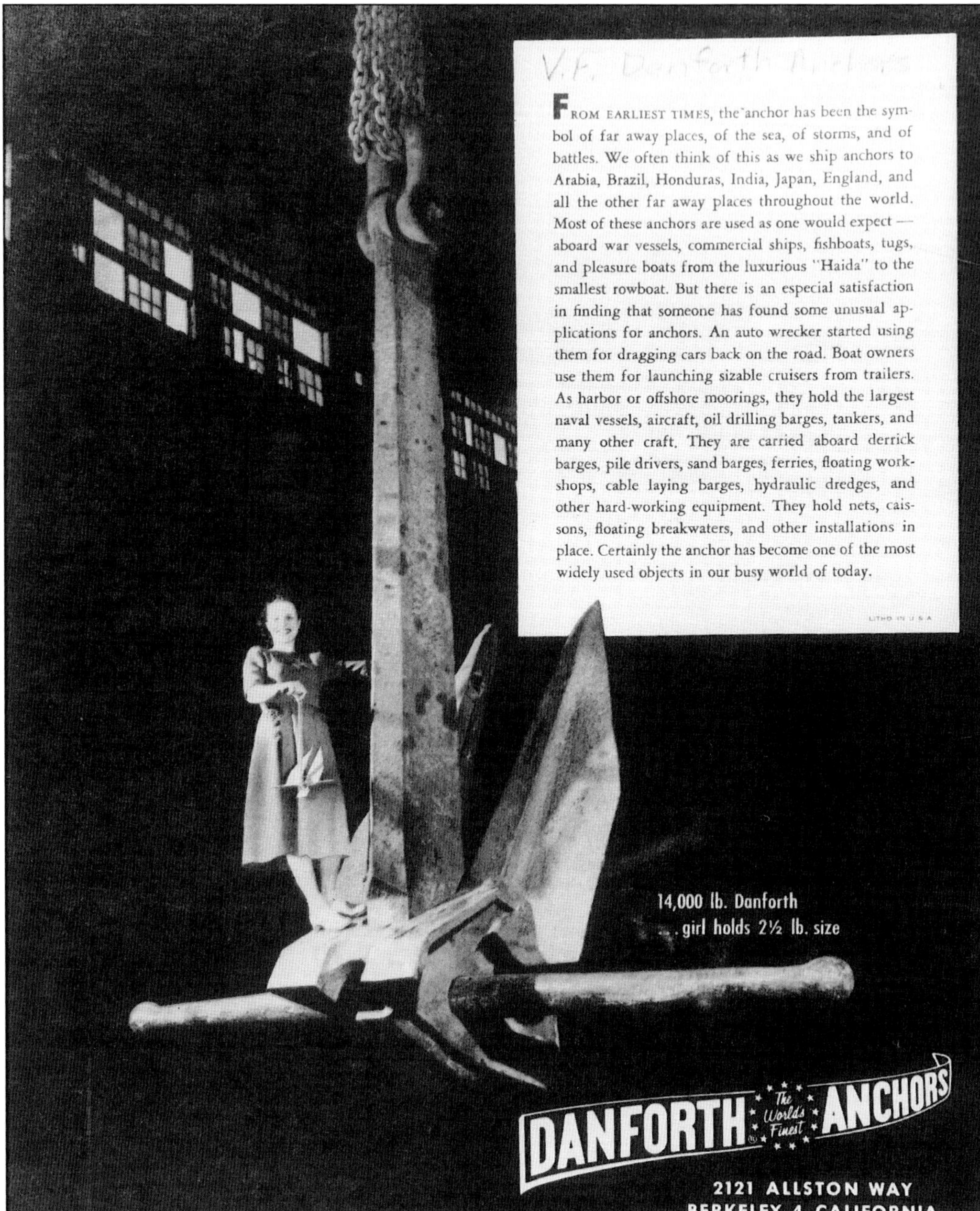

The Danforth anchor was invented and originally manufactured in Gardiner before the transfer of company operations to the west coast by Richard Danforth and his brother-in-law, Robert Ogg. This invention is still standard equipment for the navies of the world. Danforth was a member of a talented and civic-minded family. His grandfather was a justice of the Maine Supreme Court. His sister Margaret was an noted bookbinder in Boston during the Arts and Crafts Movement at the turn of the century. Through his mother, he was a descendant of Reverend Joel Clapp, ninth rector of Christ Church, and Julia Stevens, both commemorated in several stained-glass windows and woodcarvings at Christ Church. He was also a cousin of Julia Hollingsworth, whose husband established the Hollingsworth and Whitney Paper Company.

Six
Early Twentieth-Century Developments 1897–1945

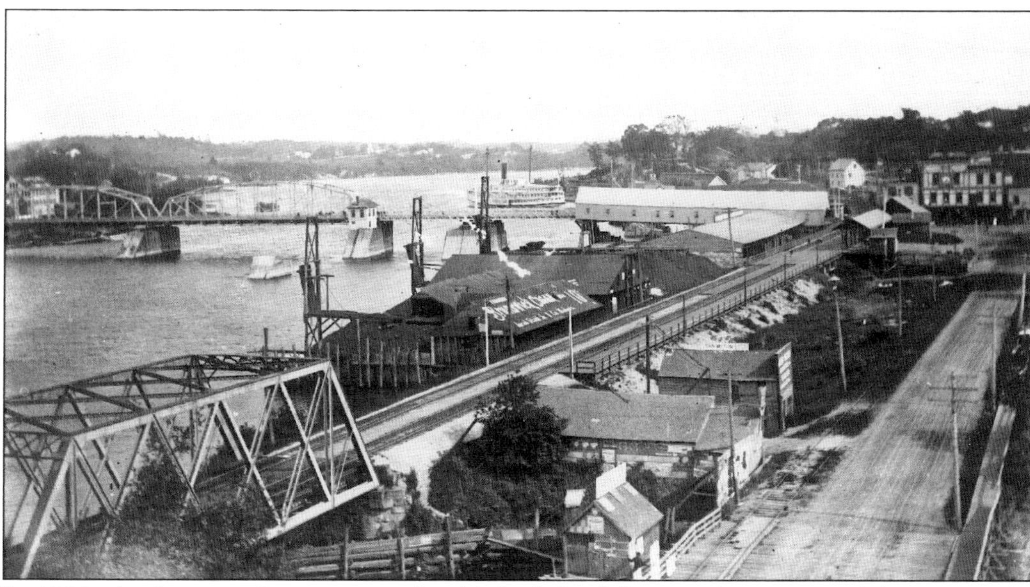

In 1922, the *Lewiston Evening Journal* published the following description of this 1902 John Gray photograph: "One will notice the old iron railroad bridge now replaced by a fine one of concrete over Cobbosseecontee Stream. Note the lock in the center foreground that conveyed the logs coming down the Kennebec River up the stream to the saw mill operated by the Gray concern . . . Just below it was the marble sheds of John Milton. Then there may be seen the Harrington Coal Sheds . . . Beyond them is the Monmouth storehouse for the reception of southern lumber which was mostly pine and was the property of the Oakland Lumber Company . . . In the background may be seen the Boston steamer wending her way down the river."

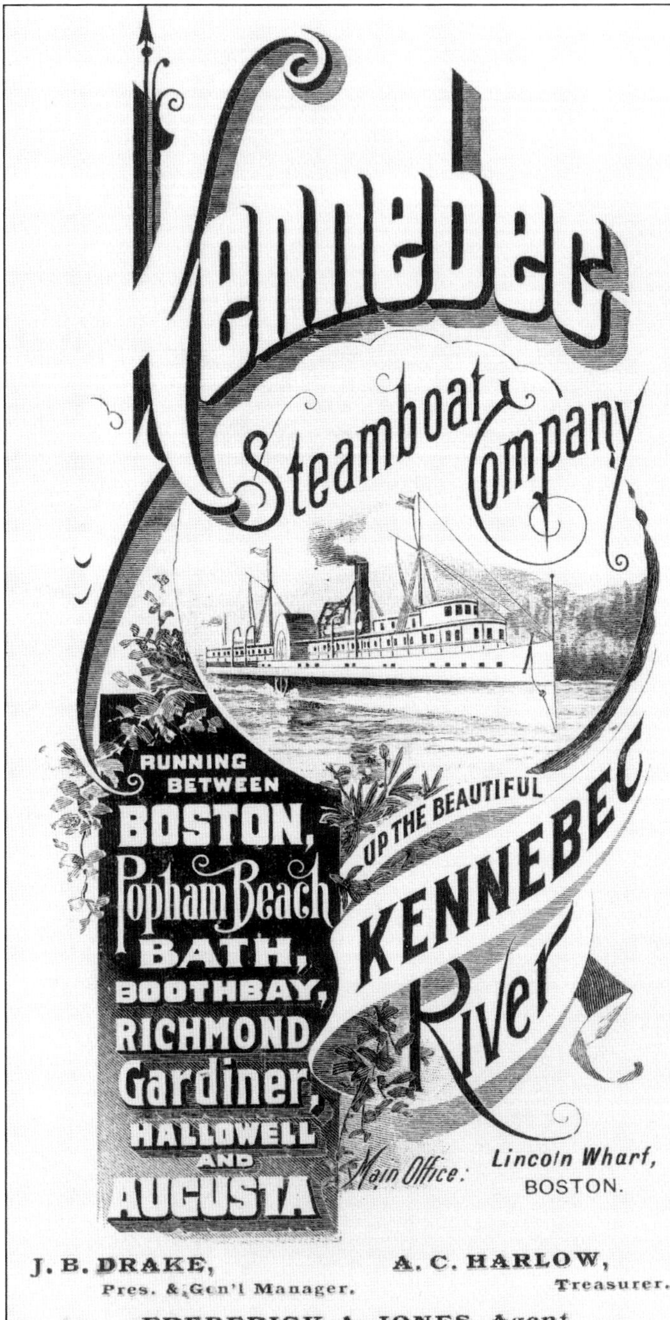

This 1890s timetable for the Kennebec Steamboat Company contains the schedules for the *Kennebec* and the *Sagadahoc*, the elegant steamers which provided daily service between Gardiner and Boston in the summer and three trips each week during the spring and fall. A 3 pm departure from the steamboat wharf in Gardiner meant a 5 am arrival at Lincoln Wharf in Boston the next morning. Round trip fare was $3.50. Private staterooms ranged from $1 to $2, and meals were 50¢ each. The brochure boasted that the *Sagadahoc* and the *Kennebec* are "noted to be the finest boats out of Boston."

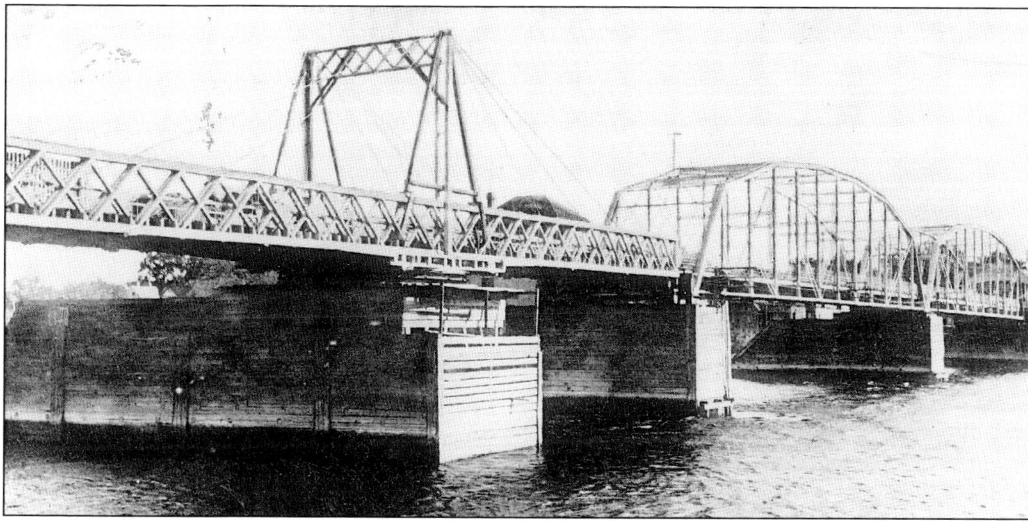

In 1896, this steel drawbridge replaced the 1853 bridge destroyed in the second highest flood of all time. High-masted ships blew a whistle to alert the bridge tender in the cabin (barely visible on the left) to open the gate. By the 1970s, traffic jams hampered the traffic flow at the intersection of Routes 1, 9, 24, 126, and 201. Since the erection of a new concrete high-level fixed bridge in 1978 about a quarter mile north of the 1896 bridge, through traffic has circled around the downtown commercial district. At the same time, the 1896 bridge was demolished.

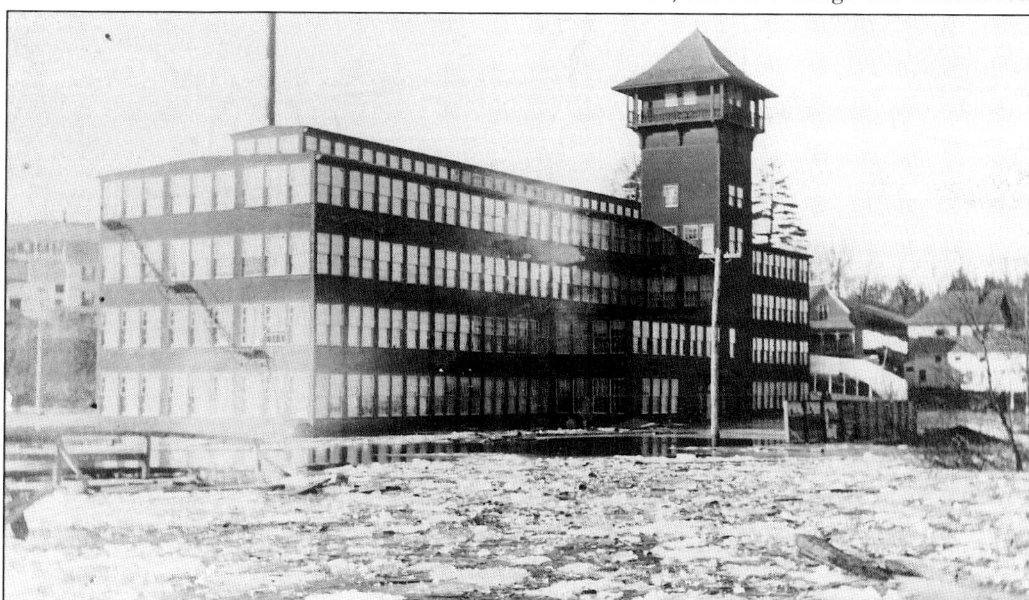

The Commonwealth Shoe and Leather Company on Maine Avenue, shown here during a spring freshet, was Gardiner's first large shoe factory. In 1897, the Gardiner Board of Trade raised $25,000 to build this plant in order to attract one of Charles H. Jones Sr.'s shoe factories to the city. A Massachusetts businessman, Jones manufactured the popular Bostonian shoe. Commonwealth's Gardiner branch thrived, resulting in plant expansions in 1906, 1913, and 1934. By the 1930s, a work force of 350 produced 1,800 pairs of shoes per day. In 1951, the board of trade built Commonwealth a new facility off Brunswick Avenue, sealing the fate of the original factory, which was demolished in 1970.

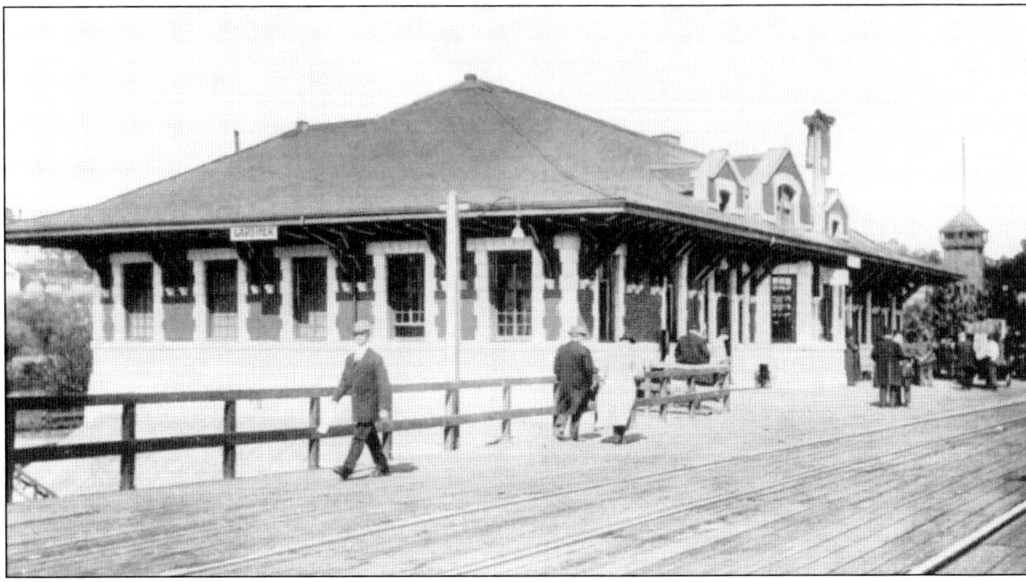

When the Maine Central Railroad replaced the 1866 wooden station in Depot Square with this impressive brick and granite structure in 1911, rail travel was at its height. Designed by Portland architect George Burnham, Gardiner's new French Renaissance-style station was located north of the old one on Maine Avenue between the two outlets of Cobbossee Stream. Costing $25,000, the building was heralded as "the handsomest on the entire system east of Portland." Within fifty years, the automobile put an end to passenger rail service in Maine, and many communities saw their stations demolished. Fortunately, this Gardiner landmark has been successfully preserved through adaptive reuse.

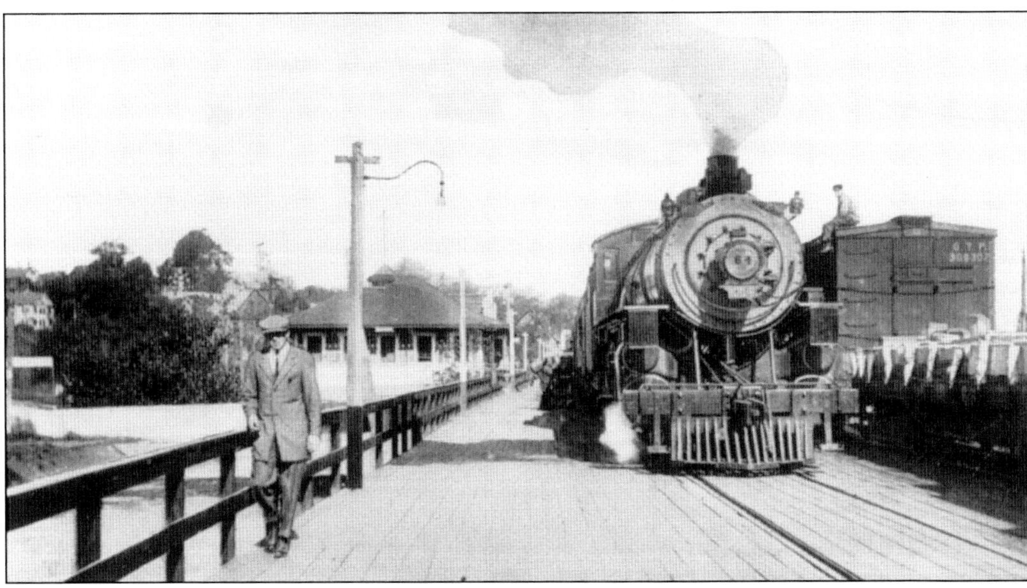

A southbound passenger train pulls out of Gardiner's new station in 1911. With a stop in Brunswick, the journey to Portland's Union Station took an hour and forty-five minutes. The Kennebec and Portland Railroad initiated passenger service to Gardiner in 1851 with the Maine Central Railroad taking over in 1870. The last passenger train left this station in June 1960.

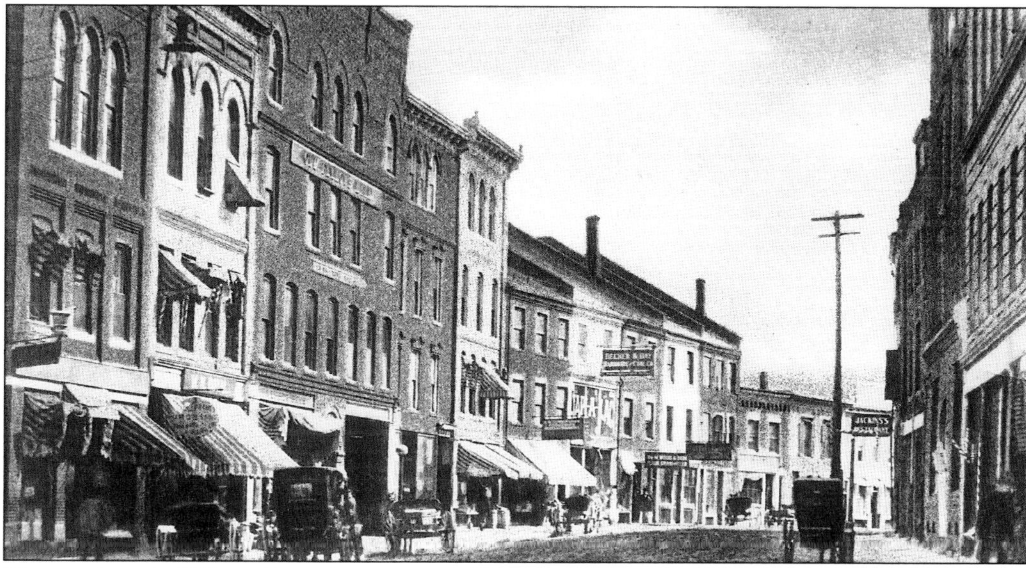

The south end of Water Street's commercial district took on a new appearance in the mid-1890s. A row of small frame and brick stores at the corner of Maine Avenue was replaced by five brick Romanesque Revival-style blocks which dominate the left half of this c. 1910 photograph. Of these, the three at the left are still standing. Built in 1895, the corner block housed Chester H. Beane's drugstore for many years. William Wood built the next block in 1896, the first tenant being H.M. Davis's clothing store. Next is the Patten Block, which was designed by Gardiner architect Edwin E. Lewis.

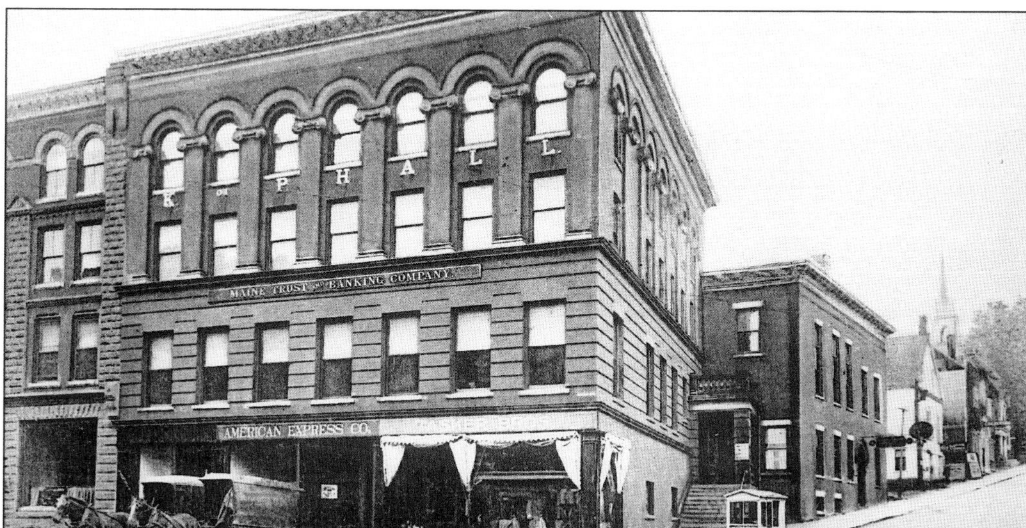

In 1903, the Gardiner Real Estate Association constructed this four-story brick block on the Water and Church Street site of the Evans Hotel, which had burned two years earlier. Designed by Lewiston architects George M. Coombs and Eugene Gibbs, the building originally housed the Real Estate Association and American Express on the first floor and the Maine Trust and Banking Company on the second floor, with the Knights of Pythias Hall occupying the third and fourth floors. City hall, the Coliseum, and the spire of the Universalist church appear to the right on Church Street in this c. 1910 view.

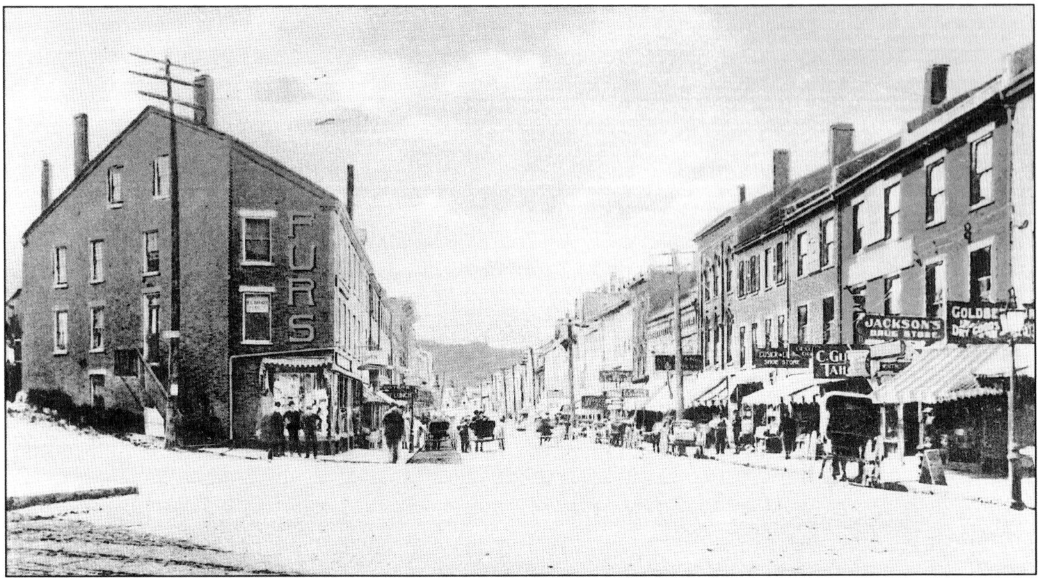

In this 1913 view looking west up Water Street from the foot of Church Street, carriages and wagons are still the main form of transportation. The large hat sign of Jacob Davis hangs at the left. Davis purchased the site from Robert Hallowell Gardiner in 1804 for $350 worth of hats. Later owners, such as H.G. Barker, continued to use the Davis hat sign into the early twentieth century. At the right, the Goldberg Brothers' Clothing Store and Jackson's Drug Store can be seen.

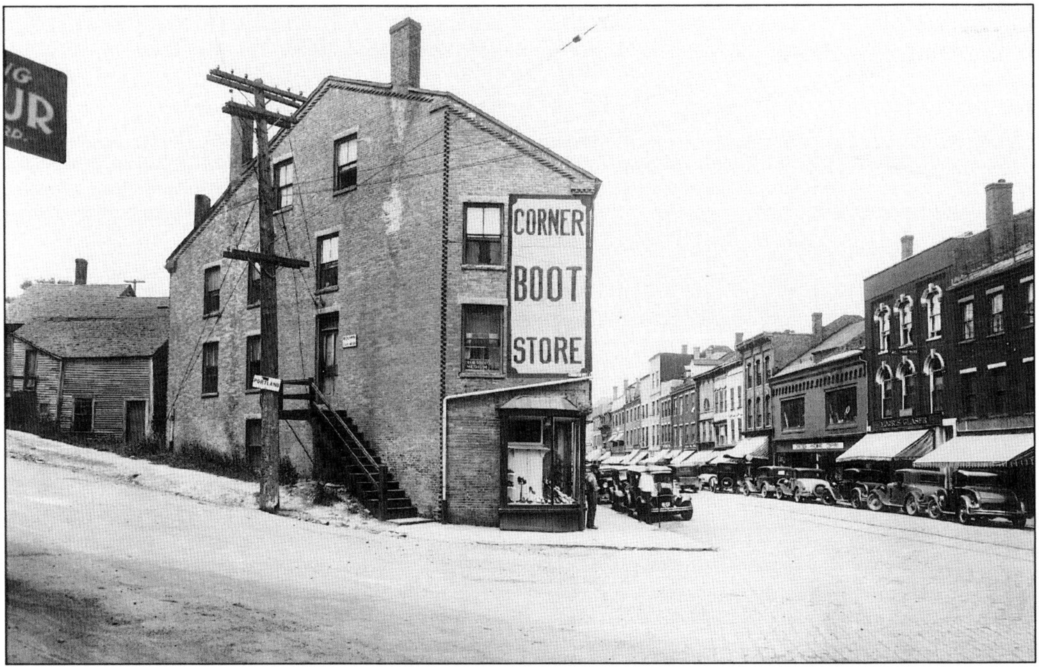

By 1931, when this photograph of Water Street was taken from the foot of Church Street, automobiles lined the street. In 1923, the Corner Boot Store opened in the Davis Block. The long tradition of a clothing business at this location continued until the 1980s, when the Corner Shoe and Clothing Store closed.

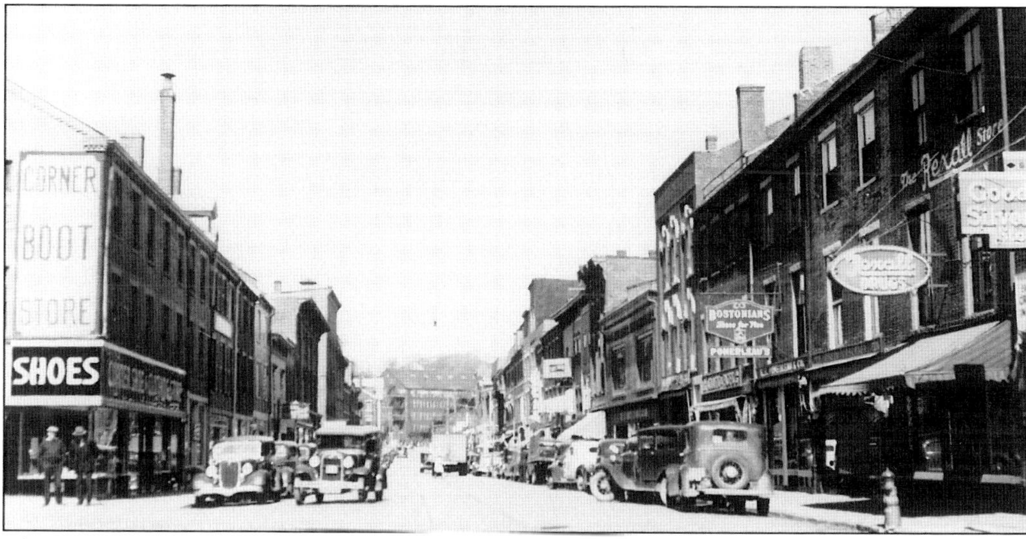

This *c.* 1935 postcard shows Water Street from the intersection of Church Street and Maine Avenue looking toward the Hazzard Shoe Factory (in the background). Henry Richards commented on the Water Street of the 1930s in his 1940 memoir *Ninety Years On*: "The contrast is startling today. Most of our remaining industries are owned and operated by outsiders, while chain stores have taken most of the retail profits out of the pockets of Gardiner men and run off to New York. It is a drying-up process, hailed as progress, which is afflicting the majority of our small towns."

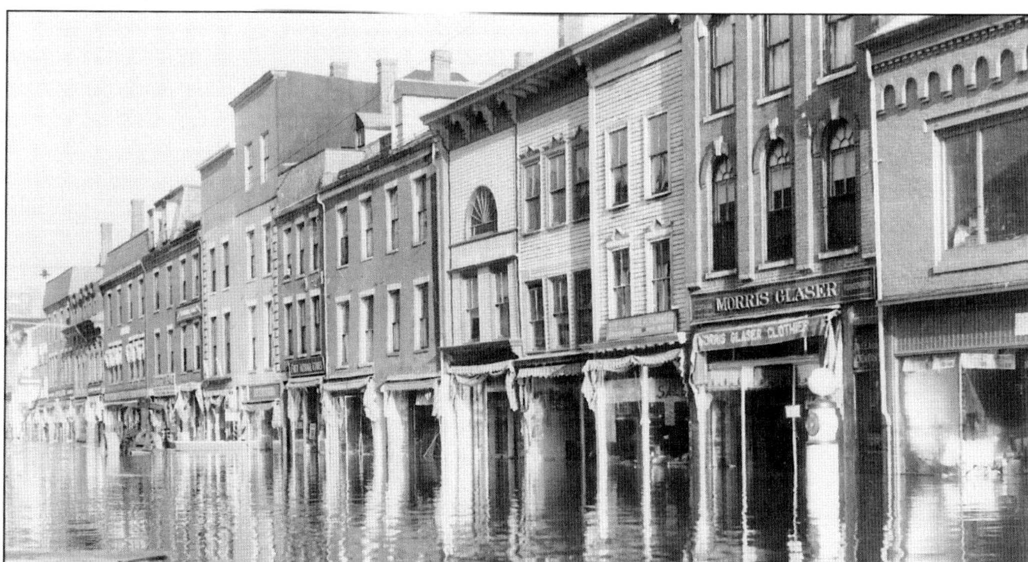

On March 16, 1936, Laura E. Richards wrote the following of the next great flood: "The flood passes into history: its consequences remain, tragic enough for the river towns. Those merchants who had cleared their cellars and thought themselves safe, rushed down, to find themselves waist-deep in street and store, in icy water, in the dark, for the power house was flooded. By such lantern light as could be come by, they worked desperately, saving what they could: little enough I fear. About eleven Saturday morning we drove down the hill, with every other car in town, to see Venice in Maine, without the palaces!"

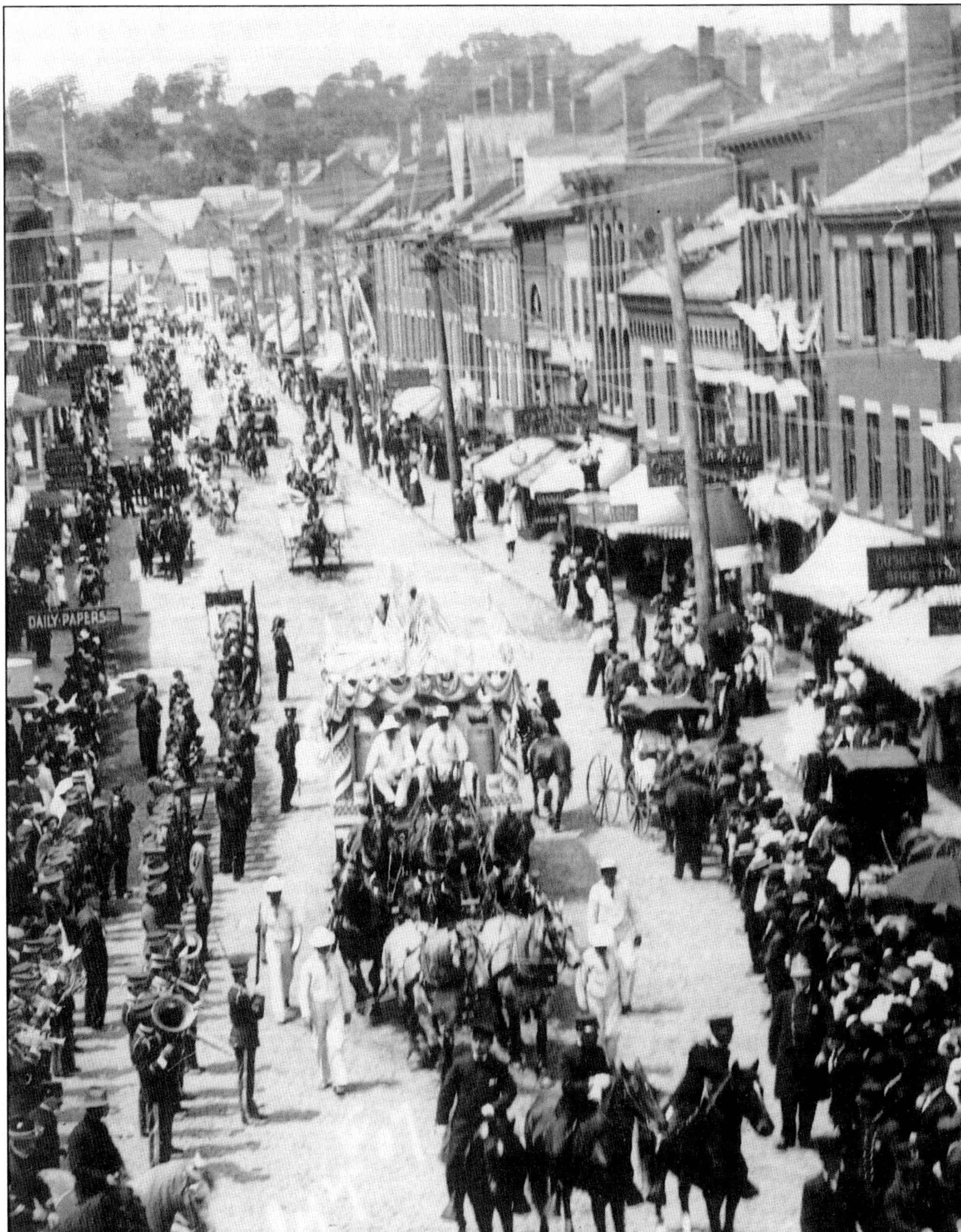

A horse-drawn float passes down Water Street in review during Gardiner's grand 1907 Fourth of July Parade. After a twenty-two year hiatus, the city decided that year to reinstitute the parade, which included military groups, fire companies, bands, and floats featuring local schools and businesses. Starting at 10:30 am the procession drew a crowd of several thousand spectators along its route. The *Daily Reporter-Journal* noted the next day that, "there were no accidents, and not so much rowdyism and drunkenness as usual, and it was a successful affair."

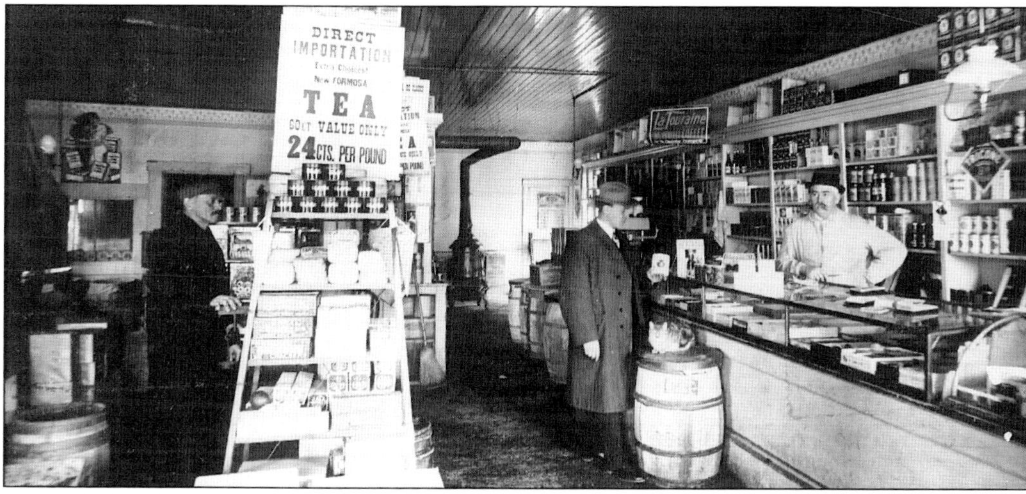

Shown behind the counter is John D. Stephenson (1854–1927), who ran a popular neighborhood grocery store on Winter Street from 1879 to 1927. Stephenson's supplier was the Portland wholesale grocery firm of Twitchell-Champlin, whose salesman, Frederick Rose, stands across the counter from the proprietor. At the left is Edwin Cole, a customer. After Stephenson's death in 1927, his son-in-law, John F. Blaisdell, operated the store until 1960. In 1923, the *Gardiner Journal* called John D. Stephenson "Gardiner's business Methusula" with a longevity record "which no brother merchant of our city now living can duplicate."

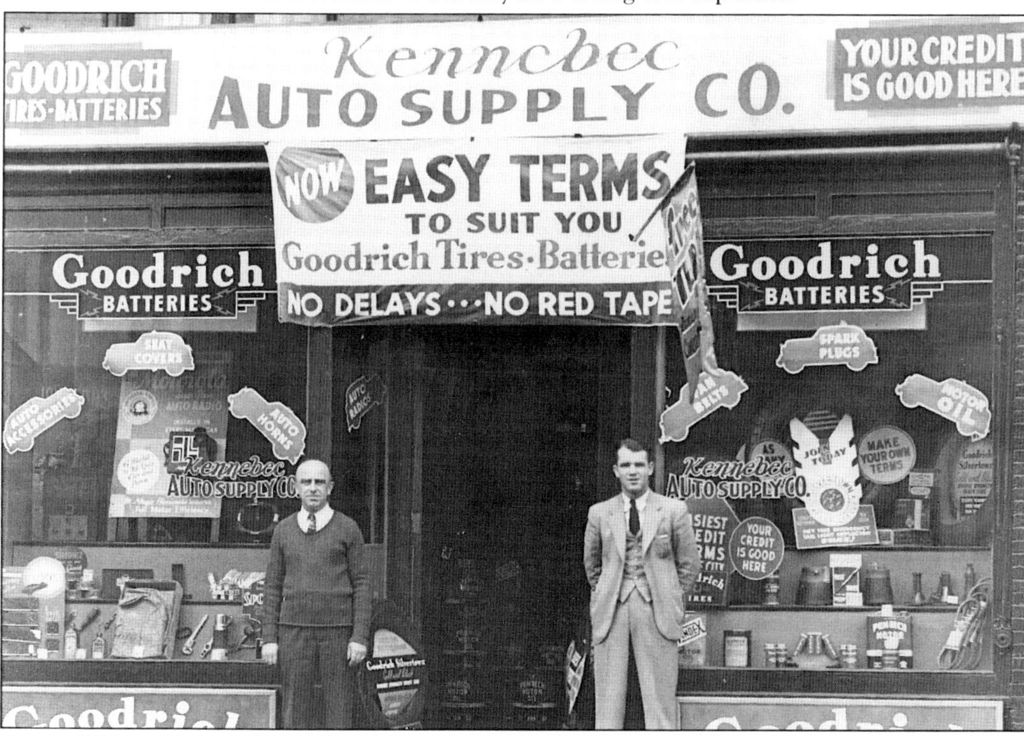

One of Water Street's short-lived Depression-era businesses was the Kennebec Auto Supply Company. Located on the first floor of 205 Water Street, this Goodrich dealership operated for approximately a year in 1935. Manager Raymond J. Compton is probably one of the two men standing at the doorway.

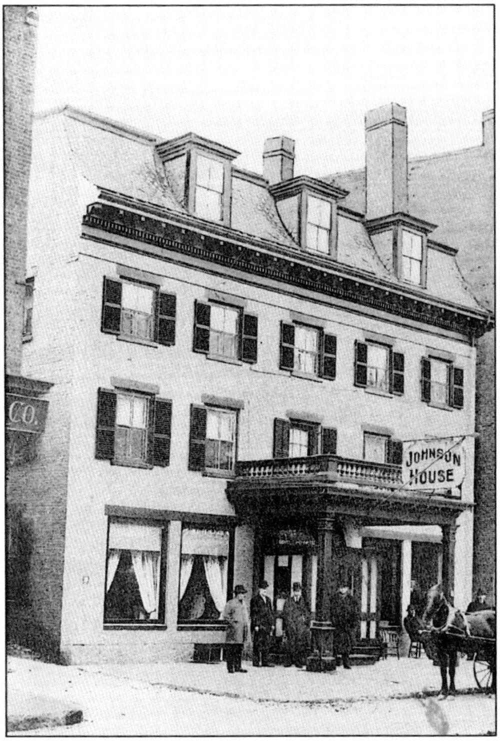

A series of new owners followed Benjamin Johnson's long management of the Johnson House on Water Street. By the time of this 1908 postcard view, the hotel was operated by the Douglas family. In 1916, Douglas' son-in-law, John Hilbert, purchased the business and ran it until his death in 1961. The Johnson House survived Hilbert by only a few years, closing in the 1960s and being demolished for a park in 1972.

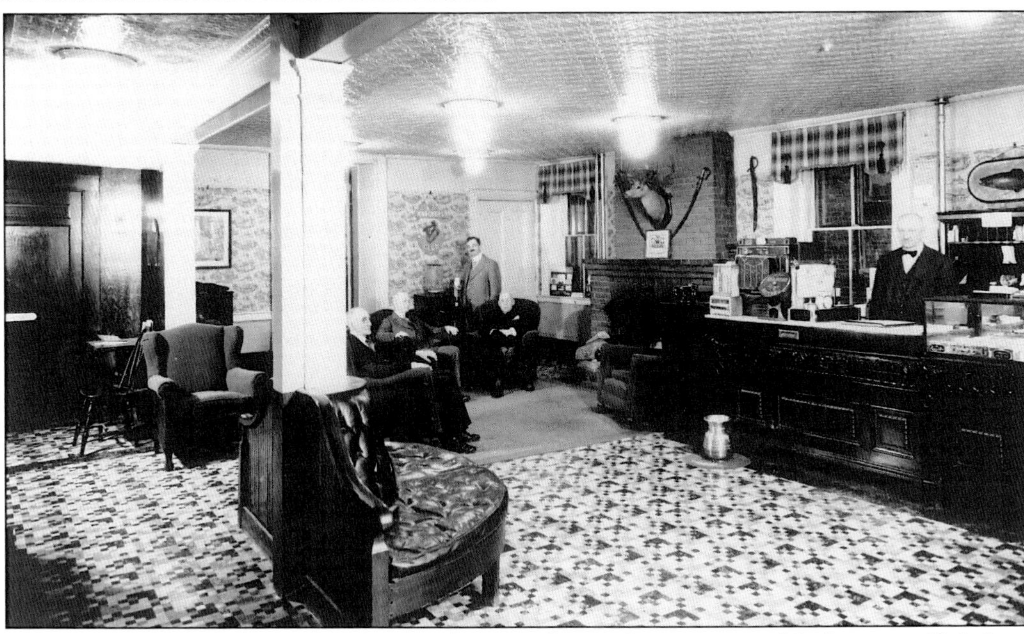

The Johnson House lobby was a favorite location for smoking cigars in black overstuffed chairs during the 1930s, at the height of John Hilbert's management of the historic hostelry. Standing in the background of this photograph, Hilbert was a native of England who devoted most of his career to operating the Johnson House. Contributing to the home-like atmosphere were a fine dining room offering complete meals for $1.50, a sword collection which hung over a lobby fireplace, and a grand piano that floated away in the 1936 flood.

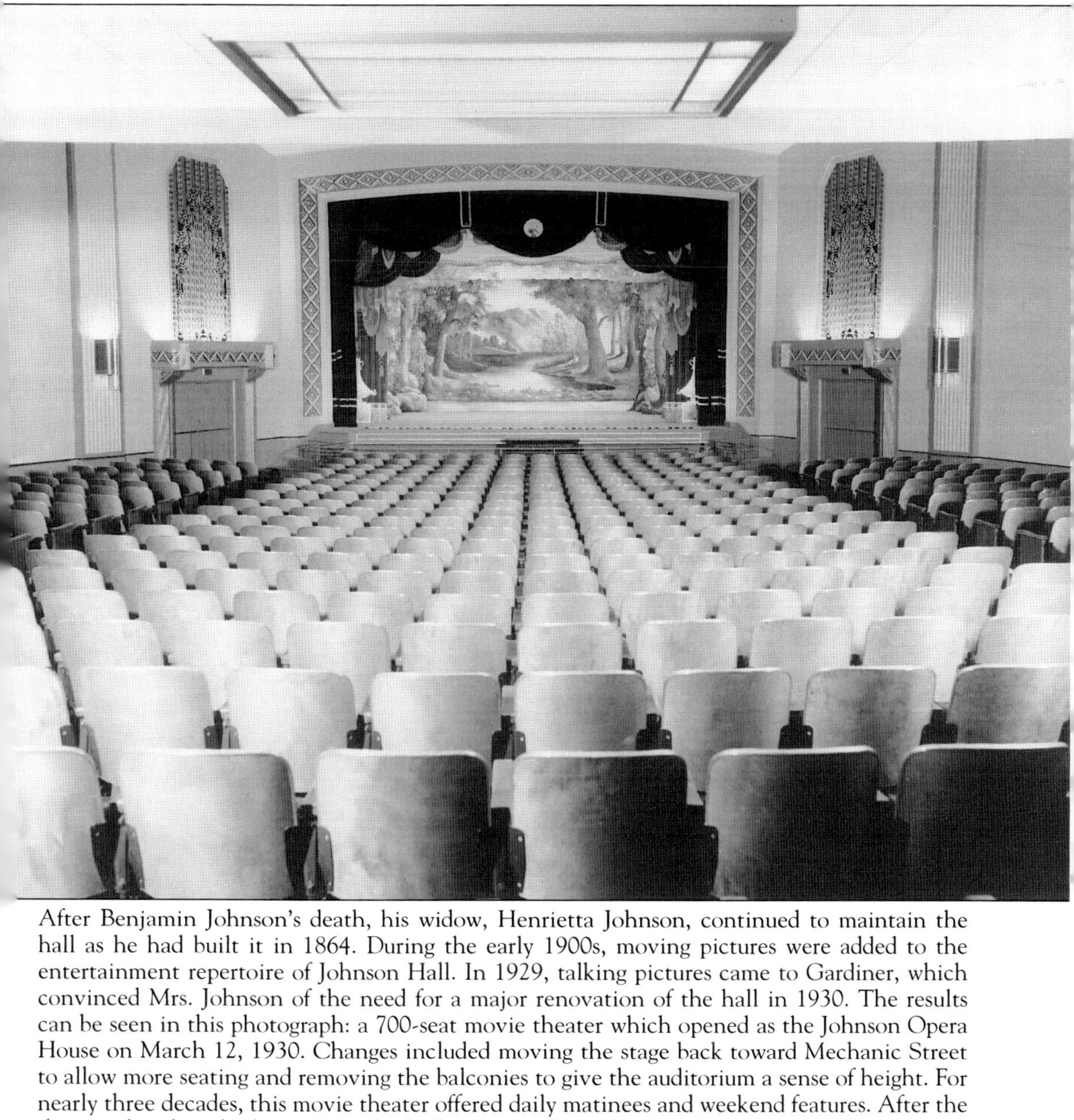

After Benjamin Johnson's death, his widow, Henrietta Johnson, continued to maintain the hall as he had built it in 1864. During the early 1900s, moving pictures were added to the entertainment repertoire of Johnson Hall. In 1929, talking pictures came to Gardiner, which convinced Mrs. Johnson of the need for a major renovation of the hall in 1930. The results can be seen in this photograph: a 700-seat movie theater which opened as the Johnson Opera House on March 12, 1930. Changes included moving the stage back toward Mechanic Street to allow more seating and removing the balconies to give the auditorium a sense of height. For nearly three decades, this movie theater offered daily matinees and weekend features. After the theater closed in the late 1950s, the hall was used for storage until its revival as a performing arts center in the 1980s by Johnson Hall, Inc., a non-profit community group.

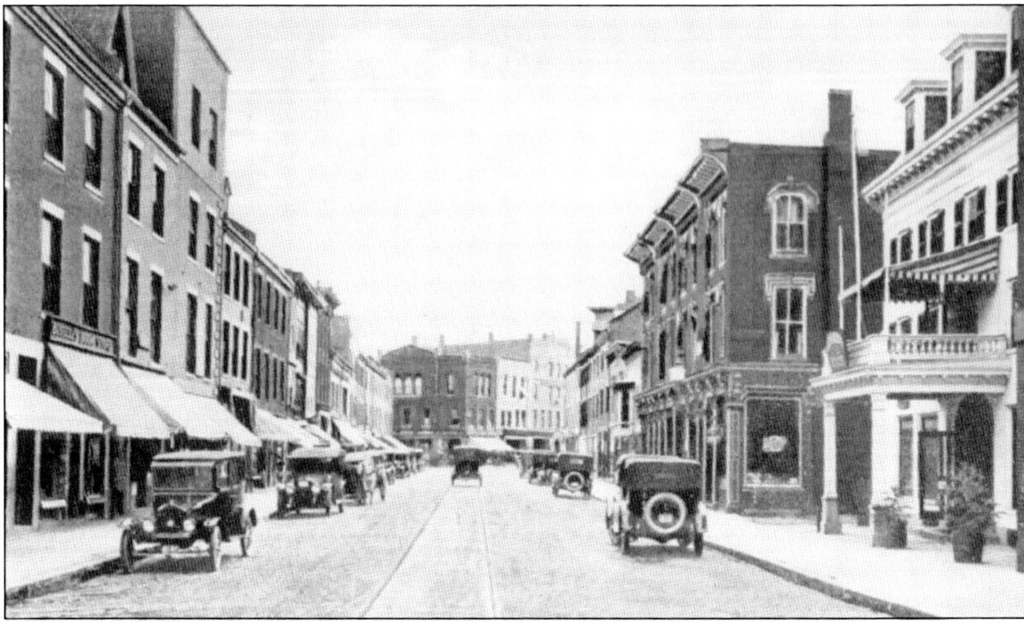

Sedans and touring cars line both sides of Water Street in this c. 1925 postcard view looking toward the intersection of Maine Avenue and Church Street. The Johnson House and the Milliken Block are at the right.

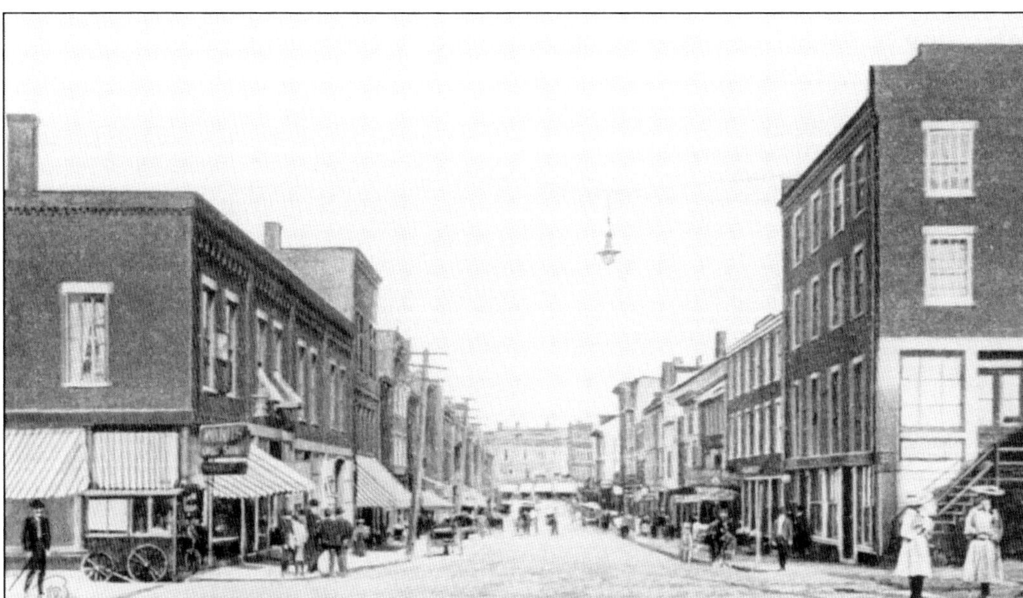

This c. 1910 postcard captured the scene looking down Water Street from the intersection of Bridge Street and Brunswick Avenue. At the left is the Maxcy, Billings, Sawyer, and Libby Block of 1860, which remains a corner landmark to this day. The Bowman Block of 1846, on the opposite corner, and the adjacent Tarbox Block of 1845 were demolished for the post office, which was constructed between 1915 and 1917.

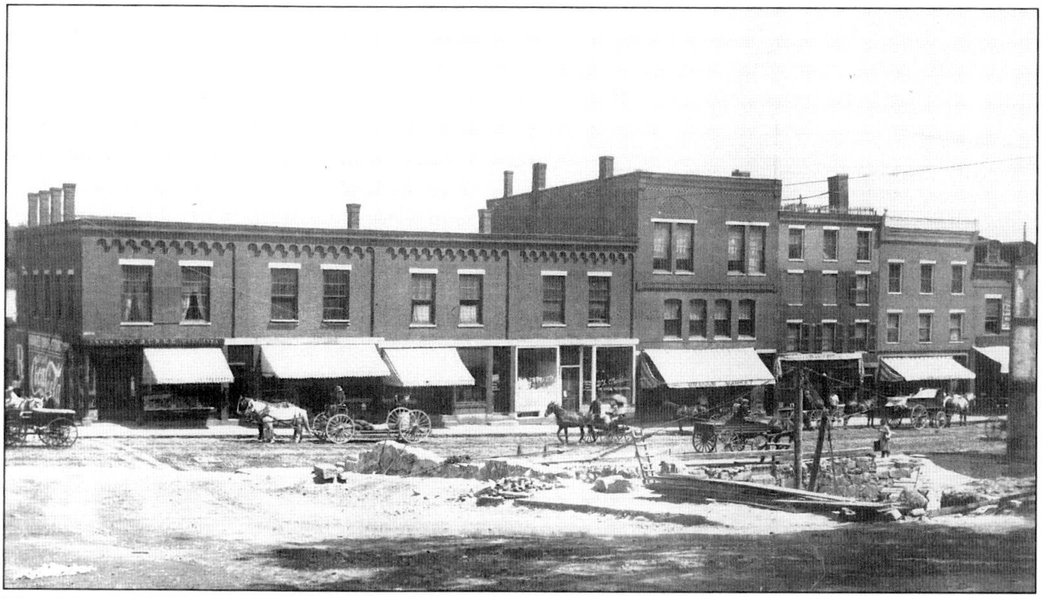

The Maxcy, Billings, Sawyer, and Libby Block of 1860 at the corner of Bridge Street and its adjacent Water Street buildings loom large in this 1915 photograph, taken from Brunswick Avenue, of the post office site.

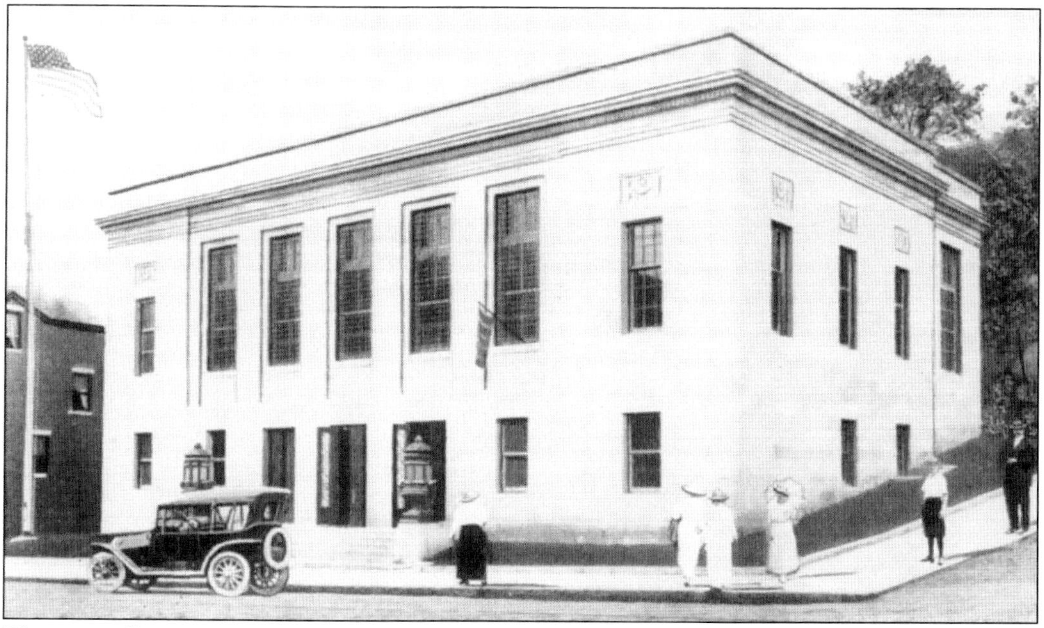

The post office at Water Street and Brunswick Avenue was built at a cost of $22,000 for the land and $56,000 for the building. This handsome Indiana limestone structure was designed by government architect James A. Wetmore. When it was completed in January 1917, some local residents thought the restrained elegance of its Classical Revival architecture too austere and requested more ornament from Washington. Relief came in March 1918, when the *Gardiner Journal* reported the following: "Due to criticism on the plainness of the recently-opened post office, Postmaster William R. Frost has obtained, through Senator C. F. Johnson, two large bronze lamps and some grill work for the unadorned windows."

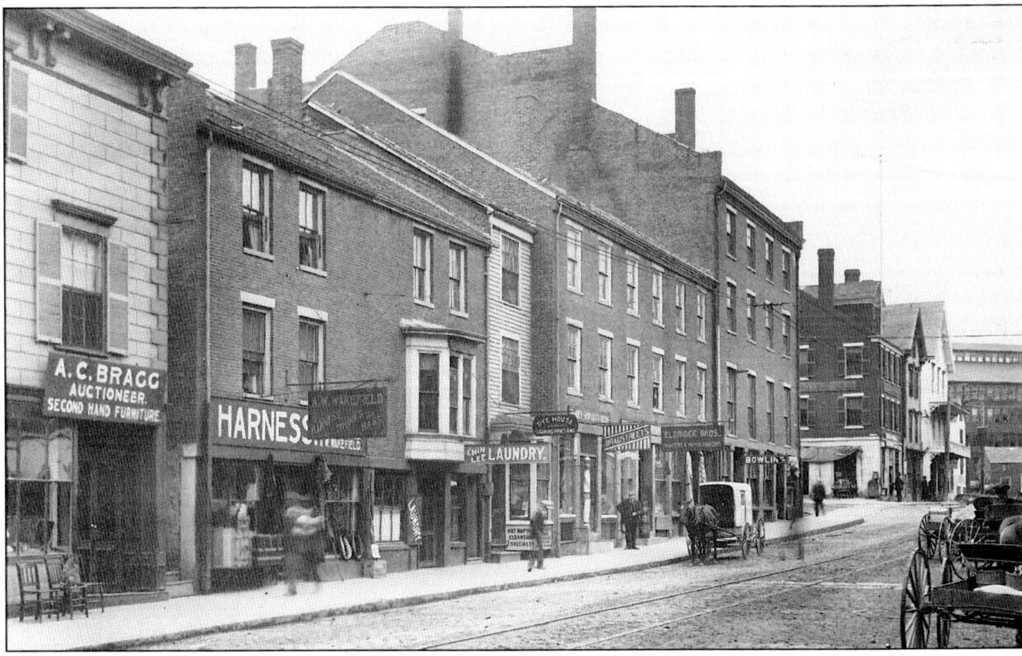

The site of the new post office had previously been home to Chin Lee's Chinese laundry and two large brick buildings, the Tarbox Block of 1846 and the Bowman Block of 1845. Excluded from the post office demolition were the two structures at left, Bragg's Second Hand Furniture Store and Wakefield's Harness Shop. In recent years the Wakefield Building was demolished for a post office parking lot, but the Bragg Building remains to this day.

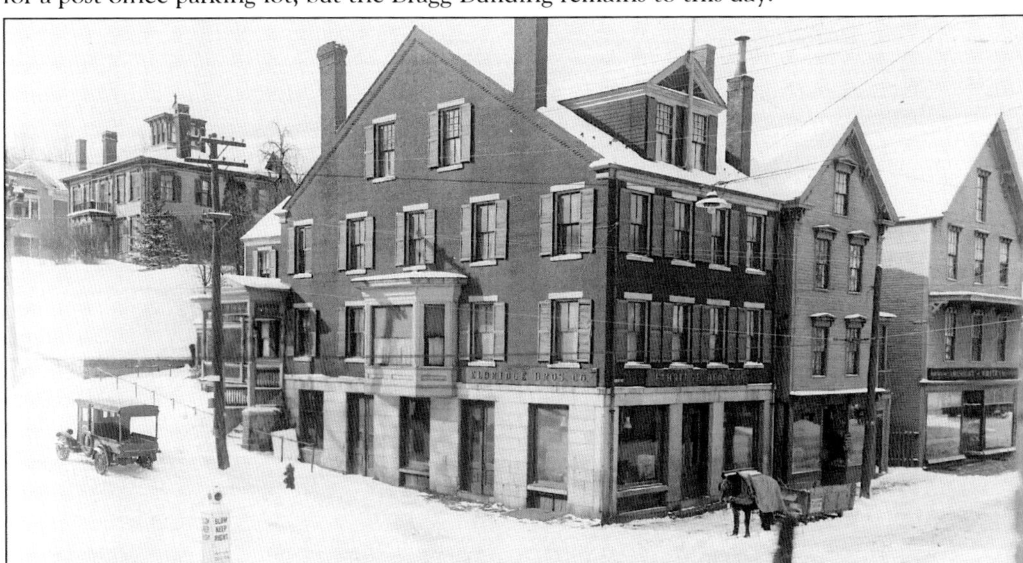

James and John Stone, dry goods merchants, constructed this substantial brick and granite block at Water Street and Brunswick Avenue in about 1850. This c. 1920 photograph shows the store where, for many years, the Stones offered, "a full and complete stock of silks, dress goods, carpeting, velvets, table linen, laces, feathers, and small wares of all kinds," in the words of an 1884 newspaper article.

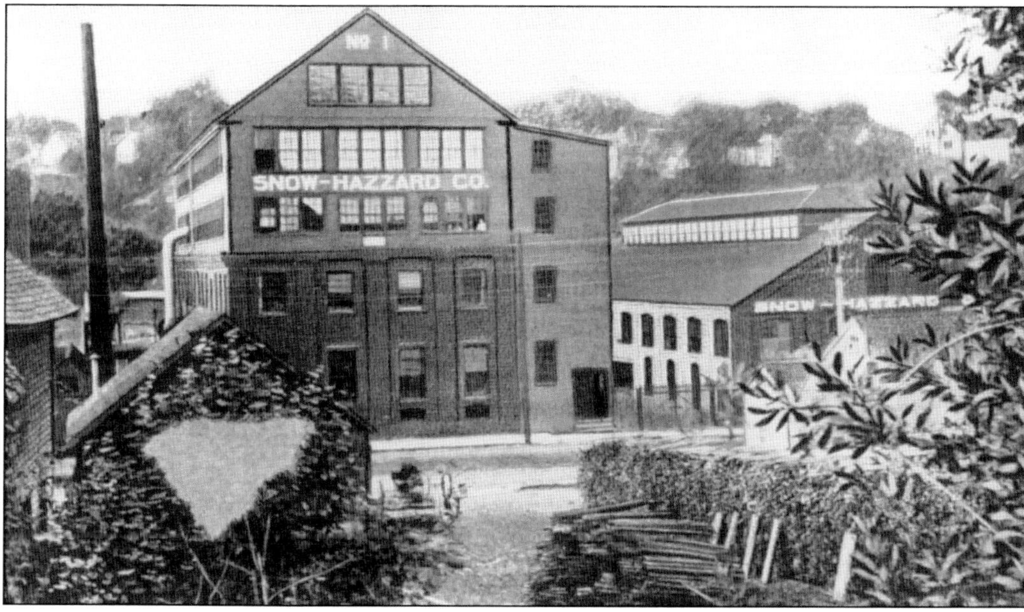

In 1906, Robert P. Hazzard, the superintendent of the Commonwealth Shoe Factory, formed a partnership with the Brockton, Massachusetts, shoe manufacturer George H. Snow to start a new factory in Gardiner. That year Hazzard convinced the board of trade to acquire the former Holmes Machine Shop and Foundry on Water Street and convert its buildings into the Snow-Hazzard Company shoe shop. The business proved such a success for Hazzard that he acquired Snow's share of the firm in 1910 and embarked upon a major expansion. This view shows the factory as it looked from 1906 to 1910.

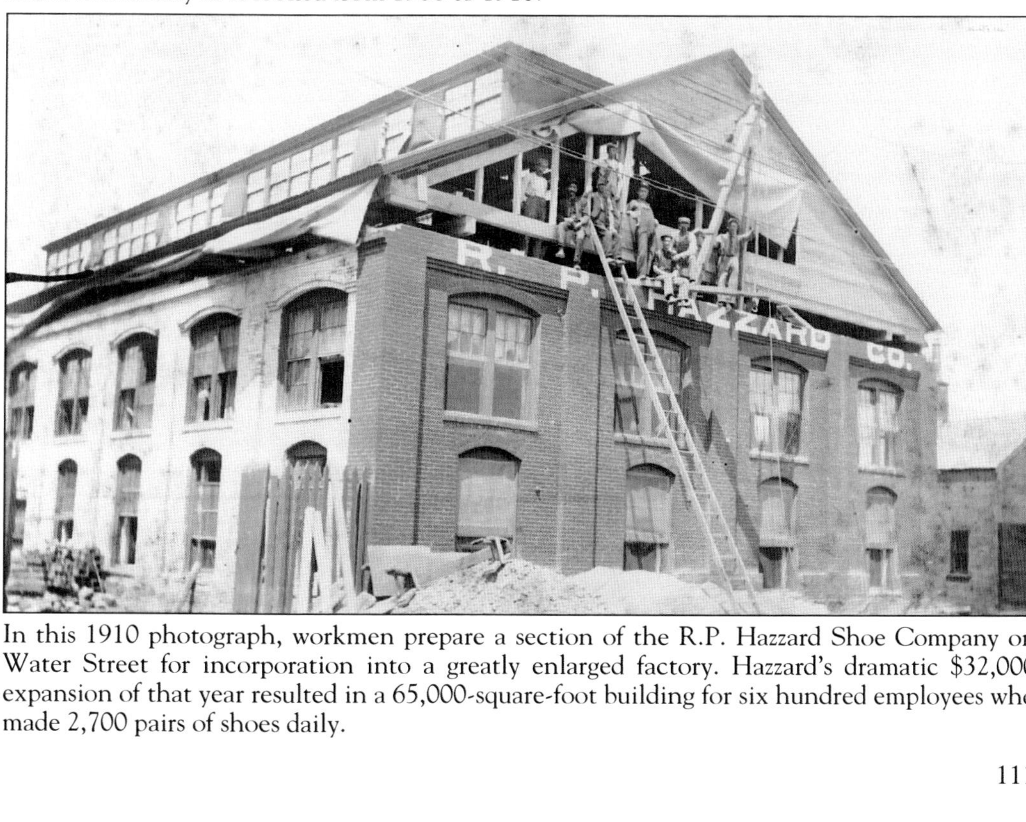

In this 1910 photograph, workmen prepare a section of the R.P. Hazzard Shoe Company on Water Street for incorporation into a greatly enlarged factory. Hazzard's dramatic $32,000 expansion of that year resulted in a 65,000-square-foot building for six hundred employees who made 2,700 pairs of shoes daily.

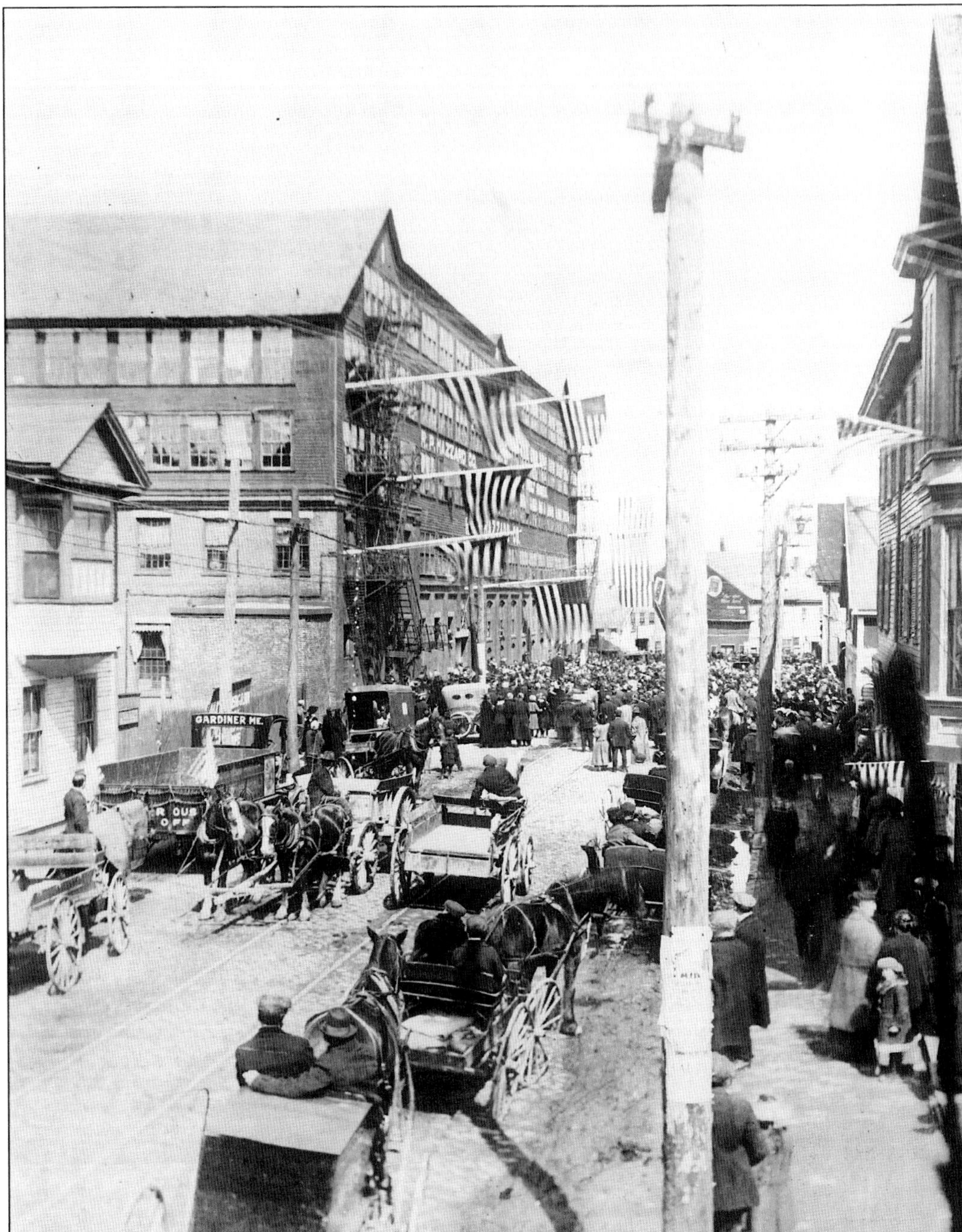

Flags fly from the six-story R.P. Hazzard Shoe Factory on Water Street in this May 1916 photograph taken at Winter Street looking toward Bridge Street. In 1913, Hazzard completed his second expansion of the factory, giving his company the capacity to produce six thousand pairs of shoes daily. A third expansion occurred in 1921 with the construction of a six-story building adjacent to the plant. These massive structures dominated this section of Water Street until their demolition in 1971.

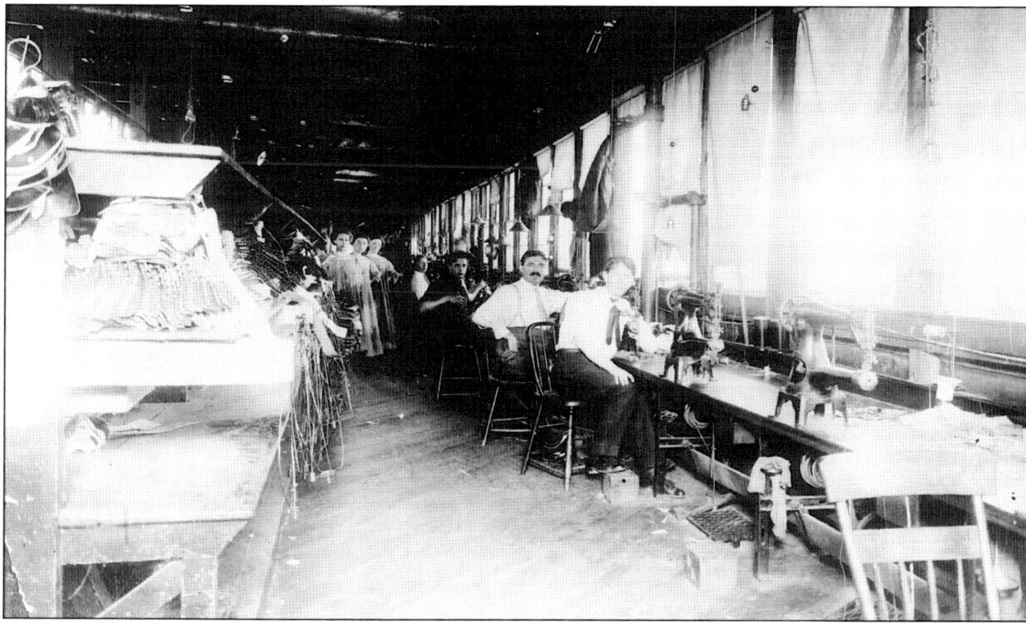

The stitching room was located on the fifth floor of the R.P. Hazzard Shoe Factory. Commenting on "the phenomenal growth of the business," the September 1913 *Industrial Journal* noted the following: "Hazzard Company employs approximately 943 hands with a weekly payroll of about $12,000, and turns out in the vicinity of 5,000 pairs daily of men's Goodyear Welts, which are sold all over the United States and exported to most foreign markets. They specialize in styles that sell and shoes that wear."

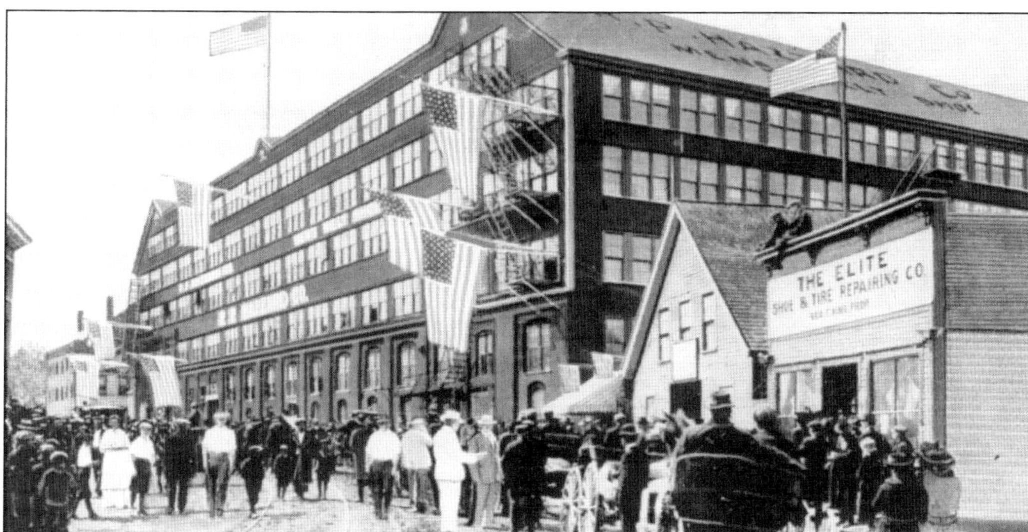

Another May 1916 view of the R.P. Hazzard Shoe Factory on Water Street, looking from Bridge Street to Winter Street. The crowd reflects a Memorial Day gathering, as well as the fact that Hazzard Shoe had become Gardiner's largest industrial operation. An August 29, 1926 *Portland Press Herald* article reported that the company "employs 1,700 men, has a payroll of $20,000 weekly, and turns out over 400 dozen pairs of shoes daily which are sold through the Hazzard chain of retail shores located in prominent cities all over the country."

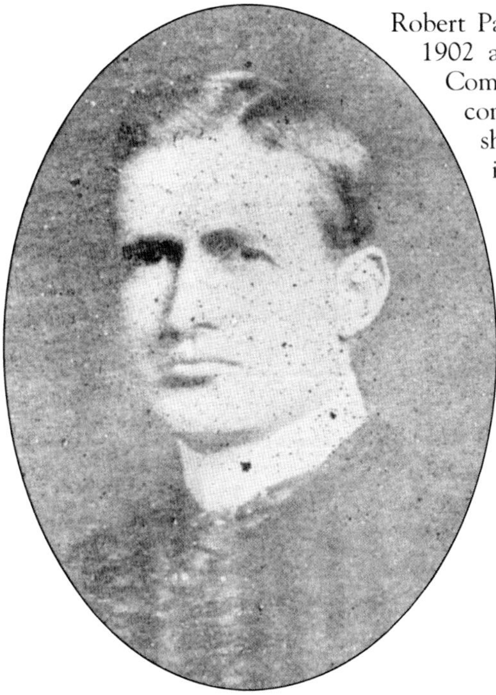

Robert Parks Hazzard (1869–1948) came to Gardiner in 1902 as superintendent of the Commonwealth Shoe Company, but four years later organized his own company, which by 1931 made 56 percent of men's shoes in Maine, or a total of 14 percent of all shoes in the state. His shoes retailed in 205 company stores across the nation. He is the common ancestor of the Shaeffer, Olmsted, Anderson, Bean, Moore, and McLaughlin families long prominent in the Gardiner area.

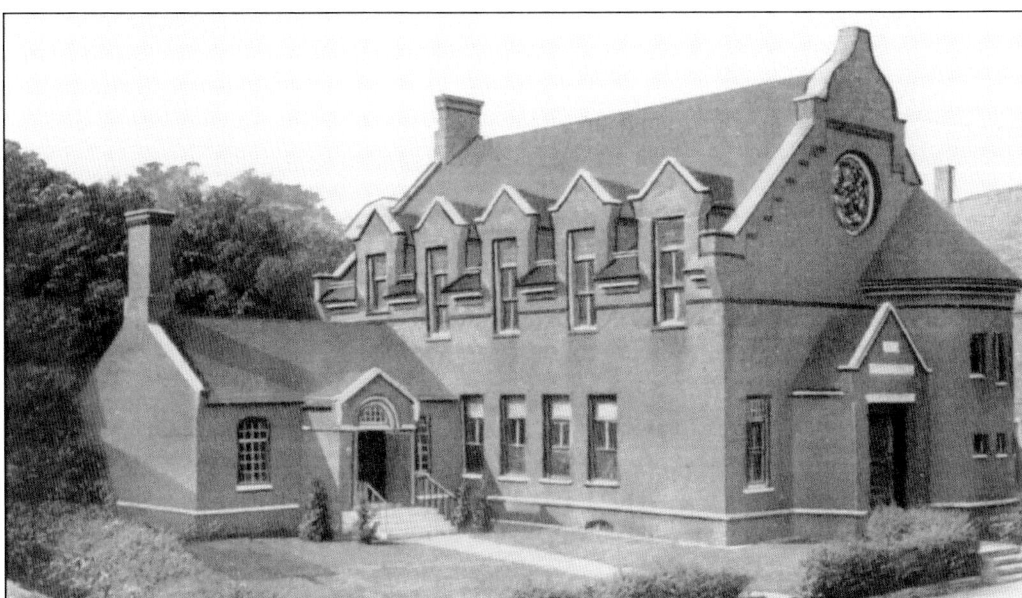

In 1929, Robert P. Hazzard commissioned Portland architect John P. Thomas to add a children's room as a 24-by-30-foot wing on the southern side of the library. The lawn in front of the wing became the Margaret Campbell Shaw Garden in 1990. Designed as a Victorian garden to compliment the building, its paths, flower beds, and an iron fence surround an armillary sphere by the late sculptor Ron Cross. The bronze tablet on the sundial honors Peg in these words: "A caring gardener, she nurtured both the tenderest shoot and the withering rose."

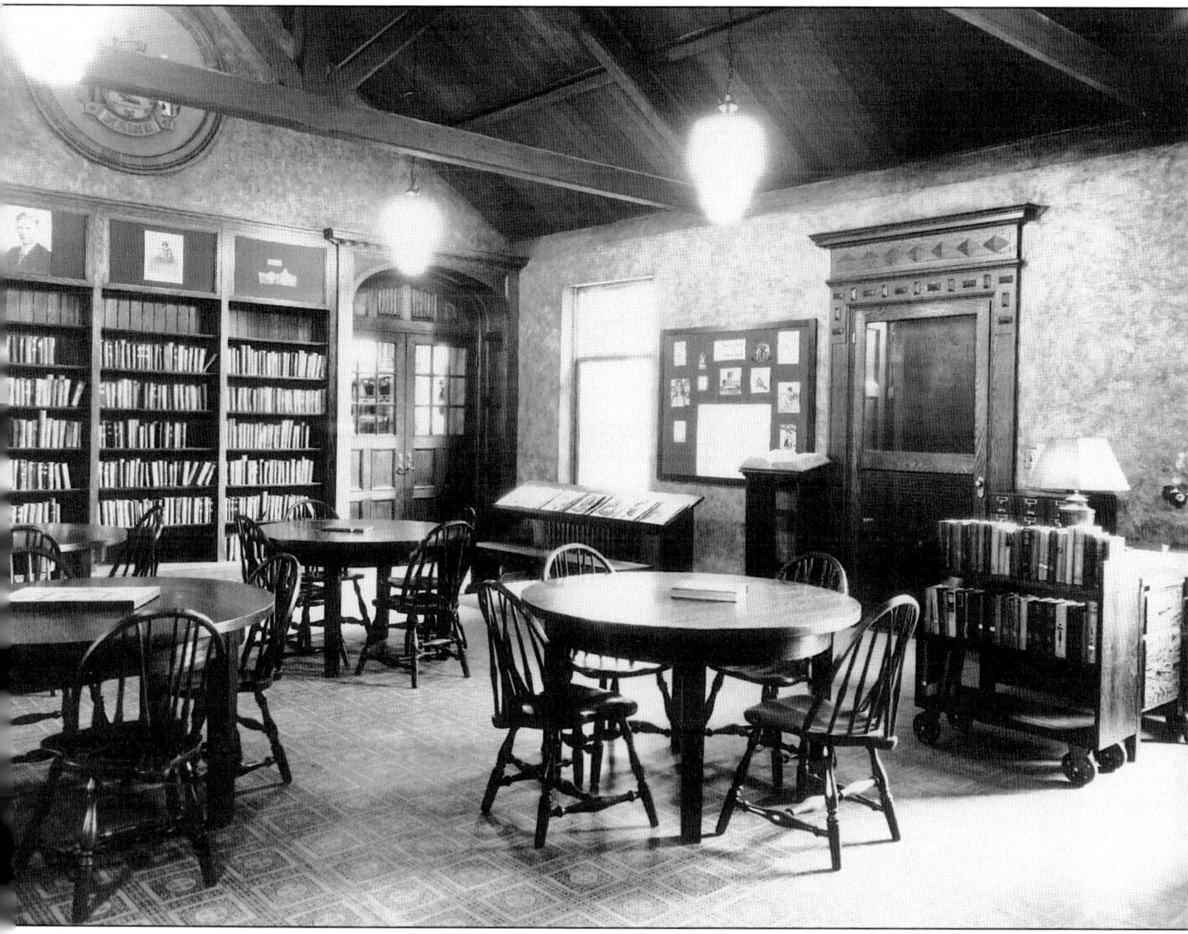

The interior of the Robert P. Hazzard wing of the Gardiner Public Library opened as a children's room on May 20, 1930, and in 1977, Hazzard descendants funded its conversion to a reference room. The Elizabethan interior, with its fine oak paneling and mantelpiece, draws inspiration from Breccles Hall, County Suffolk, England, which was built in 1583. At the same time in 1977, the second floor opened as a children's room as a gift from Hazzard's daughter, Mrs. Clarence McLaughlin, in memory of her son, Burress Moore III. As this book goes to press, the lowered ceiling installed during the energy crisis of the 1970s is being removed to reveal the original splendor of the ceiling and the State of Maine seal painted by Hazzard's sister, Miss Sarah Hazzard of Jamestown, New York.

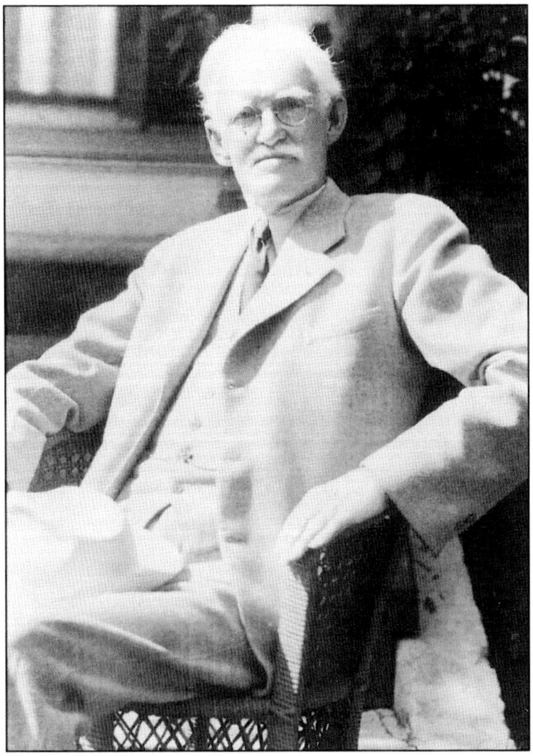

The career of Josiah Smith Maxcy (1854–1936) mirrored that of his namesake father so closely that the contributions of the two men to this city seem to span one continuous lifetime. A second-generation manager of his family's insurance firm and bank president, he was the principal founder of the Gardiner General Hospital. In his will he left many trust funds for the benefit of civic causes, the hospital, and Christ Church.

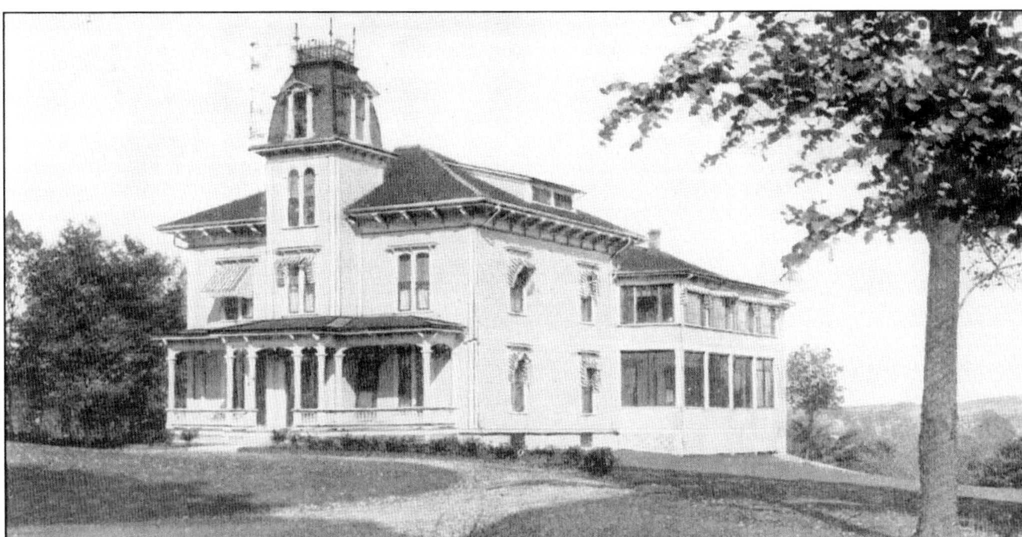

Because of advances in medical science, especially surgery, communities perceived the need for hospitals by the turn of the century. Dr. A.B. Libby, the leading physician in this city, acquired the Dunphy House on River Avenue and moved it to this site on Dresden Avenue to be used as a private hospital. At the same time, Josiah S. Maxcy and the Richards family, after many public appeals, raised sufficient money to enable Dr. Libby to open it as a public hospital, just in time to receive the many seriously ill patients during the great influenza epidemic in 1919. This view shows the handsome mansard-roofed building which served as the hospital for ten years until a devastating fire in 1928.

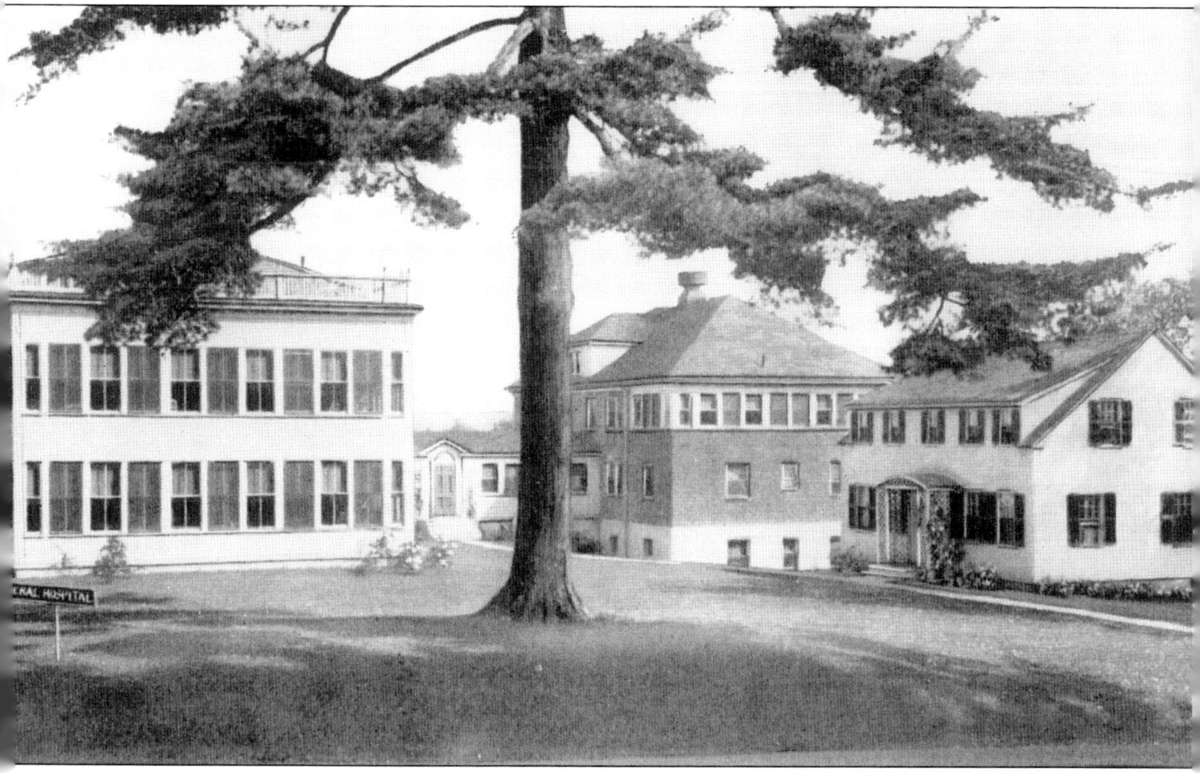

Mercifully, all the patients in the hospital on January 6, 1928, were safely evacuated when faulty electrical wiring in the attic started a fire. Now the community appreciated the hospital, and within days, civic leaders raised the necessary money to build an expanded hospital according to architectural plans submitted by Henry Richards. This view shows the old Dunphy House shorn of its Victorian features and transformed into a Colonial Revival structure with a glassed-in porch on front. The brick block (at right) housed the new maternity ward, which was connected to the old building by a corridor. In 1968, the hospital had become obsolete, and the new building, started in 1970, was completed four years later. The old hospital was razed; only the 1928 brick building remains. Shortly before the erection of the high school at the corner of Pleasant and School Streets, the old Williamson House was moved to the hospital grounds for use as the nurses' residence (shown on the right).

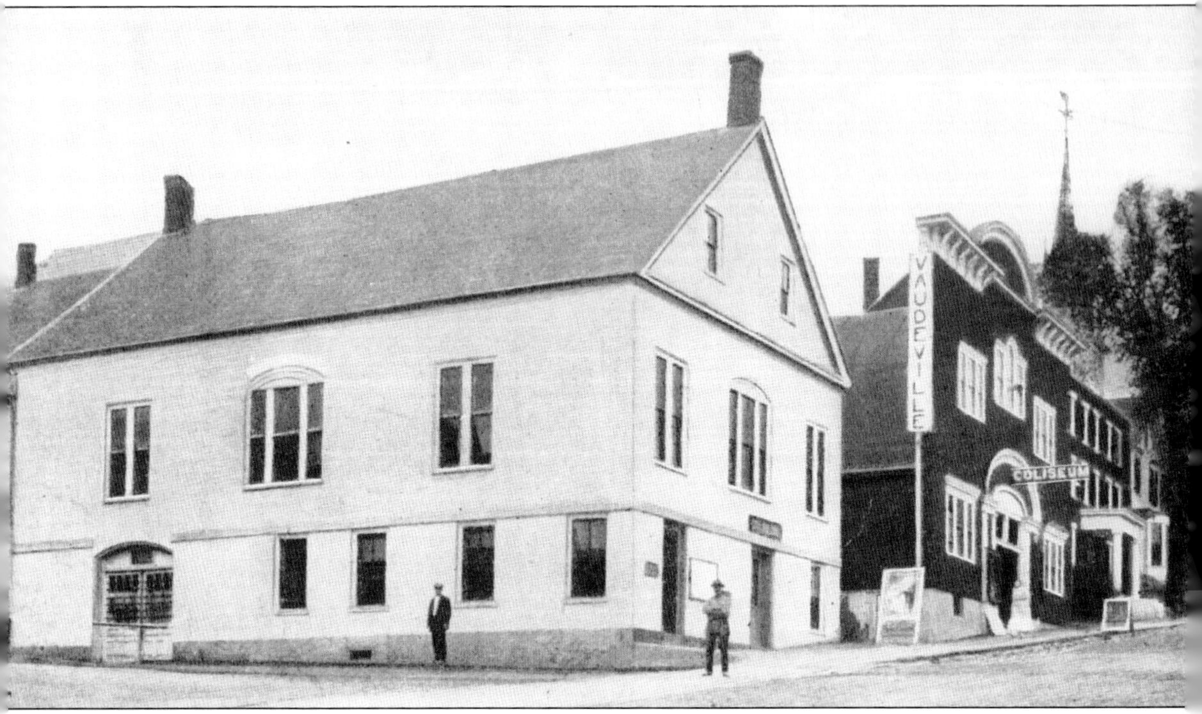

After the old meetinghouse next to Christ Church burned in 1834, the town fathers soon erected the municipal building shown at the left. This building, with a door to the municipal court on the left and a door to the local liquor agency on the right, served as city hall until 1969, when the present brick, steel, and glass structure was built. Next up the hill is the Coliseum, replacing the one which burned at Depot Square in 1904. In 1908, the Gardiner Realty Corporation commissioned Langdon G. Paul to transform the old Smith carriage factory into an auditorium for fairs, sports events, and vaudeville. Later it became a movie theater, but after falling out of use, this second Coliseum was razed in 1942. Still further up the hill are the Berry and Trask Houses, later broken up into apartments. They were razed in 1965 in anticipation of the 1969 city hall and fire department complex.

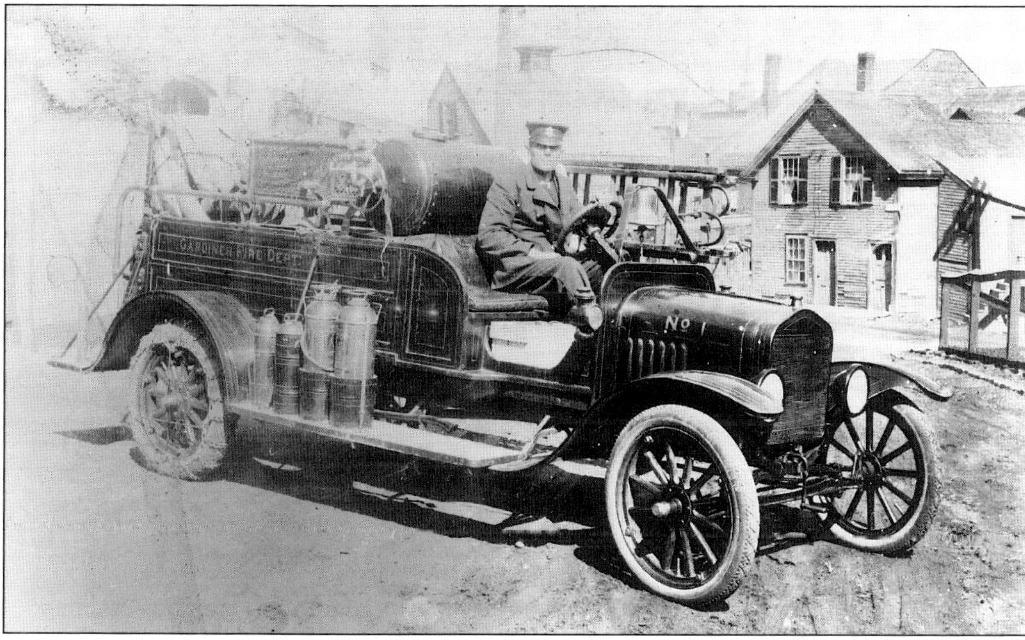

The Gardiner Fire Department's first motorized piece of apparatus was this combination hose and chemical truck. Dating from about 1919, the truck is shown parked at the firehouse on Church Street. The driver is believed to be Albert C. Hinckley.

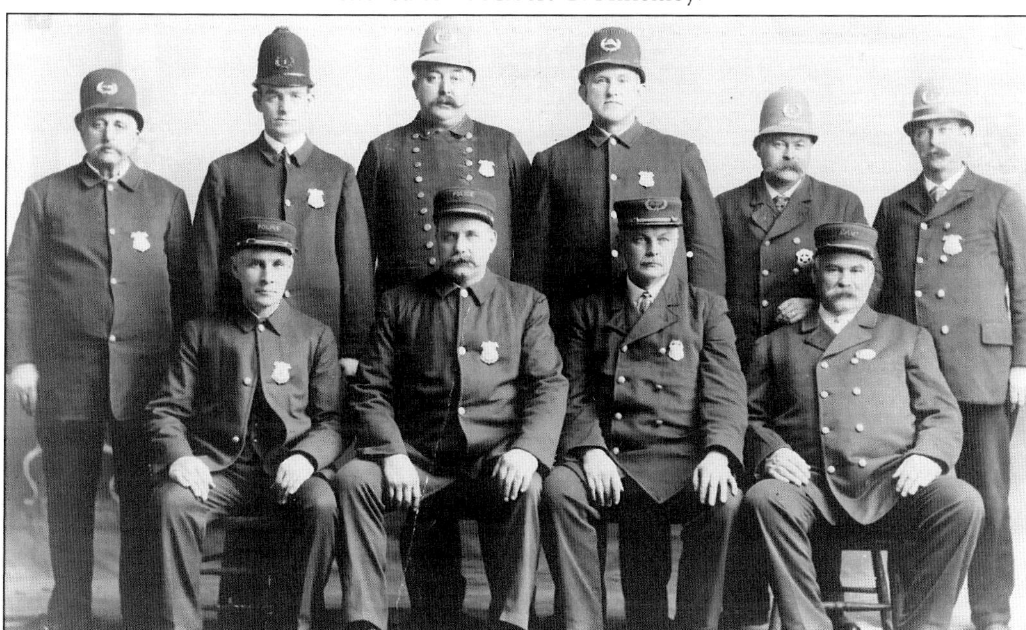

In 1911, the Gardiner Police Force won a nationwide contest in newspapers by weighing in on a hay scale at 2,800 pounds, or a 280-pound average. These ten officers individually weighed from a low of 192 to a high of 296, borne by Mike Cusick, "The Living Derrick," who, when he "got his hands on a wrong-doer, he went along." From left to right are: (front row) Warren Tozier, Fred Merrill, Chief Walter Wakefield, and Charles Blaisdell; (back row) Henry King, Frank Annis, Byron Buzzell, Mike Cusick, Ren Peacock, and Forest Wiles.

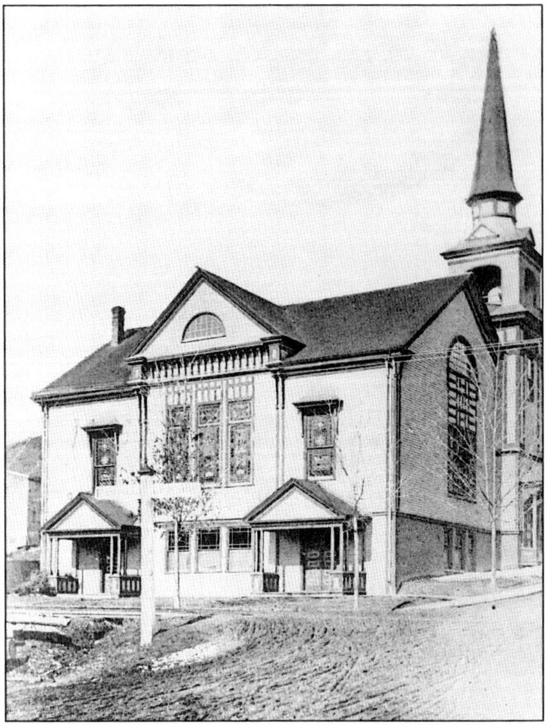

The Winter Street Baptist Church was built in 1846 by the Free Will Baptists at a cost of $3,100. In 1892, Gardiner architect Edwin E. Lewis drew the plans which gave the church its present Queen Anne-style appearance.

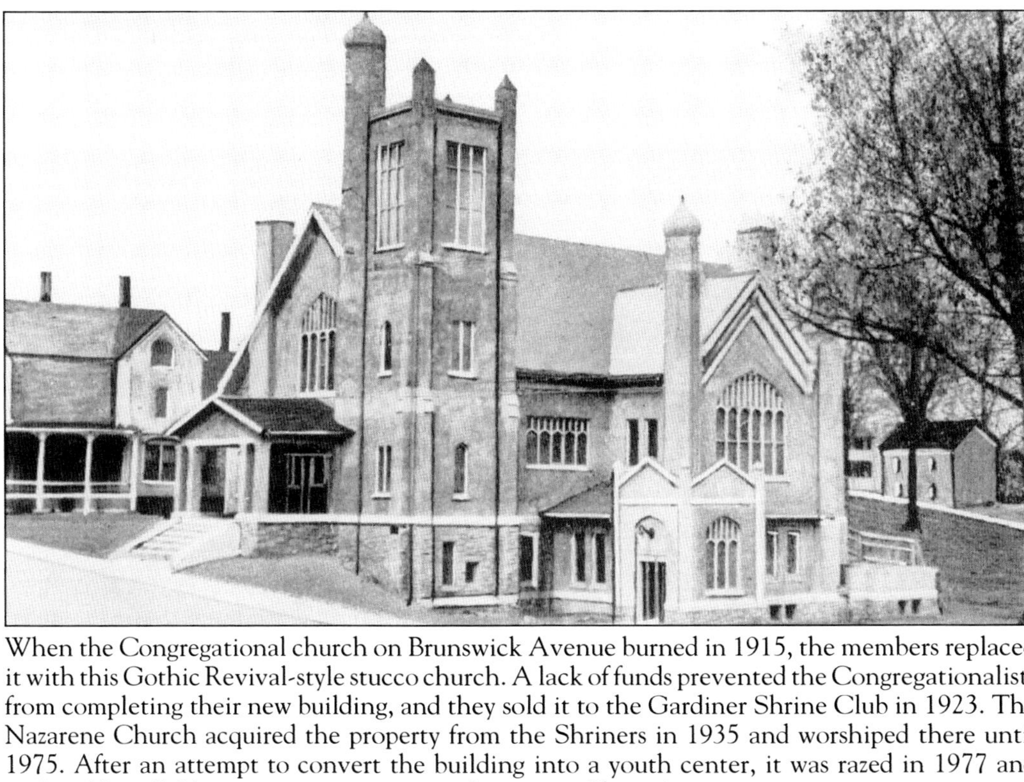

When the Congregational church on Brunswick Avenue burned in 1915, the members replaced it with this Gothic Revival-style stucco church. A lack of funds prevented the Congregationalists from completing their new building, and they sold it to the Gardiner Shrine Club in 1923. The Nazarene Church acquired the property from the Shriners in 1935 and worshiped there until 1975. After an attempt to convert the building into a youth center, it was razed in 1977 and replaced by a 7-11 convenience store, now known as Christy's.

Erected in 1905 on Lincoln Avenue, this Shingle-Style church with Gothic windows was Maine's first Christian Science building. Gardiner's Christian Science church was the gift of Mr. and Mrs. Palmer Noyes, with Mrs. Noyes designing the building. After the last Christian Science service in 1962, the church was used by the Assembly of God and as a sheltered workshop before its conversion into apartments in the 1980s.

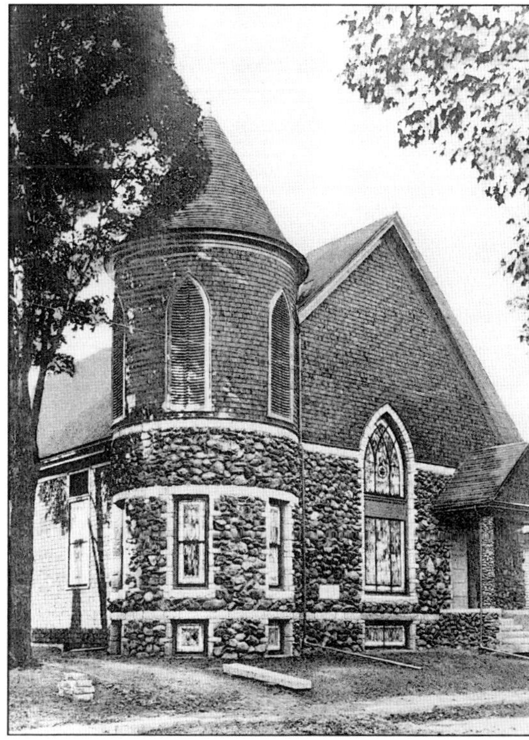

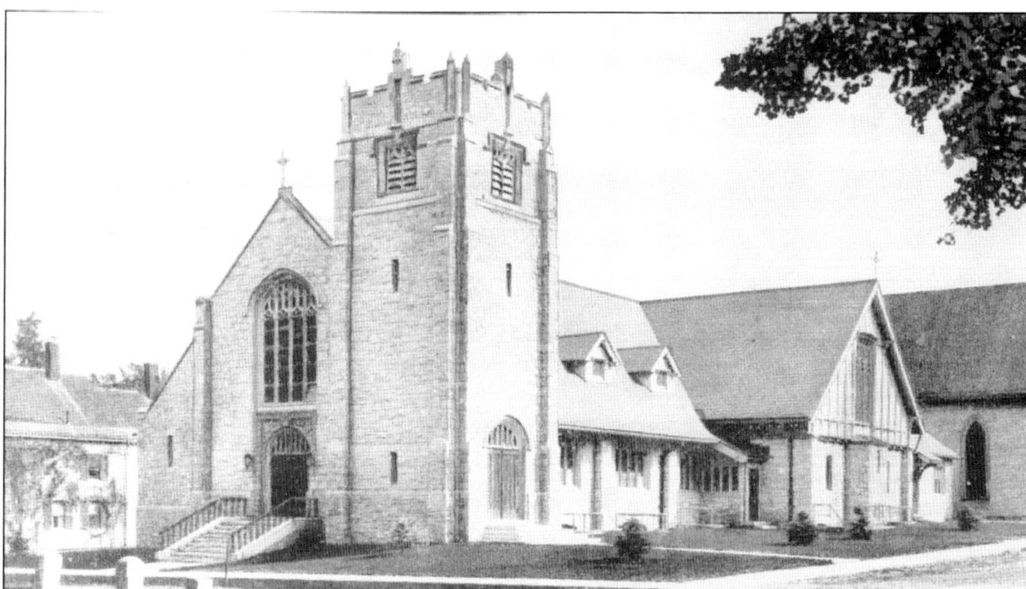

St. Joseph's Catholic Church was built at School Street and Lincoln Avenue between 1914 and 1916, at a cost of $150,000. Designed by Boston architect Edward Graham, this handsome Gothic Revival building was constructed of Hallowell granite. Graham also designed the 1931 stone rectory across the street. A glimpse of the first St. Joseph's can be seen at the right behind the present church. The original wooden church of 1858 continued to serve as a parish hall from 1916 until its demolition about 1933.

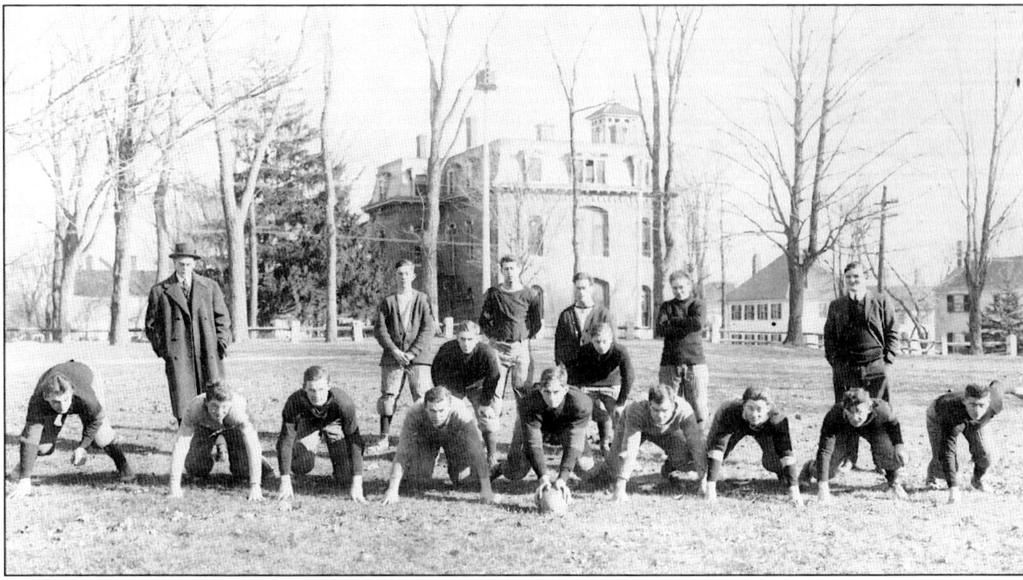

The Gardiner High School football team of 1915 posed on the Common, with the mansard-roofed building that served as the high school from 1870 to 1921 in the background. Organized football in Gardiner dates from 1892 when the Gardiner "Tigers" first challenged their traditional rivals, the Cony "Rams" of Augusta. In 1915, the score was Gardiner 13, Cony 0.

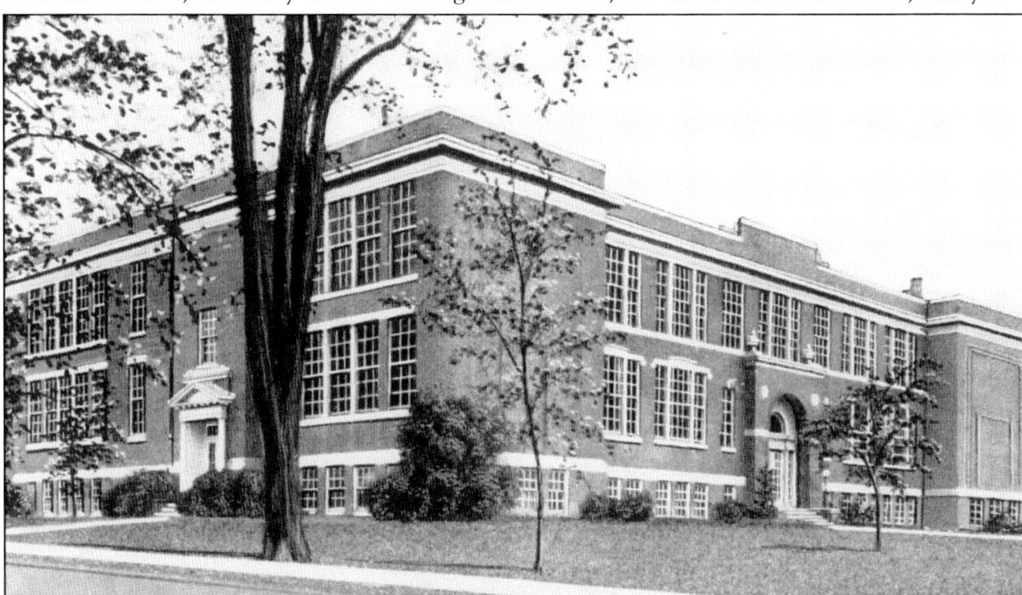

Between 1917 and 1919, Laura E. Richards spearheaded fund-raising to enable the city to commission Lewiston architect Harry Coombs to design this building in 1920. At the corner of Pleasant and School Streets, it housed the Gardiner High School classes from 1921 to 1963. In December 1971 it was renamed to honor O.C. Woodman, who served the city as a teacher and superintendent from 1927 to 1961. It was the junior high school, and later the middle school, from 1963 until its closing in 1992. Since then, the city has rented space to the alternative education project known as Evergreen School and retained gymnasium space for the youth recreation program.

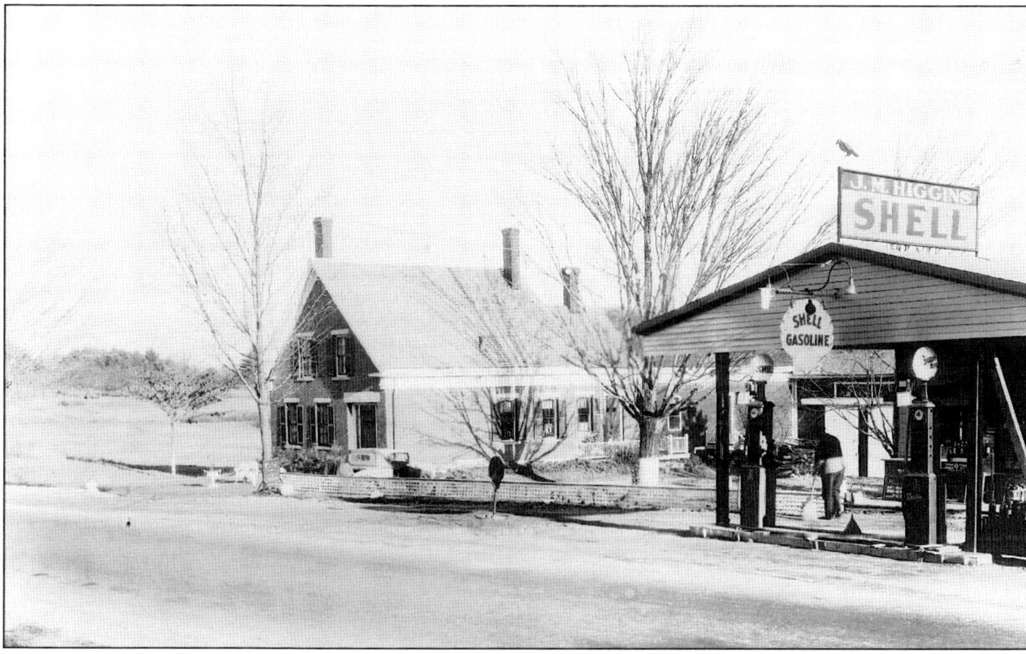

Filling stations first appear in the city directories in 1927. This photograph captures the brief time when Joseph and Marie Higgins managed a Shell station doubling as a grocery store in 1931 on Brunswick Road. Alvan McCausland, Harry Poole, and Morrill Totman operated other filling stations on Brunswick Road through 1952, shortly after which time the traffic rerouted to the new Route 201 cut them off from through traffic. The road then became the Old Brunswick Road.

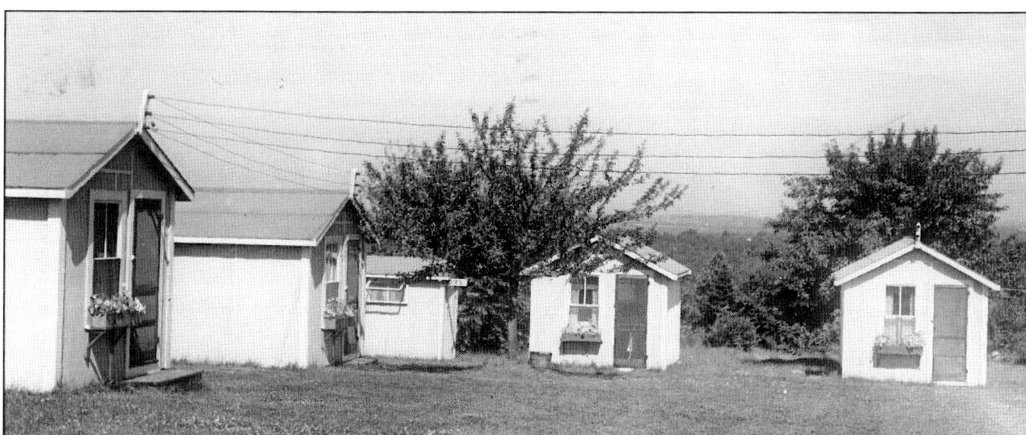

The appearance of roadside cabins near major traffic arteries in the state heralded the availability of automobiles between the two world wars. Elmer J. Clark opened a confectionery business on Brunswick Road on the outskirts of the city in 1929 and supplemented his income by building these inexpensive lodgings for motorists in 1931. By 1933, Edwin R. Leonard acquired them and was followed by Clarence Thompson in 1936, who by 1941 called the vacation spot the Rendezvous. By 1945 Thompson worked full-time at Bath Iron Works and closed the cabins, a sign of the devastation which war-time gas rationing brought to all forms of recreation business. Similar roadside cabins at Grant's Crossing in Farmingdale were demolished in 1965.

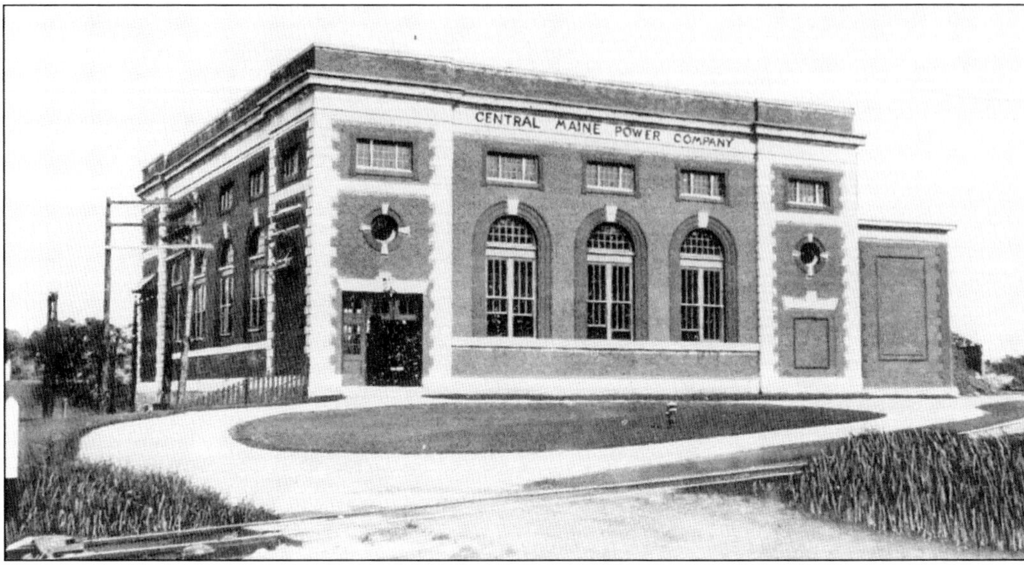

Since 1912, this handsome Georgian Revival-style power station has stood on Bowman's Point in Farmingdale. Built by the Central Maine Power Company from designs by the Portland architectural firm of Miller and Mayo, the station originally generated 2,500 kilowatts of electricity by hand-fired coal-burning steam turbines. White's 1952 *History of Farmingdale* noted that the plant "employed as many as 26 men to keep it going. In the so-called good old days during a period of heavy runs, 56 tons of coal were fired in the 4 boilers in 14 hours, which meant shoveling a ton of coal per man per hour."

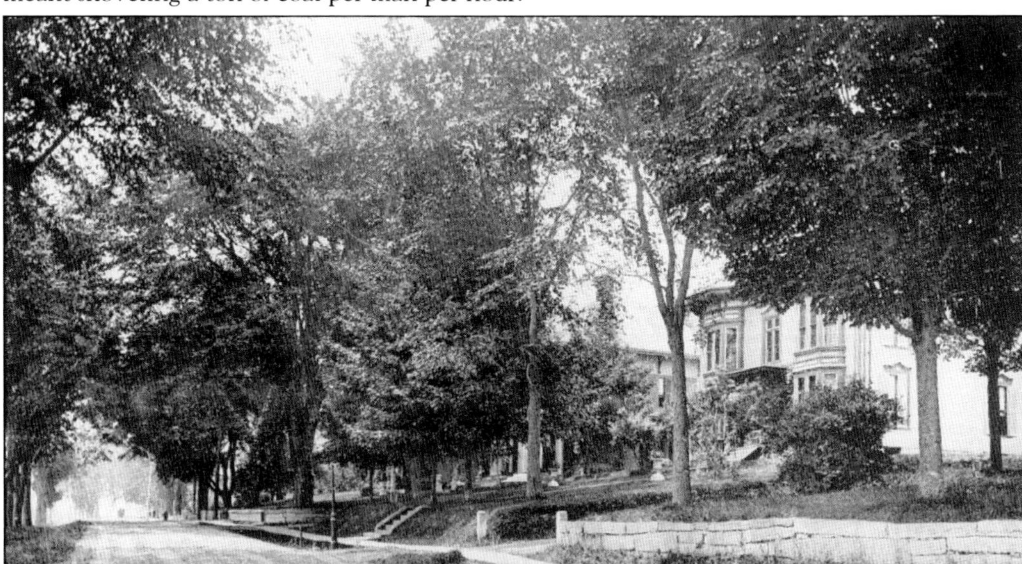

In 1787, only one house stood on the bridle path between Hallowell and Cobbossee Stream in Gardiner. The General Court of Sessions established the road in 1799, relocated it in 1807, and finally commissioned an elaborate engineering plan in 1823 from which time settlers rapidly built houses on what is now Route 201, known locally as Maine Avenue. This photograph, from *Picturesque Gardiner* (1896), shows the facade of the Italianate mansion popularly known as the Dr. Carroll Church House.

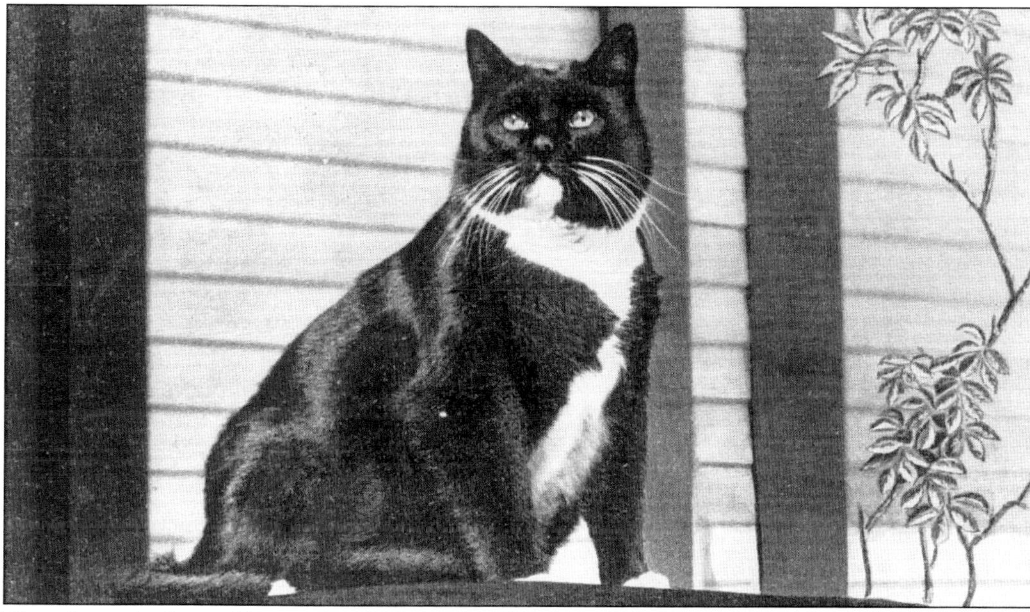

This fierce-looking feline named McKinley lived in Farmingdale when Warren W. Seavey photographed him in 1907. Weighing 35 pounds, McKinley was billed as "the largest domestic cat." This claim may have been true at the time, considering that the average male cat weights 8.6 pounds, and the largest cat on record died in 1986 at 46 pounds, 15.25 ounces.

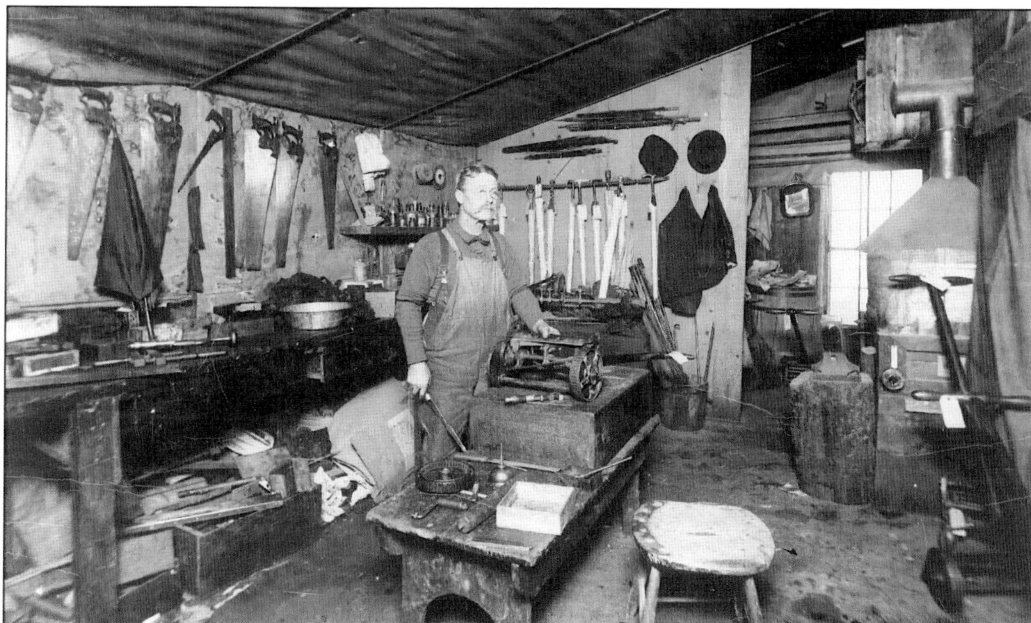

Joseph C. King (1836–1904) returned to Gardiner from service in Company I of the 24th Maine Regiment and started his career as a carpenter and cabinetmaker. Understanding the need for good saws, King repaired saws and made keys in this shop at the corner of Bridge and Water Streets from about 1880 to the time of his death. This photograph contains a clue about a development in his own work and in society at large: a lawn mower on the repair bench. In Victorian times, most home owners started to maintain finely manicured lawns.

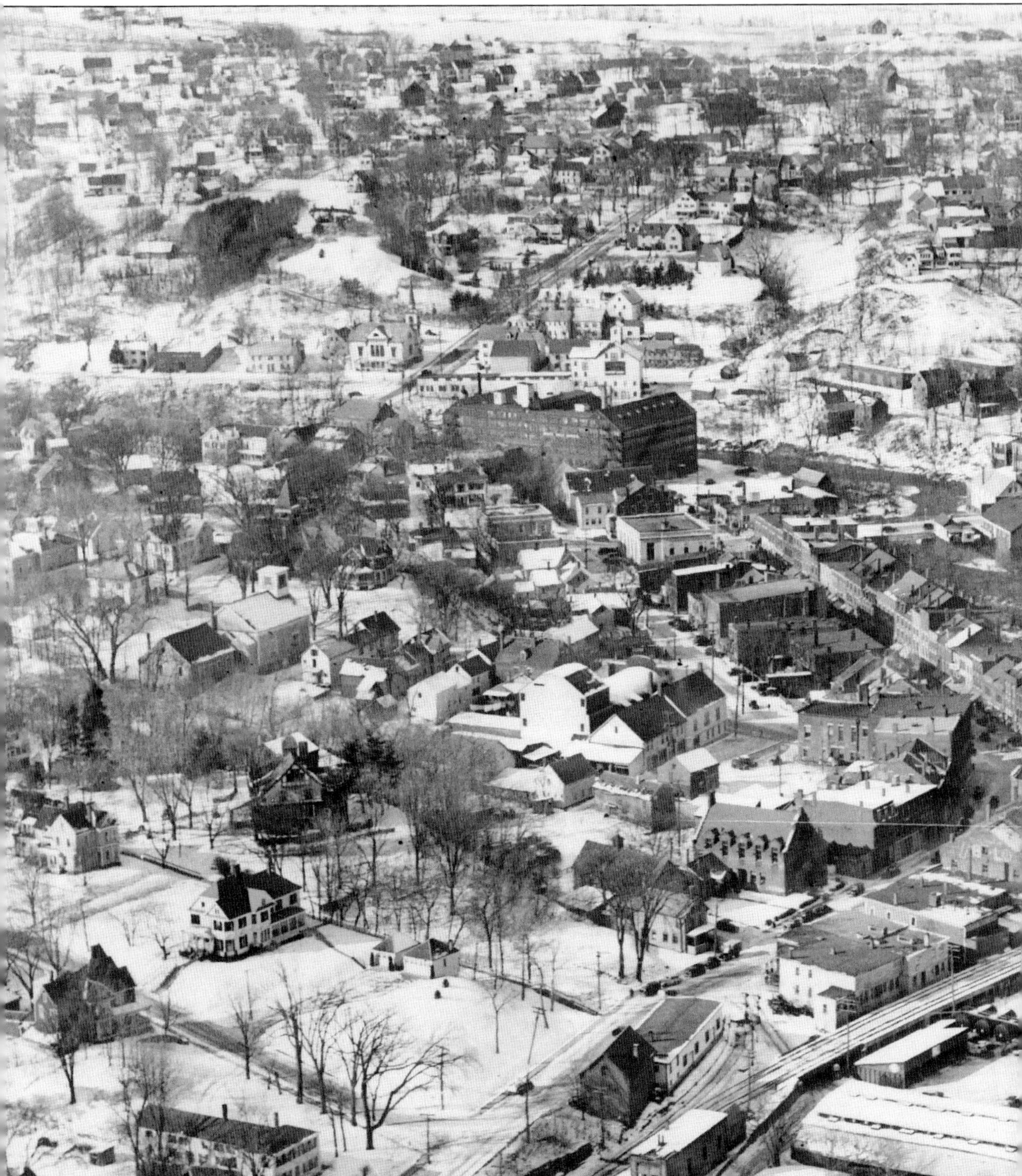

In 1937, aerial photographs enabled city planners to articulate their hopes for the commercial district. A continuous rim of restaurants, hotels, and stores line the curve from old Depot Square to the stream bank. The Commonwealth Shoe Factory (on the right) sits next to the completely filled-in Mill Pond some thirty years before the shopping center first competed with, and then

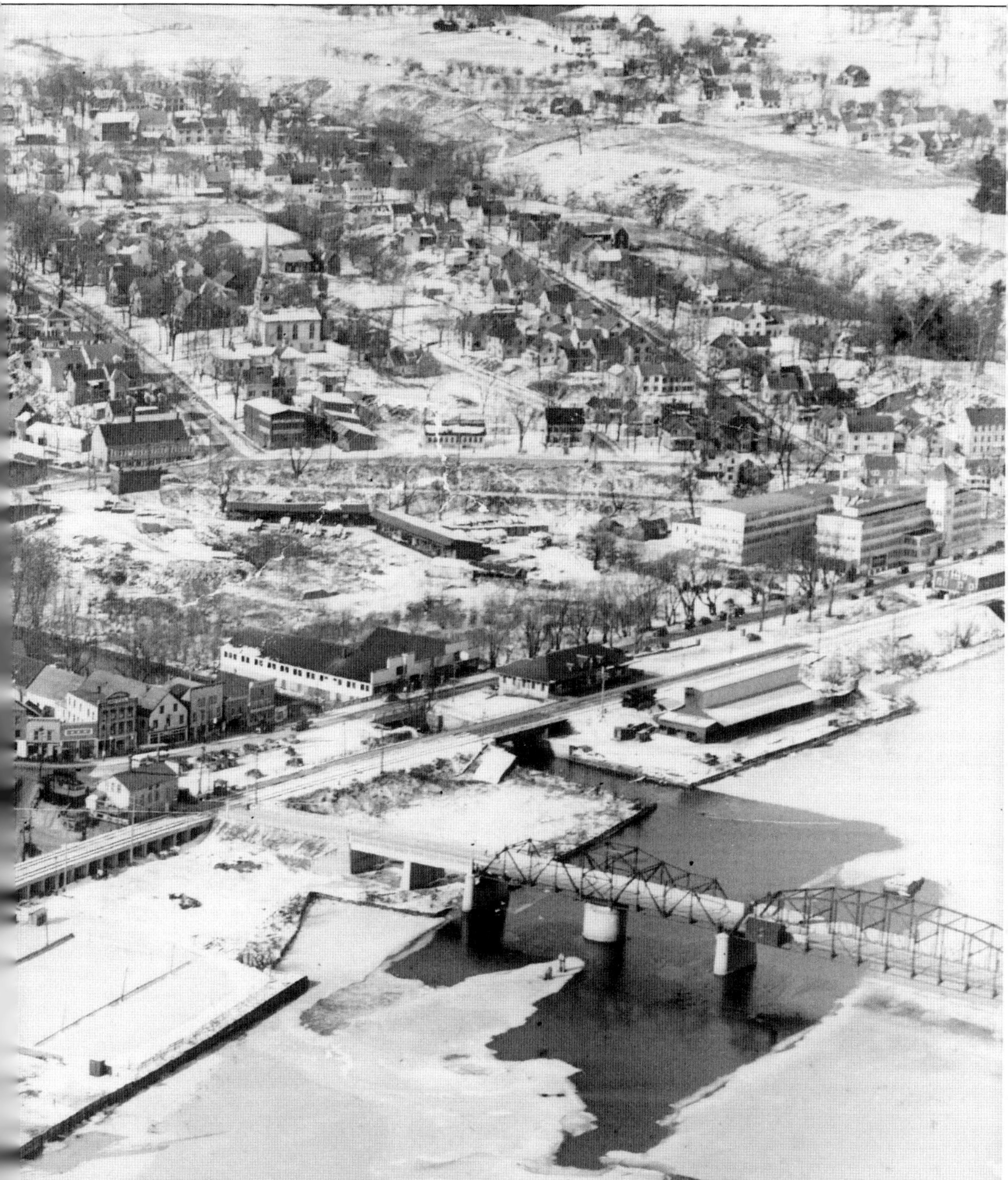

closed, the grocery stores and pharmacies on Water Street. The Hazzard Shoe Factory, known after 1930 as the Gardiner Shoe Company, appears as a giant "E" in the left center. Many storage sheds occupy the present parking lot between the library and city hall. Most surprising is the stream bed stretching under all three spans of the bridge on Bridge Street.

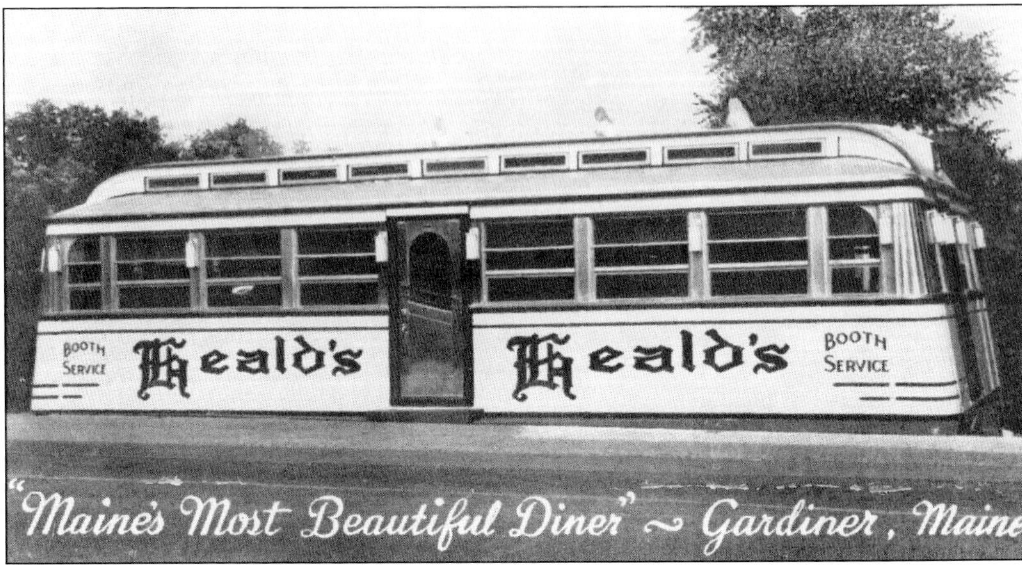

One of Gardiner's more recent landmarks is the diner on Bridge Street, which has served countless numbers of hungry customers during the last fifty years. The city already had a history of portable lunch carts on Water Street, as well as a diner on Depot Square during the 1930s. Eddie Heald acquired this streamlined Art Deco diner from the Worcester Lunch Car Company in 1946. Heald sold his business in about 1953 to Morris Wakefield, from whom Albert Giberson purchased it in 1979. Since 1988, Giberson's son Michael, and Neil Anderson, have operated the diner under its present A-1 name. Giberson and Anderson's combination of traditional diner fare and more adventuresome dishes has earned the A-1 Diner a widespread following as it enters its next half-century.

Acknowledgments

Acknowledgment for help in securing data and photographs is made to: William Bunting, Joanne D. Clark, Michael A. LaPlante, the Gardiner Public Library, the Maine Historic Preservation Commission, the Maine State Library, and the Maine State Museum. The portrait of General Henry Dearborn by Gilbert Stuart is reproduced with the permission of the Portland Museum of Art.